A

DICTIONARY

OF

CONGREGATIONAL USAGES AND PRINCIPLES

ACCORDING TO ANCIENT AND MODERN AUTHORS:

TO WHICH ARE ADDED

BRIEF NOTICES OF SOME OF THE PRINCIPAL WRITERS, ASSEMBLIES, AND TREATISES REFERRED TO IN THE COMPILATION.

BY

PRESTON CUMMINGS,

OF LEICESTER, MASS., LATE PASTOR OF THE CONGREGATIONAL CHURCH, BUCKLAND, MASS.

NINTH EDITION.

BOSTON:

S. K. WHIPPLE AND CO.

161, WASHINGTON STREET.

1857.

BOSTON:
PRINTED BY JOHN WILSON AND SON,
No. 22 School Street.

PREFACE.

It has been said that a good book needs no Preface. Had this fewer defects, it would require less apology. The origin of this work was a supposed want of copious references to many points of frequent practical use in councils, church-meetings, and private duties. It was undertaken at the request of the Franklin Association, but without a due counting of the cost by the compiler.

Three full years of close daily application has sufficed only to discover the magnitude of that subject, which lies at the foundation of the whole fabric of our civil as well as religious liberties. Even Hume, with all his scorn, admits that to the principles and efforts of the Puritans the English owe the whole freedom of their Constitution.

The reader will make no new discovery when he finds that there are many and great defects in this work. The necessary hurry of consulting so many treatises; creates a constant liability of giving a wrong shade to the views of their authors. To express those views in full is impracticable; and brevity or irrelevancy very often forbids introducing both sides of the argument. All that can reasonably be expected, in such a case, is a striking or elucidating extract or epitome; while the copious references direct to chapter and page, where the author cited has treated the subject at length.

The reader should never judge of the general character of a book by a mere reference to it in this compilation. The work may be valuable, notwithstanding one supposed or real inconsistency; and, on the other hand, of comparatively little worth, though it contains some important admissions or illustrations.

With sincere aim to be a faithful lexicographer, this book must still have very much the shade of the compiler's sentiments. Selecting those points which to him seem most important, those which seem paramount to people of different views are sometimes necessarily excluded. Still, through an endeavor to avoid this evil, our differences may sometimes appear greater than they are; because the views of the few who may be but semi-Congregationalists thus get a prominence disproportioned to those of the multitudes who are agreed. The aim has been to state facts as they are, and let the consequences care for themselves. This has led to some slight change of the author's views on a few points of order; but he may sustain himself from any probable charge of fickleness, with the reply of an old convert to Nonconformity, "He that can long and closely contemplate a subject with no modification of his own views shall not have me for his competitor."

Some clamor for a work of undoubted authority in our churches. We have one, and can have but one, such work, viz., the Holy Scriptures. Our ecclesiastical government is a pure theocracy, administered by the people, who can remove their officers whenever they cease to rule — that is, to moderate — according to the divine constitution.

The churches are confederated only by fraternal ties, and the great common charter of their existence. Do any, then, inquire of what use is it to consult opinions and precedents? It is answered, To learn truth, not to be dictated by fallible men. He who relies implicitly on commentaries is a mental slave: he who discards the use of them is an ignorant egotist. It is with every uninspired book as Richard Mather said of a decree of a council: "It has just so much force as there is force in the reason of it."

The reader should be apprised, that the references to books in the several libraries, contained in the Notices at the end of this volume, is incomplete. It was also found impracticable to give a particular notice of every work and author referred to in the Dictionary.

With all its faults, this book is now sent into the world. If men will be excited to examine the originals, even to detect its errors, one great end of its publication will be gained. These originals contain vast funds of sound learning, by men who knew whereof they affirmed, and who many of them suffered, and even died, for the maintenance of those blessed truths and principles through which we now enjoy rest, liberty, and prosperity. May this work be instrumental in leading Christians to the law and the testimony as the ground of their faith and practice, and contribute its mite towards advancing spiritual to the overthrow of formal religion; and the praise be to Almighty God for ever!

The first edition of this work, published last April, was exhausted early in the winter. In preparing this stereotype edition, nearly all the passages have been collated with the originals. A few new topics and many new references have been added; chapters and sections have been often substituted for pages; and the references to the works of John Robinson conformed to the recent American edition.

Grateful acknowledgments are due to ministers, who have so universally aided the author, both by friendly criticisms and recommendations of the work to their people.

LEICESTER, April, 1853.

CONTENTS.

DICTIONARY.

ACCUSATION, *in discipline, should not be received, unless on the testimony of two or three witnesses.** [1] — Mere rumor may justify inquiry on the part of the church, but is not a sufficient basis on which to proceed to formal acts of discipline.[2] A question has been raised, whether the testimony of several witnesses, each to a separate act of the same general nature, should be received, and made the basis of church action.[3] Some modern writers have maintained, that charges may be entertained, founded on general rumor;[4] but, however the usages of other denominations may sanction such a course, it seems inconsistent with the spirit and usages of Congregationalism. Cotton Mather[5] asserts, that, should a member fall into scandalous transgressions, and it be at once a matter of public fame, the pastor *inquires into it*, and brings it im-

* By parity of reason, we infer that an accusation ought not to be brought, nor be suffered to be brought, unless there are two or three witnesses. It seems that this is one of the reasons why one or two brethren are to be taken with the accuser, in the second step, viz. that they may either be witnesses themselves, or see that there are competent witnesses of the facts specified.

2

mediately under ecclesiastical cognizance. — See ACCUSED, *Rights of;* DISCIPLINE; ELDER, *Accusation against.*

[1] Goodwin, Ch. Gov. 129; Mitchell, Guide, 103. [2] Ib. [3] Ib. note. [4] Congregational Manual, 35, 36. [5] Rat. Dis. 141, 142.

ACCUSED, *Rights of.* — There is great lack of definiteness on this point in our treatises on church government. One reason for this may be the universally admitted principle of Congregationalism, — Whatever is the dictate of nature is the law of God. Their right to a distinct specification of the charges to be brought against them, of the witnesses to be confronted, to a proper time to prepare for their defence, and to a trial and decision without unnecessary delay; in a word, to all the privileges which appertain to persons justly adjudged at other tribunals, belongs to them. Mitchell[1] says charges should be distinctly specified and seasonably communicated to the accused, commonly in writing. Crowell, in his Church Member's Manual,[2] shows that he must not be condemned but on the testimony of some witness besides the complainant; and Cambridge Platform[3] and other treatises show conclusively that they have a right to the first and second steps pointed out in Matt. xviii., though some make an exception in case of public offences. — See DISCIPLINE; SUSPENSION.

[1] Guide, 102. [2] Pages 234—237. [3] Chap. xiv.

ADMONITION *was formerly considered as an indispensable act of the church, preceding excommuni-*

cation.[1] — The Puritans in Holland "practised no church censures but admonition, and excommunication for obstinate offenders."[2] The nineteenth article of the Savoy Declaration says: "The censures appointed by Christ are admonition and excommunication." It directs that those who know the facts "first admonish the offender in private;" and, in case of non-amendment, "the offence being related to the church, and the offender not manifesting his repentance, he is to be duly admonished in the name of Christ by the whole church, — by the ministry of the elders of the church."[3] Cotton Mather[4] describes the manner in which public admonitions were performed in his day in the New England churches, by the pastor (in behalf of the church) summoning the delinquent, and the church proceeding to excommunicate him, provided he contemptuously refused to appear and be admonished. He gives the substance of a form of such public admonition, and says that private Christians then visited "the delinquent, and followed up *the good effects* of the admonition upon him." Letchford[5] says that "the admonished must abstain from communion and satisfy the church, else excommunication follows." Dr. Dwight[6] says: "Should the accused person be found guilty of the fault laid to his charge, it becomes the duty of the church solemnly to admonish him of his sin, and the absolute necessity of atoning for it, by making proper reparation, with the spirit of the gospel." Upham[7] and Cambridge Platform[8] assert, that "if the church discern him to be willing to hear, yet not fully convinced of his offence, as in case of heresy, they are to dispense to him a public admonition; which, declaring the offender to lie under the public offence of the church, doth thereby withhold or suspend him from the holy fellowship of the Lord's supper, till his offence be removed by public confession." (This supposes the first and second steps to have been taken.) "If he still continue obstinate, they are to cast him out by excommunication." Punchard[9] says: "But if unsuccessful (i.e. the measures of the church to reclaim the offender), the church, after suitable delay, proceed to admonish him, to suspend him from their communion, or to excommunicate and cut him off from all connection with the church."

[1] Discipline of Visible Church, by Clyfton or Smith, in Punchard, Hist. 371; Hanbury, i. 32. [2] Apol. Nar. of Indepen. in W. Assembly in Neal's Pur. i. 492, and Han. ii. 224. [3] Han. iii. 547. [4] Rat. Dis. 145—148. [5] In Mass. Hist. Soc. Col., series iii. vol. iii. 73. [6] Works, Serm. clxii. [7] Rat. Disc. 139. [8] Ch. xiv. sect. 2. [9] View, 179.

AFFINITY, *is it a sufficient cause for either multiplying churches in the same place, or transferring members to other churches?* — It often occurs that diversities of opinion and practice, in matters not strictly fundamental, cause a portion of the church to feel, that they had better either organize into a distinct church, or transfer their relations to some other church. It is a mooted question, whether this alone is a sufficient ground for such organization or such transfer of relation. John Robinson and William Brewster give it as their opinion, in council, on the Ainsworth and Johnson controversy, that it would have been better to have dismissed in peace than to have made their brethren their adversaries.... The Johnsonians insisted, that, if the Ainsworthians were dismissed, they should remove out of the place. The latter pleaded a pecuniary necessity for remaining.[1] Cambridge Platform[2] says: "If a member's departure be manifestly unsafe and sinful, the church may not consent thereunto; for, in so doing, they should not act in faith. ... If the case be doubtful, and the person not to be persuaded, it seemeth best to leave the matter to God, and not forcibly to detain him." The authors of the Congregational Manual recommend leaving such a case to a council.[3] Cleveland's Narrative and Conduct of the Fourth Church in Ipswich maintains, that, if particular persons cannot agree with the major part, they may withdraw, if the church refuse to dismiss them.[4] So Owen. — See WITHDRAWING *to other churches.*

In these cases, personal liberty is usually pleaded, on the one hand, and the evil of separation, with the wrong which the church would sanction by dismissing, on the other. This practical difficulty is most satisfactorily obviated in the Answer of the New England Elders to the nine positions sent out to them by divers reverend and godly ministers in England. They show,[5] that in such a case the churches dissuade from removing, and show the sin, and *do not consent* if it seem wrong to them, but "suspend their vote against him, as not willing, against his will, to detain him, abhorring to make our churches places of restraint and imprisonment." This was made a practical rule with our forefathers. It was applied in several cases, and once to no less a personage than John Davenport (see remarks on his case in art. PASTORS *not lightly removed*). An adjourned ex-parte council in Concord, in 1743, advise the church, in failure of bringing their pastor to repentance, "to withdraw from his ministry, and *seek gospel ordinances elsewhere*." T. Goodwin advocates the same principles.[6] Isaac Chauncy asserts[7] that "a church may deny a dismission to one under church dealing, or when he desires it at large to the world or to a false church. But if he asks a dismission to a church of the same order, and gives no satisfactory reason, and remains peremptory, the church ought not to refuse the granting of it. For this is to make a church a prison, to lord it over God's heritage, to lay a stumbling-block in his way, tempting him to schism, destroying his edification; for he cannot edify by means he is forcibly kept under. It is contrary to the golden rule, and may cause a root of bitterness that may affect many. If, upon all due means, the church will grant no dismission, the member refused may join another church as a non-member." — See DISMISSION, *may a church receive members without?* SCHISM, SEPARATION.

[1] Testimony of the Elders of the Church in Leyden, in Han. i. 255; and Works, iii. 471—475. [2] Chap. xiii. sec. 3. [3] Page 33. [4] Page 38. [5] Page 74. [6] Ch. Gov. 394, 395. [7] Divine Institution of Congregational Churches, 120, 121.

AGREEMENT *of Congregationalists.* — We are often represented as peculiar for disagreement among ourselves, relative to our own distinctive principles. We, however, challenge an instance of more perfect agreement among the people of any other denomination. Cotton Mather[1] comments on five distinctive points, on which he affirms that we are all agreed. In substance they are these: The right of Christians to associate for the worship of God — Those thus associated are an instituted church — Their chosen pastors have a right to administer the sacraments — Churches ought to pay great regard to the *advice* of other churches; and, "The Sacred Scriptures are the *sufficient* rule for *belief*, *worship*, and *manners* among the people of God." Minor differences, particularly about the application of the Scripture standard to individual cases, of course exist where there is a perfectly acknowledged right of private judgment; but there is equal diversity relative to the application of the particular standards of other denominations. Some, who take hold of our skirts and would be called by our name, would impose on us other standards than the Scriptures; but from the beginning it was not so. Even the framers of the Saybrook Platform did not claim to be strict Congregationalists.[2] Ainsworth retorts on those who taunted on him the disagreement of Congregationalists, "Your persuasions are to make us believe, that, because there are sins in Zion, there are none in Babylon."[3] Rev. C. Upham[4] quotes Gov. Endicot's letter to Gov. Bradford, showing that he learned from Dr. Fuller that they of Plymouth held the same doctrine with himself, "being far from the common report that hath been spread of you." Punchard[5] says: "After a somewhat careful examination of the writings of all those worthy men, our ecclesiastical ancestors, I feel justified in saying, that, although they differ among themselves, and from modern Congregationalists, on some *minor* points, yet in the essentials of our polity there is a most remarkable agreement among them all with what is now deemed sound Congregationalism." — See CONGREGATIONALISM, *epitome of principles.*

[1] Rat. Dis. Introduction, pp. 8—10. [2] Trumbull's Hist. of Conn. i. 486, 487, 493. [3] In Han. i. 99. [4] Note in his Dedication Sermon, 43. [5] View, 27.

AMUSEMENTS. — The old Puritan Congregationalists have always been distinguished for their aversion to vain amusements. They made a stand against the Book of Sports of King James I., which, to please the rabble and break down the discipline of the godly, authorized such sports even on the Lord's day.[1] Though Prynne and other godly Presbyterians were valiant for and suffered deeply in the same cause, yet it was the Independents who suffered most deeply as a body. They fully approved of Prynne's "Histrio-Mastix or Player's Scourge, wherein it is evidenced, by divers arguments, that popular stage-plays are sinful, heathenish, lewd, and ungodly spectacles."[2] This had much to do with exiling them to Holland. Hence they came here, not only loathing such amusements in their consciences, but smarting under the effects of them on their own religious liberties and privileges. The Histrio-Mastix was published in 1,006 pages quarto, and shows, even from multitudes of heathen writers, that stage-plays were of the most infamous origin, and were most pernicious in their effects, condemned by the moral, and productive only of sensuality and crime. He shows that they were prohibited by a multitude of early councils, and that members were excluded from the primitive churches for either participating in them or attending them. He also incidentally shows the same of dancing, in numerous instances, as may be seen by reference to the table at the end of his volume. He admits [3] that we may sometimes need recreations, — as after sickness or fatigue or hard study, but denies that we need it in plays, or in any unlawful employments. In the whole work he calls up the united testimony of heaven, earth, and hell, to show the iniquity of theatres and vain amusements. For this he lost his ears. Dr. John Rainolds (or Reynolds), in his "Overthrow of Stage Plays," shows their libidinous and other evil tendencies, abundantly demonstrating their injurious effects by the testimony of heathen writers, as well as of holy writ. He also incidentally shows that promiscuous dancing tends to the same evils.

Dr. Ames [4] says: "If there were any that did not dare to be at stage-plays, nor swear lustily on trivial occasions or in ordinary discourse, nor drink wine until he stared in pledging the cup, nor frequent masking, dice, or revelling, he should presently have no other name than Puritan." Prince informs us,[5] that the same Dr. Ames was obliged to flee to the continent for preaching against playing cards and dice. Philip Stubbs, in his "Anatomie of Abuses," strikingly illustrates the evils of promiscuous dancing, stage-plays, cards, dice, &c. Rev. T. Allen, afterwards of Charlestown, Mass., refused to read the Book of Sports, when the clergy were required to do so, and lost his parish (St. Edmunds, in Cambridge, Eng.) by order of Bishop Wren.[6] President Chauncy displeased Bishop Laud, by preaching against the Book of Sports, &c.[7] — See DANCING.

[1] Han. i. 358, 359. [2] Han. i. 512. [3] Pages 945—948. [4] Pref. to Bradshaw's English Puritanism. [5] Chronology, 29. [6] Eliot, Biog. Dict. 20. [7] Ib. 98.

ANOINTING *with oil.* — Thos. Goodwin (styled the Father of Congregationalism, though it is believed to have had even a far more illustrious origin) devotes the eleventh chapter of the seventh book of his treatise on Church Government[1] to this subject. He maintains that the healing promised in James, v. 14, 15, was not miraculous, but only a blessing accompanying the prayers of the elders, in the use of an appointed ordinance, which he argues to be still in force. Isaac Chauncy[2] maintains that the directions for anointing were, by a synecdoche, equivalent to requiring the use of outward means, to be accompanied with prayer. Goodwin, in his Catechism,[3] however, admits that the ordinance has ceased, and that the promise never was of universal application, though it put great honor on the elders to be thus the medium of special blessings to the sick. From this time, anointing, as an ordinance, seems to have become perfectly obsolete in the Congregational churches.

[1] Pages 387—390. [2] Ans. to Goodwin, 3—30. [3] Page 22.

APOSTLES *not bishops.*—John Milton[1] shows conclusively, that the apostles *could* not *possibly* have been bishops by office, i.e. moderators or governors of the churches, and so that modern diocesan bishops are no successors of the apostles. Dr. Bacon, in his Church Manual, most happily illustrates this point, showing that though they had certain duties to perform, yet they were not officers in any churches. They had "Bishoprics" according to the Scriptures; but these had little or no analogy to the supposed duties and prerogatives of modern prelates.—See BISHOPS.

[1] Eikonoklastes, 135. [2] Pages 30—36.

APOSTLES, *English bishops cannot trace their succession from.* — Hanbury[1] shows that this is admitted by Archbishop Usher, Geraldus, and Stillingfleet; and by them their succession is made to depend only on common fame, owing to the loss of records in the English church. It would be an endless task to attempt even a synopsis of the controversies on this point. I therefore only give the above admissions of episcopal champions.—See BISHOPS.

[1] Vol. i. 166.

APPEALS *from the decision of churches are unnecessary.* — Thomas Goodwin[1] shows that they are not required by the law of nature; for they did not exist either in the patriarchal or the Jewish code. Neither do they exist in some of the reformed churches of Europe, nor even in matters of life and death in civil courts. They cannot consistently go before sentence; for this would deprive the church of the power of sentence, and the delinquent will lack the means of his conversion, until the matter has run through all the courts of appeals. Nor can they follow the sentence, because it is bound in heaven, unless the delinquent repents,[2] and also because the church would thus give up the authority with which Christ has entrusted them.

J. Davenport shows[3] that they are endless in their practical application; for, if the principle is once admitted, there is no consistent stopping-place short of a general œcumenical council, which may not assemble for an age. Richard Mather and W. Tompson[4] press the same argument concerning appeals to discipline churches. John Wise,[5] doubtless referring to Matt. xviii., says: There is apparently some great fallacy in the objection (i.e. to the ultimate power resting in the church), or certainly our blessed Saviour did not state his cases right." Hanbury[6] speaks of T. Edwards, in his Reasons against the Independents, as resting the necessity of a court of appeal on the precedent of the church at Antioch, "but forgetting that they were not members of that church that caused the dissension." Katharine Chidley, in her answer to

Edwards,[7] says: "This chapter (Acts xv.), above all the chapters that I can find, proves Independency. The church of Antioch judged it an unequal thing for them to judge the members of the church of Jerusalem."

Dr. Emmons[8] says: "Christ here gives no direction to the censured person to appeal to any higher tribunal, . . . nor to the church to call a council for advice. The censured person has no right of appeal, . . . because there is no higher tribunal on earth to which he can appeal. . . . There must be a final decision, and the church must make it." His reasoning looks like not allowing the aggrieved a right to seek admission to other churches; but this was not probably his meaning.

[1] Ch. Gov. 197—200. [2] See EXCOMMUNICATION, *what?* [3] Power of Cong. Churches, in Han. ii. 65. [4] In ib. 174. [5] Vindic. 54. [6] Vol. ii. 103. [7] In ib. 109. [8] Platform estab. by the Lord Jesus Christ, in Works, v. 454.

APPEALS, *how far allowed in strict congregational discipline.* — John Wise, in his Vindication,[1] shows that the first trial is at the bar of the delinquent's own conscience: "If he hear thee, thou hast gained a brother;" thence there is an appeal to one or two more; and, if he neglect to hear them, there is an appeal to the church, which is the highest tribunal known in the word of God. Thomas Goodwin[2] acknowledges the right of appeal to other churches, in case of mal-administration; but their decision is not to be received with implicit faith. Upham[3] recognizes the right of appeal, in the last resort, to the churches at large, through the medium of an ex-parte council. A thousand and one disquisitions, maintaining juridical appeals, may be found, fathered by so called Congregational writers; but almost or quite every one of them bears date as late as the commencement of the eighteenth century. — For the whole subject of appeals, see further, COUNCILS, SYNODS.

[1] Pages 52—54. [2] Ch. Gov. 202. [3] Ratio Disciplinæ, sec. 175.

APPROBATION *to preach.* — When candidates for the pastoral office go out to preach the gospel, it is desirable that they have letters of commendation from some who are known to the churches. Formerly, the churches thus recommended those who went out from them.[1] About the year 1705, "Proposals" were made by certain ministers to have the churches give their power to do this into the hands of ministerial associations.[2] This custom has now, by innovation, generally prevailed among the New England Congregationalists; some associations giving a mere recommendation, and others a formal license, to preach the gospel. It is, however, an encroachment on ancient usages and principles, which maintain that it was not a matter of necessity; and that to hold it necessary was "to deny Christians their liberty, and assume the infallible chair."[3] Stoddard (who differed from most New England ministers) argues in his Instituted Churches,[4] that it belongs to synods to appoint persons to examine candidates for the ministry, yet not to abridge the churches of their liberty. In the petition of the church and town of Woburn to the General Court, Aug. 30, 1653,[5] they say: "If a church has liberty of election and ordination, then it has the power of approbation also." The result was a repeal of an order which had passed the General Court, that ministers should be approbated by a council, or by the county court.[6] Punchard says[7] that the first suggestion on this subject, so far as he has discovered, came from the united brethren, Congregational and Presbyterian, in England, in 1692; but the above petition shows an earlier date by a Massachusetts law, which was subsequently repealed. John Owen,[8] in his Duty of Pastor and People, chap. vii., asserts that private Christians have a right to make known whatever is revealed (i.e. made clear) to them, and, if called in Providence (as, for instance, being shipwrecked on an island), to preach the gospel. — See Punchard's View, 199, 200; and Upham's Ratio Disciplinæ, 55, 117—123. See also ASSOCIATIONS, LICENSE (in particular), PROPHESYING, PREACH *who may?*

[1] Wise's Quarrel of the Churches Espoused, 124—128. [2] Ib. [3] Oliver Cromwell, in Neal's Hist. Puritans, ii. 116. [4] Page 34. [5] In Mass. Hist. Soc. Col., series iii. vol. i. 42. [6] Ib. 39. [7] View, 199. [8] Works, xix. 43—47.

ASSOCIATIONS, *their rise and province.* — About the year 1675, perhaps earlier,* after great

* President Stiles, says about 1670. Note to Convention Sermon, page 68. A manuscript-book has been recently deposited in the library of the Mass. Hist. Soc. by Rev. Dr. William Jenks from the Hon. Judge White, of Salem, containing the constitution and records of an association formed in Bodmin in Cornwall,

desolations by the Indian wars, the neighboring ministers in several counties in New England met together to pray; and subsequently they began to discuss subjects of common interest at their meetings. At length, some "presbyterially inclined" ministers began to dignify their meetings with the name of "Classes." Thus matters progressed until, in 1705, an effort was made by one of these associations to combine all the ministers in the country into similar bodies, for the purpose of establishing a consociation with powers similar to those afterwards claimed by the consociations of Connecticut. They issued their proposals, bearing date Nov. 5,

Sept. 9, 1655. Their record of proceedings continues till May 4, 1659, which was on the eve of the restoration. Charles Morton, afterwards of Charlestown, Mass., was one of the members. They voted to ordain three ministers in December and January, 1656-7, "being satisfied with their qualifications." But whether they were ordained as pastors or evangelists, the record does not inform us.

The same volume also contains the constitution and records of Cambridge Association, which was formed at the house of the same Charles Morton, in Charlestown, Mass., Oct. 13, 1690. On the records are found votes, passed Feb. 23, 1690-1, recommending the ordination of evangelists; and that the candidates for such ordination be "recommended by the churches of which they are members to the adjoining eldership for their ordination." MS. p. 40. It appears that they received a communication from "the ministers of the county of Essex, Nov. 2, 1691." MS. p. 41. March 6, 1692, "Voted that letters be written to the *other* associations," &c. The records in this volume continue till 1701, and contain some scattered notes of a later date. This is doubtless the association from which issued the "Proposals" referred to above. In these records are the originals of most of the votes of the ministers at Cambridge, reported by Mather in his Magnalia, book v. vol. ii. pp. 212—237.

1705.[1] These proposals were successfully resisted by "divers godly ministers" at the time,[2] though they afterwards prevailed, by the interference of state authority, in Connecticut. In Massachusetts, however, associations from this time became general,* but have neither held nor claimed any ecclesiastical authority, such as was designed in the "Proposals," with the single exception of examining and licensing candidates. Two attempts have since been made to give ecclesiastical authority to ministerial associations; but they have been signal failures. John Cotton, in his Book of the Keys, alludes to the desirableness of such associations; and Goodwin and Nye, in their dedicatory epistle to that book,[3] speak of his asserting the necessity of so guarding them that they shall not "*intrench or impair the privilege of* ENTIRE *jurisdiction* committed to each congregation." Mitchell[4] says: "It is the province of associations to license candidates for the ministry," which is true in practice; "but from the beginning it was not so." I am informed that the American Baptist and English Independent churches all stand fast in their liberty on this point.

Eliot, in his Ecclesiastical History of Massachusetts,[5] informs us that Roger Williams and others opposed ministers' meetings, lest it should grow to

* Punchard, View, 196, quotes Cotton Mather, Rat. Dis. 179—181, affirming that the proposals for associations had not been universally complied withal in 1726. Upham, Rat. Dis. 153, shows from the Magnalia, that they, however, began to be formed as early as 1690.

presbytery; but this fear was without foundation, as they were *all* clear on this one point, that no church or person can have power over another church.[6] The Answer to the Hampshire Narrative asserts that[7] associations are not so much as named in the Platform: it is free and voluntary how far people will refer to them for advice. It expresses hope[8] that "a new contention will not arise about the rights of associations and the liberty of the churches in calling and ordaining pastors." The association had interposed in a case in Springfield, and the civil authority had a warrant for arresting part of the council, assembled against the wishes of the association. And they actually did imprison the candidate for an alleged breach of the peace in the matter.[9] The council[10] blame the association for setting up authority over the church in Springfield. Their answer was imputed to the pen of the Rev. William Cooper, of Brattle-street Church, Boston.[11] — See APPROBATION, LICENSE.

[1] See them in Wise's Quarrel of the Churches Espoused, 77—80. [2] See CONSOCIATION. [3] Page 7. [4] Page 232. [5] In Mass. Hist. Soc. Col. x. 16. [6] See the same corroborated in Eliot's Biog. Dict. 434, art. SKELTON. [7] Page 5. [8] Page 55. [9] Pages 79—82. [10] Page 77. [11] Eliot's Biog. Dict. 129.*

AUTHORITY, *human, renounced.* — Robinson, in his answer to Bernard,[1] is very positive on this point.

* The author has been requested to give an article on the tenure of the connection of members with their associations. Finding nothing on the subject, he can report nothing, save the obvious principle, that, in such a case, the tenure is limited to a strict construction of the given associational constitution.

"Not to prove and try what is offered to the contrary of any man's judgment, in the balance of the sanctuary, is to honor men above God, and advance a throne above the throne of Christ." J. Cook[2] thinks that "nothing more hinders reformation than taking things upon trust, not supporting authority by solid reasoning; as if an argument from authority were any proof to a wise man." In Foxcroft's Century Sermon,[3] it is asserted that "there was, in the infancy of the Reformation, a set of men who appealed to the law and to the testimony; renounced all implicit credit to human teachers, and all human imposition in divine worship. One hundred of these pleaded their separation before the Lord Mayor and Bishop Sands, and fourteen or fifteen of them were imprisoned in 1557." — See Watts's Hymns, b. ii. hymn 149, stanza 5. SCRIPTURES *a sufficient guide to order.*

[1] In Han. i. 208; and Works, ii. 52. [2] What the Independents would Have, in Han. iii. 259. [3] Page 8.

BAPTISM, *proper subjects of.* — Visible believers and their households have always been held by Congregationalists proper, to be proper subjects of this ordinance. The early and most of the late Congregationalists hold these the only proper subjects of it. John Robinson says:[1] "It doth no more belong to the seed of godless parents than doth the comfort flowing from the righteousness of faith unto the parents themselves." His defence of infant-baptism is condensed from his answer to Helwisse in Punchard's History of Congregationalism.[2] Ainsworth maintained the same: his views may be seen at length in Hanbury.[3] The elders of the New England churches, in their Answer to the Nine Positions,[4] quote John Alasco: "None ought to be driven back who is a member of the church, nor admitted to baptism who is not a member. . . . We do baptize their infants alone who have joined themselves to our churches." John Cotton argues:[5] "If one of the parents cannot claim a right to the communion, they cannot claim baptism for their children." He maintains[6] that it can only be on account of the next parent or pro-parent, otherwise it may be extended even to Turks and infidels. Cotton afterwards changed his mind on some points relative to the subjects of baptism; and what is claimed to be his retraction is bound with a copy of his treatise on the Holiness of Church Members, in the Antiquarian Library, Worcester; but, instead of advocating the half-way covenant, he seems only to retract a former opinion, that being in covenant was unnecessary to communion in either seal. This point seems to have been one of those which led to the separation of the New England Puritans from the English church; and "Mr. Davenport left Amsterdam because he could not conscientiously baptize all sorts of infants."[7] He had a controversy with the Dutch divines, and also in New England, whether the children of communicants only should be admitted to the ordinance.[8] Isaac Chauncy[9] says: "No non-member can plead right to any seal, the seals being given to the church." The Apology of the Overseers, Elders, and Deacons of the English Church at Amsterdam maintains[10] that baptism is only for the faithful and their seed, or those under their government. The Principles of the Robinson Church assert[11] that baptism is only for visible believers and their unadult children. Increase Mather maintains[12] that adopted children of believers may be baptized, and shows that Ames and Cotton taught the same. Dwight[13] argues, at length, for confining it to the households of believers, from the constitution of the Abrahamic church; from Matt. xix. 13, 14, Acts xx. 38, 39, and 1 Cor. vii. 14; from the Scriptures not presenting two sets of qualification; from the tenor of the Christian covenant precluding it; and the presumption that it would introduce disorder into the Christian church to admit it. The adverse principles seem to have begun to prevail in New England about 1660, though a foundation for them had previously been laid. In the Answer of the Elders and Messengers to the General Court in Boston in 1662, they argue largely in favor of receiving the children of those who were baptized in infancy and own the covenant.[14] Dr. Increase Mather at first opposed the doctrine of this synod, but soon changed his mind, and published "the First Principles of New England concerning Baptism," in which he declares that the half-way covenant was the doctrine of the first fathers of New England,[15] and claims[16] John Cotton as on that side of the question. But the argument was either overstrained through the testimony of posthumous letters, or else Cotton's opponents justly charged him with contradicting himself.[17] He did, however, maintain that the children of those not in covenant might be baptized, provided the parents would resign their education to responsible church members, as grandparents, &c. This proviso, however, destroys by implication the right of those not conforming to it. His doctrines on this point amount to little else than that of the admitted right of baptism to the adopted children of believing householders.

Among the noted defenders of confining baptism to the households of believers was President Chauncy, who wrote his famous Antisynodalia for this purpose, in which he takes this ground:[18] "Visible believers, and converts in full communion, in an instituted church (being unbaptized), *together with their next seed in minority*, are the proper subjects of baptism."* These are an account only of disputes about the extent of the ordinance, while the writings of those who agree on the validity of infant-baptism are too numerous to admit even a synopsis in this work. Dwight[19] and Emmons[20] have given us their views at large on the general subject. Robinson says:[21] "We require of them (Anabaptists) proof how the grace of God is so straitened by Christ's coming in the flesh as to cast out of the church the greatest part of the church before,—the infants of believers."—See Half-way Covenant.

* Enough to vindicate him from the charge of antipedobaptist sentiments, though he held to immersion.

[1] Apology, in Han. i. 375; and Works, iii. 19. [2] Pages 342, 343. [3] Vol. i. 152, 408—416. [4] Page 71. [5] Way, 81. [6] Ib. 87, 88. [7] Trumbull's Hist. of Conn. i. 492, and Han. i. 526—546 [8] Eliot, Biog. Dict. 149. [9] Divine Institution of Cong. Churches, Preface ix. [10] Page 71. [11] In Prince's Chronology, 91. [12] First Principles of New England concerning Baptism. [13] Works, Serm. clix. [14] Prop. v. 97—108. [15] Page 1. [16] Pages 2, 5. [17] See Han. ii. 560—583. [18] Page 16. [19] Vol. v. Serm. clvii.—clix. [20] Vol. v. 482—500. [21] Ans. to Helwisse, in Han. i. 270.

Another question closely connected with the foregoing is — Does

BAPTISM *admit the baptized to the churches?* — The advocates for national establishments, and also the abettors of the half-way covenant, of course, maintain the affirmative; while the separating Congregational Puritans advocate the negative, and the Baptists many of them advocate the affirmative, seemingly on the principle that extremes meet. Some of the early Congregational lights wrote with great clearness to prove their position. John Robinson says,[1] "The church was not given to baptism, but baptism to the church;" and argues, that, if admission to the church be by baptism, then casting out of the church must be unbaptizing. The same doctrine is taught in Hooker's Survey,[2] Richard Mather's Church Government and Church Covenant,[3] J. Owen's Answer to the Review of the Nature of Schism.[4] John Robinson[5] inquires to *what* church Helwisse, Smith, and others were admitted. They rebaptized themselves. The same question will apply to Roger Williams and the American Baptists. Prof. Knowles[6] attempts to avoid the dilemma, by assuming that a voluntary agreement makes a church; and then they may ordain a minister, and he may baptize the members. This is true Congregational doctrine; but how does it comport with the Baptist doctrine, that baptism is indispensable to church membership?

[1] Ans. to Helwisse, in Han. i. 266, 267; and Works, iii. 167. [2] Part i. 55. [3] Pages 12—21. [4] In Han. iii. 460. [5] Ans. to Helwisse, in Han. i. 267; and Works, iii. 168. [6] Life of Roger Williams, 168.

BAPTISM, *does it make infants members?* — This question is so blended with the foregoing, that the same persons, if Congregationalists, must, to be consistent, maintain either the affirmative or the negative of both. Richard Mather[1] approvingly quotes Zepperus and Parker, showing that they were not received as members till they made a profession of their own faith. Higginson and Brewster agreed to the same doctrine.[2] Cambridge Platform takes the same ground.[3] J. Owen[4] shows how, though no members, they are still, by covenant with the parents, under the watch and care of the church; a very important distinction and doctrine. Cotton Mather[5] quotes Flavel as maintaining, that the fierce disputes about infant-baptism are punishments for neglecting our duty to the baptized.

Lord King, on the other hand, says:[6] "In general, all those that were baptized were looked upon as members of the church, and had a right to all the privileges thereof." He then excepts those who were guilty of gross, scandalous sins. The Answer of the Boston Synod of 1662[7] maintains their membership, so as to claim membership for their households, though not to full communion without public personal profession. The Gospel Order Revived, in answer to Dr. I. Mather, says:[8] "For he (Dr. M.) has taught us that adult baptized persons are of the church." In Dr. Mather's own copy of that work (in the Antiquarian Library, Worcester) is written in the margin against this sentence, "*false.*" It is in the doctor's own handwriting. Shepard, in his Church Membership of Children, adduces all the usual arguments in favor of their membership. Dr. Dwight[9] maintains that they are members of the church general, in the same sense that the eunuch was a member. He gives his opinion,[10] that such persons cannot be excommunicated; that, during their minority, their discipline is committed wholly to their parents and guardians; that the church thus possesses an indirect control over them; and that they are bound to reprove and admonish baptized persons, whom they see in the commission of sin.

[1] Apology, 34, 35. [2] Han. ii. 166. [3] Chap. xii. sect. 7. [4] Original of Churches, chap. iv. in Works, xx. 188. [5] Magnalia, ii. 459. [6] Enquiry, part i. 100. [7] Pages 72—108. [8] Page 19. [9] Serm. clvii. [10] Ib. Serm. clxii.

BAPTISM, *is it indispensable to communion?*— Robert Hall, a Baptist,[1] has cogently argued that it is not *per se* indispensable, because the first communicants had not received *Christian* baptism; and the evidence preponderates, that others, as Apollos, had communed previously to receiving it.

4

From various other considerations, he also demonstrates the same point. The Encyclopedia of Religious Knowledge[2] gives the arguments of Mr. J. D. Fuller, on the other side, which may be thus epitomized: The difference in the baptisms practised before and after Christ's death were circumstantial, and not essential. The commission in Matt. xxviii. makes baptism as essential to communion as faith to baptism. The apostles uniformly baptized converts previously to their admission. Conformity to the commission thus explained is not *schism*, but promotive of Christian union. The mutual forbearance required does not involve the surrender of Christian institutions. It is not inconsistency, but charity, to unite with Pedobaptists in acts not implying the abandonment of the commission. It is better to suffer imputations of uncharitableness than to sin by abandoning Christ's commission. — See COMMUNION, *Terms of;* BAPTISM, *does it admit the baptized to churches?**

[1] Works, i. 292—351; ii. 202—230. [2] Page 396.

BAPTISM, *may it be administered without a church?* — The affirmative of this question is maintained by Goodwin[1] on the ground of the case of the Ethiopian eunuch; of John the Baptist, requiring only faith and repentance; of Peter, at the Pentecost; and of the jailer and his household. Owen maintains[2] that professing believers and their households have a right to baptism, whether they

* A large portion of the Congregationalists now hold baptism to be indispensable to communion.

are joined to any particular church or not. John Cotton, on the contrary, did not baptize his child at sea, because he believed that it should be done in a church, and that a minister could not give the seal but in his own congregation.[3] This was also the long-received doctrine in the New England churches, and precluded baptisms out of the church. — See MINISTERS, *may they administer seals, &c.?*

[1] Ch. Gov. 233, 377, 378. [2] Review of Nature of Schism, in Han. iii. 460. [3] Winthrop's Journal, i. 110; New Englander for August, 1850, p. 410.

BAPTISM *should be public.* — Dr. Sparke and Mr. Travers, in their conference with Archbishop Whitgift,[1] object to three things in the practice of baptism in the English Episcopal church: Its being done in private; being done by laymen and women; and being held necessary to salvation. Cotton Mather[2] offers reasons to show why the New England churches did not practise private baptism; one of which is, "that, as the church owe *special duties to the baptized*, they think it reasonable that they should see the baptism." Increase Mather, in his Order of the Gospel Professed and Practised in the New England Churches, shows[3] that they disallowed of private baptisms. Upham[4] says that they are commonly, but not necessarily, performed before the whole congregation; sometimes in those meetings which are open only to church members; and sometimes, when there is urgent and satisfactory reason, in private houses.

[1] In Neal, Hist. Pur. i. 166. [2] Rat. Dis. 72—74. [3] Page 62. [4] Rat. Dis. 218.

BAPTISM, *who can administer valid?* — Lord King says,[1] that in the primitive churches it was usually performed by "bishops and pastors;" and that it was permitted to "presbyters and deacons, and, in cases of necessity, even to laymen, to baptize." Thomas Goodwin[2] maintains, that a minister, who is not a pastor, may administer it. This was long controverted by many of the old Congregationalists. (See MINISTERS, *may they administer seals in a church of which they are not pastors?*) This is, I believe, now universally admitted, and has been since the synod of 1648, which virtually admitted it in the fifteenth chapter of the Platform. There is a manuscript letter of Cotton Mather in the Antiquarian Library in Worcester, which cites a case where baptism administered by an Anabaptist deacon was held to be valid. By this it is not meant that it is in order for others than ministers to baptize. The New England elders say,[3] that the administration of the seals is given to ministers, as the stewards of the mysteries of God. John Robinson says,[4] that baptism, "by an unlawful minister, of an unfit subject, and in an unsanctified communion and unlawful manner, is true baptism. unlawfully and falsely administered." This he illustrates by the case of a profane oath, which binds him who takes it. The Genevan disputants say:[5] "The force of the sacraments doth in nowise depend on the person of the minister who delivereth them, but upon the ordinance of God, only so that the same be observed by a public person, rightly called, or at least exercising a public function by a common error. . . . The Donatists, therefore, and such like, did err, who taught that the sacraments, administered by evil ministers, were of no force." "Neither[6] did those spots (papal additions), though filthy and loathsome, annihilate baptism." This is argued at length by Anthony Thysius, "a Low-country man."

[1] Enquiry, part ii. 44. [2] Ch. Gov. 377, 378. [3] Answer to Nine Positions, 67. [4] In Han. i. 269; and Works, iii. 186. [5] Page 165. [6] Page 174.

Here arises another question, viz.

BAPTISM, *is popish, valid?* — This seems to have been admitted by all the early Congregationalists.[1] Francis Johnson maintains the affirmative on this question,[2] because, where God requireth his people to come out of Babylon, "he doth not require them to leave whatsoever is there had, but requireth them to have no more communion with her sins." Henry Johnson argues[3] that the church of Rome must be a true church to render her baptism valid. This is the doctrine of rigid Separatists.

[1] Han. i. 310, 311. [2] Treatise against Two Errors of the Anabaptists, in Han. i. 169. [3] Ib. 320—324.

BAPTISM, *mode of?* — Sprinkling has always been considered by Congregationalists as a valid mode of baptism. So says Cotton Mather in his Ratio Disciplinæ.[1] He gives a description of the ancient manner of baptizing,[2] which is the same as that now in general use. Dwight[3] maintains that it may be administered indifferently, either by sprinkling, affusion, or immersion. Emmons[4] maintains the propriety of sprinkling or pouring, but admits the validity of immersion. In Ware's History of the Old North and New Brick Churches, Boston,[5] there is a record of the baptism of a child by immersion, in 1781, at the particular request of its mother.

[1] Page 79. [2] Ib. 75. [3] Vol. v. 330—342. [4] Vol. v. 473—482. [5] Page 59. Much succinct information on the several points connected with the subject of Baptism may be found in Upham's Ratio Disciplinæ, 212—224.

BENEDICTION. — Coleman, in his Primitive Church,[1] shows at length that there is a great deal of superstitious reverence for a sacerdotal benediction, growing out of the error of a vicarious priesthood in the Christian church. He maintains that it properly means no more than a benevolent wish and an appropriate prayer for a blessing on the people. He asserts[2] that there are no traces of its having been used in the primitive churches during the first and second centuries.

[1] Chap. xiv. pp. 412—426. [2] Ib. 416.

BISHOPS, *same as presbyters.* — Wickliffe is bold to assert that they were the same in the apostolic age.[1] Ærius had maintained the same doctrine several centuries before him.[2] The same was maintained even by the reforming Puritan Episcopalians;[3] and even the then Archbishop of Canterbury asserted[4] that bishops and priests were but one office in the beginning of Christ's religion. See the same doctrine advocated by Lord Brooke,[5] Thomas Hooker,[6] and Cotton Mather.[7] See also Neander, Church History, i. 106. Gibbon, in his Decline and Fall of the Roman Empire,[8] calls them "two appellations, which in their first origin seem to have distinguished the same office and the same order of persons." Dwight discusses the subject at length.[9] See Answer of the Divines to his Majesty's Reasons why he cannot abolish Episcopal Government, 3—8; and their Answer to his Majesty's Second Paper, 1—38.

[1] Punchard, Hist. 162; and Neal, Pur. i. 29, note. [2] Punchard, Hist. 75, 78. [3] Ib. 195, 196. [4] Ib. 198. [5] In Han. ii. 118. [6] Survey, Part ii. 22, 33. [7] Rat. Dis. 200—207. [8] In Han. i. 7. [9] Serm. cl. cli.

BISHOPS, *diocesan, not jure divino.* — This was long ago maintained by even Bellarmine.[1] Lord Brooke[2] maintained the same in the discourse cited in the last article. And John Owen says:[3] "Sir Edward Coke will satisfy any in the rise and fall of Episcopal jurisdiction." The defence of M. Henry's Inquiry into the Nature of Schism[4] says: "The word of God nowhere asserts that bishops are a superior order to presbyters." And,[5] "Though some reformed churches admit a kind of Episcopacy, yet they never pretend a *jus divinum* for it." Mr. Baynes[6] shows that Christ and his apostles did not ordain ordinary ministers with power over others. Macaulay says:[7] "The founders of the Anglican church had retained Episcopacy as an ancient, a decent, and a convenient ecclesiastical polity, but had not declared that form of church government to be of divine institution. In the reign of Elizabeth, Jewell, Cooper, and Whitgift . . . never denied that a Christian community without a bishop might be a pure church."

[1] See Goodwin's Ch. Gov. 67. [2] Han. ii. 118. [3] In ib. iii. 442. [4] Page 17. [5] Page 32. [6] Diocesan's Trial, 24—77. [7] Hist. Eng. i. 58, 59.

BISHOPS *diocesan, not successors of the apostles.* — This follows, of course, from the arguments of the last article, "unless" they succeed them, as says John Robinson,[1] "as darkness succeeds light." Burton pertinently answers Prynne, even to Presbyterian claims to legislative power:[2] "If they who pretend to succeed the apostles will challenge the same liberty which the apostles had, they must first of all show their immediate commission from Christ." — See SUCCESSION, *ministerial, interrupted or uninterrupted?*

[1] In Punchard, Hist. 333; and Works, ii. 436, 437. [2] In Han. ii. 400.

BISHOPS *originally had the care of but one church.* — So Mosheim in Hanbury.[1] Wise[2] quotes Tertullian, Irenæus, Eusebius, Justin Martyr, and Cyprian, to the same point. Punchard, in his View,[3] also quotes Mosheim: "A bishop had charge of a single church, which might ordinarily be contained in a private house. NOR WAS HE ITS HEAD, BUT WAS IN REALITY ITS MINISTER AND SERVANT."

He had no power to ordain or determine any thing, except with the concurrence of the presbyters and brotherhood.

[1] Vol. i. 10. [2] Vindication, 10—12. [3] Page 144.

BISHOPS *should be chosen by the people.* — Wise asserts[1] that they always were thus chosen in the primitive churches. — See PASTOR *chosen by the people.* Congregationalists hold pastor and bishop to be exactly synonymous.

[1] Vindication, 13.

BROWNISTS. — I introduce this article to inquire how far they differed from Congregationalists. Punchard says:[1] "It is evident, that in its essential features it (Brownism) corresponded with Congregationalism as established in New England." Yet the early Congregationalists took great pains not to be identified with the followers of Robert Brown. In an important point they obviously differed. The Brownists did not acknowledge the churches of England to be true churches,[2] whereas this has never been denied by true Congregationalists. It has perhaps been generally supposed that the Brownists held to the utter independency of the churches; but Punchard shows[3] that they held that one church might give advice, counsel, and even reproof, to another; and, if need be, even withdraw fellowship from it, which is all that is ever claimed either by English Independents or strict American Congregationalists. It is highly probable that they often supposed themselves to differ where they were really agreed, as was the case with the churches in Salem and Plymouth, who afterwards found that they were one in sentiment. — See AGREEMENT *of Congregationalists.*

They, however, always kept aloof from the exclusive spirit of the Brownists; and, as these were proscribed, no one wished to identify himself with them further than his own conscience required. Baillie (who wanted a Scots army, 15,000 strong, to promote Presbyterianism) speaks of Robinson[4] as "the most learned, polished, and modest spirit which that sect ever enjoyed." He says: "It would have been truly a marvel if such a man had gone to the end a rigid Separatist. But, alas! his new doctrine, though it was destructive to his old sect, became the occasion of a new one, not very good." Robinson's sentiments he styles Semi-separating Independency. He says: "No Independent will take it well at any man's hand to be called a Brownist." Dr. I. Mather[5] makes the distinction between Brownists and Congregationalists to consist in the question, whether a valid church act can be consummated without the concurrence of both the elders and the brethren; but whoever is much conversant with these subjects can hardly fail to refer this assertion to special pleading. Paget[6] says, Brownists are of three kinds: "Some separate from the church of England for corruptions, and yet confess it and the church of Rome to be a true church, as the followers of Mr. Johnson. Some renounce the church of England, and yet allow of private communion with the godly therein, as Mr. Robinson. Some renounce all communion with that church, as Mr. Ainsworth." — See POWER, *church, is it installed in ministry or brethren?*

[1] Hist. 248. [2] Neal, Puritans, i. 149. [3] Hist. 248. [4] Han. iii. 132. [5] Disq. Ecc. Councils, Preface, iv. [6] Arrow against Separation, in Han. i. 325.

CALLING *of a minister, in what does it consist?* — Congregationalists have ever held that it consists, not in ordination, by the imposition of hands, but in the election of the people; that the ordination is nothing but the recognizing of the election, and not the substance of it.[1] Hence their doctrine is, that it is the lifting up of the hands of the brethren,[2] and not the laying on of the hands of the elders, which constitutes the essence of the pastoral relation. Isaac Chauncy,[3] after speaking of an immediate call, as of the apostles, says a mediate call is that which Christ makes by the instrumentality of a church. The consummation of the call is made by the free acceptance of the person called. — See PASTOR, ORDINATION, IMPOSITION OF HANDS, ELDERS, MINISTER, *calling, what?*

[1] R. Mather's Ans. to Rutherford, in Han. ii. 187; Goodwin, Ch. Gov. 195. [2] Greek of Acts xiv. 23, in opposition to King James's and the Bishops' garbled translation of the passage. [3] Divine Institution of Congregational Churches, 64, 65.

CATHOLICISM *of Congregational churches.* — A very prevalent error is the belief that the early Congregationalists were very exclusive in their religion. One of the dividing points between them and the Brownists was the question of fellowshipping the English and Reformed churches (see BROWNISTS). This was also one of their great points of controversy with Roger Williams.[1] Cotton Mather[2] quotes the words of "a worthy man who walked in our way: 'I will be one with every one that is one with Christ.'"[3] He says the churches of New England endeavor to make their ecclesiastical state a visible sermon to the world upon the requisites of men's being received into heaven at the last. Governor Winslow says[4] that Mr. Parker and Mr. Noyes of Newbury, and Mr. Hubbard of Hingham, were for Presbytery, yet were never molested; Presbyterians might have a complete Presbytery near Ipswich and Newbury, and it was answered affirmatively by the court that they might have one. One minister denieth the baptism of infants, and divers of his congregation are fallen in with him, and the government only moved the elders to try to convince and reclaim him. — See CONFESSIONS OF FAITH, COMMUNION, CREEDS, SEPARATION, SCHISM, TOLERATION.

[1] Winthrop, i. 53. [2] Rat. Dis. 37. [3] Ib. 142. [4] Nar. in Young's Chron. of the Pilgrims, 402—405.

CENSURES, *power of, in the church.* — The Savoy Declaration[1] says: "Every church hath power in itself to exercise and execute all those censures appointed by him (Christ) in the way and order prescribed in the gospel." — See ADMONITION, SUSPENSION, EXCOMMUNICATION, APPEALS, CHURCHES *subject to no jurisdiction out of themselves*, CONSOCIATIONS, JURISDICTION, KEYS; POWER, *church*.

[1] Inst. of Cong. Churches, art. xviii. in Han. iii. 547.

CEREMONIES. — Bradshaw[1] argues strongly against conformity to these, for instance the sign of the cross in baptism, because conforming to them is not keeping ourselves from idols. Robert Parker wrote a volume "Against Symbolizing with Antichrist in Ceremonies, especially the Cross in Baptism." He powerfully argues that a host of evils grow out of it. Dr. Osgood[2] says "We had no consecrated churches, no burial or matrimonial service; . . . because we had nothing but the Bible, they (Episcopalians) were confident that we had no religion." Dr. Ames, in his "Fresh Suit against Human Ceremonies,"[3] asserts that "the Waldenses made much the same objections to human ceremonies which we do." He quotes one of their prominent men: "All customs in the church, which in the gospel they don't read, they do contemn; they affirm that those things which are appointed by the bishops and prelates are not to be observed, because they are the tradition of men, and not of God."[4] "Even the inquisitor Sylvester says, that to interpret human precepts, in the court of conscience, belongs to every one as touching his own practice." John Howe says:[5] "Stillingfleet complains because we dare not consent with them to the additions which belong not to religion. While they (Dissenters) cannot judge the ceremonies lawful, how can they apprehend themselves bound to be without the means of salvation which Christ's charter entitles them to?" Pierce, in his Vindication of Dissenters,[6] quotes Wickliffe: "All human traditions, that are not taught in the gospel, are superfluous and wicked." He shows[7] that the Bishop of St. David's inquired in the Hampton Court Conference how he should answer certain objections against the ceremonies, as the sign of the cross; and was forbidden to reply to the answer given him. He shows[8] that the church has no right to impose kneeling at the sacrament, . . . and then refuse it to those that will not conform. Ames, in his Marrow of Sacred Divinity, says:[9] "No worship instituted is lawful, unless it hath God for the Author and Ordainer of it. . . . Of like kind with images are all those ceremonies which are ordained of men for mystical or religious signification." One of the Genevan Disputants says:[10] "Whosoever do break out into that boldness, that either they do coin new sacraments, or *add* unto those that were appointed of the Lord, or detract any tittle from them, they are guilty of treason against the Majesty of the Highest." Another of them says:[11] "It is not lawful for an angel in heaven to ordain any new sacramental rites." Hence he condemns the "curious additions" to the sacrament of baptism. — See Habits, Kneeling, Authority *human*, Indifferents, Idolatry, Liberty of Conscience, Non-conformists, Prayer *prescribed*, Schism, Separation, Uniformity.

[1] Treatise on Worship and Ordinances, 98—116. [2] Dudlean Lect. 30. [3] Page 8. [4] Ib. 79. [5] Works, 170, 171. [6] Pages 4—6.

[7] Ib. 158—163. [8] Ib. 490. [9] Pages 271, 274. [10] Page 162. [11] Page 173.

CHAPLAINS. — "Private chaplains, to minister to families or neighborhoods in time of divine service of the churches where they dwell, is considered disorderly."[1] "Though the communicants in the churches of New England are not constantly tied to their own pastors, yet, if they should not ordinarily hear them when they are able to do it, the omission would be thought a disorder."[2] John Milton says:[3] "Scripture knows no chaplains; and, the church not owning them, they are left to the fate of the sons of Sceva the Jew. . . . Public prayer did not pertain only to the office of a priest: David, Solomon, and Jehoshaphat might pray in public, even in the temple, while the priest stood and heard. . . . What ailed the king that he could not chew his own matins without the priest's *ore tenus?*"

[1] C. Mather, Rat. Dis. 62. [2] Ib. [3] Eikonoklastes, 163, 167.

CHRISTIANS, *the weakest, to be received to the churches.* — "It is not eminency of holiness that we look to in the entertainment of members, but uprightness of the heart."[1] — See MEMBERS, *church.*

[1] Hooker's Survey, part i. 23.

CHRISTMAS. — This, with other holy days, is rejected by Congregationalists, on the ground that they are enjoined on no higher authority than that of men. Indeed, they do not see cause to believe that it is appointed on the true anniversary of the birthday of our Saviour.[1] — See HOLY DAYS, CEREMONIES, IDOLATRY, AUTHORITY *human*.

[1] Ainsworth's Arrow Against Idolatry, in Han. i. 237.

CHURCH, *what constitutes one?* — It was the united opinion of the early Congregationalists, that any number of persons, united together by a covenant either expressed or implied, for the worship of God, constitute a church. John Robinson says:[1] "And for the gathering of a church I do tell you, that in what place soever, whether by preaching the gospel by a true minister, by a false minister, by no minister, or by reading and conference, or by any other means of publishing it, two or three faithful people do arise, separating themselves from the world into the fellowship of the gospel, they are a church truly gathered, though never so weak." In his Apology[2] he defines a church to be a company of faithful, holy people, with their seed, called by the word of God into a public covenant with Christ, and among themselves, for mutual fellowship, in the use of all the means of God's glory and their salvation. Burton[3] says: "*Ekklesia*, the church, is properly a congregation of believers called out from the rest of the world; for so saith the Lord, 2 Cor. vi. 17." The Saint's Apology says,[4] this consent or agreement ought to be explicit, for the well-being, but not necessarily for the being, of a true church; for it may be implied by frequent acts of communion, &c. Dr. Ames says:[5] "The first thing that doth make actually a church is calling; whence also it hath taken both its name and definition." Jacob's Church Confession says:[6] "They (the English congregations) are a true political church, as they are a company of visible Christians, united, by their own consent, to serve God; . . . therefore we commune with them upon occasion." Euring says:[7] "Search the Scriptures, and you shall find that every true visible church of Christ must consist of a company of people separated from the froward generation of the world by the gospel, and joined or built together into a holy communion and fellowship among themselves." The voluntary covenant, either expressed or implied, our fathers considered a *sine qua non* to a regular church organization. They therefore rejected the ideas of a national church, and of the full communion of those not in voluntary personal covenant.[8]

In Burton's Modest Answer to Prynne's Full Reply in 1645, it is shown[9] that a mere implicit covenant is sufficient to the being, though not to the well-being, of a church. Thomas Goodwin argues,[10] that a church must be composed of those who not only make confession, as Peter did, but are united together for divine worship, ordinances, and church government; and[11] that it is "a holy nation, . . . a household of faith, . . . a holy temple," and thus is an organized body; and[12] that it is an instituted body, assembling in one place, built by a special covenant. In his Catechism[13] he shows that the ancient converts *joined* themselves to the church, and that a covenant is implied in their authority to judge and discipline their members, as they have no power to "judge them that are without." Bradshaw says:[14] "They hold and maintain, that every congregation or assembly of men, ordinarily joined together in the true worship of God, is a true visible church of Christ." Penry says:[15] "This church (Christ's) I believe to be a company of those whom the word calleth saints, which do not only profess in word that they know God, but are subject to his laws and ordinances indeed." The Confession of the Low Country Exiles, art. xxxiii., says:[16] "Christians are willingly to join together in Christian communion and orderly covenant; and, by free confession of the faith and obedience of Christ, to unite themselves into peculiar and visible congregations." J. Davenport[17] says: "The church of Christ arises from the coadunition or knitting together of many saints into one by a holy covenant, whereby they, as lively stones, are built into a spiritual house, 1 Pet. ii. 4, 5. Though church covenant be common to all churches in its general nature, yet there is a special combination which gives a peculiar being to one Congregational church and its members, distinct from all others." — See also, for corroboration of the same sentiments, Burrough's Irenicum, in Han. iii. 115; Bartlett's Model, in ib. 239; Savoy Declaration, in ib. 545, 546; Camb. Platform, chap. 2, sect. 6, and chap. 4; Wise's Vindication, chap. 2; Lord King's Enquiry, part i. 3, 7; Hooker's Survey, part i. 46; Hutchinson's Hist. Mass. 370, 371; Hall's Puritans, 294; S. Mather's Apology, 2; Increase Mather's Dis. Ecc. Councils, preface; Owen's Complete Works, xix. 213, 505, and xx. 370, 371;

Watts's Works, iii. 198, 250; Cotton Mather's Rat. Dis. 10, 11; Eaton's and Taylor's Defence, 44; Letchford's Plain Dealing, epistle to the reader; Dwight, Serm. cxlix.; Emmons, v. 444—446; and Principles of Church Order by the Congregational Union of England and Wales, art. i. in Hanbury, iii. 599. — See COVENANT.

[1] Ans. to Bernard, in Punchard's Hist. 331; and Han. i. 214; and Works, ii. 232. [2] Ib. 389, note; and Works, iii. 427. [3] Protestation Protested, in Han. ii. 73. [4] Ib. 231. [5] Marrow of Sacred Divinity, 135. [6] Art. viii. in Hanbury, i. 296. [7] Answer to Ten Counter Demands, ib. 367. [8] Richard Mather's Apology, 5—25, and Church Gov. and Church Cov. 9, 11; Ans. of the N. E. Elders, 75; Cotton's Way of the Churches, 2. [9] Page 25. [10] Ch. Gov. chap. iii. 49—54. [11] Ib. 242. [12] Ib. 249, 251, 256. [13] Pages 7, 8. [14] English Puritanism, in Neal's Puritans, i. 248. [15] Declaration of Allegiance to her Majesty, in Han. i. 81. [16] Ib. 95. [17] Power of Congregational Churches, in ib. ii. 62.

CHURCH, *of what constituted?* — Lord King defines it:[1] All professors of religion; — a particular church; — a meeting-house; — once only in the Fathers, a collection of churches; — and sometimes the invisible church. Isaac Chauncy[2] shows that the word *church* is derived from *Kuriou oikos*, — House of God; that there is no just ground for applying such a trope (church) to a house for a public assembly; that men's laws cannot establish churches, but they must be built after the pattern which God shows; that a true church may be discovered by its being on the foundation, Jesus Christ; by the visible matter, living stones; by the form, fashion, and frame, according to the gospel

It is no church if either of these be wholly wanting; faulty where these are defective. Lobb[3] quotes Humphrey, a great anti-separatist: "The Congregationalists stand here. The church of Christ is a number of truly faithful, regenerate persons." Dr. Emmons[4] says: "There is an invisible and a visible church. The invisible church comprehends all real saints. By a visible church we are to understand a society of visible saints." Greenwood,[5] being asked, "Is not the whole land, as now ordered, a true church?" answered emphatically, "No." For this and similar sentiments, he became a martyr. Dr. Hopkins says,[6] that the word *church* "signifies an assembly of men, called and collected together for some special purpose. The church of Christ on earth consists of those who are united together as professed friends to Christ and believers in him, are under explicit engagements to serve him," &c. . . . "Whenever a number of persons voluntarily unite together, under profession of holiness in Christ, to attend to his institutions and ordinances, they are a church." The second chapter of Cambridge Platform establishes the same position.

[1] Part i. 2—5. [2] Divine Inst. Cong. Churches, 1—8. [3] True Dissenter, 98. [4] Vol. v. 444. [5] In Han. i. 62. [6] System, ii. 224, 225.

CHURCH, *mode of constituting.* — A summary of the usual ceremonies in constituting a church is given in Cotton's Way of the Churches,[1] and Cot. Mather's Ratio Disciplinæ,[2] which does not essentially differ from those now generally practised, save that the brethren of the churches invited, nominated as many delegates as they chose. In Cotton's time, however, the candidates appointed one of their own number to read the covenant, and one of the council to give them the right hand of fellowship. Whoever reads the more ancient treatises on Congregationalism, and proceeds to the more modern ones, will perceive a gradual increase to the prerogatives claimed by councils. "*Facilis descensus.*" Letchford[3] says: "At gathering of churches, one of the messengers examines the candidates; and, on acknowledging their covenant, he pronounces them a true church, and gives them the right hand of fellowship. So did Mr. Welde at the founding of Weymouth Church." A church was gathered at Lynn[4] for Long Island. He quotes[5] from the Answer of the Elders in Boston, to a question which he put to them: Though it be not usual, "yet it is lawful to gather a church without other churches and ministers to advise." Dr. Harris[6] states that the first church in Dorchester was gathered in Plymouth, England. Mr. White preached in the forenoon, and in the afternoon Messrs. Wareham and Maverick were chosen and separated to the care of the intended congregation, and they preached in the afternoon. The formation of Richard Mather's church in Dorchester was for a time delayed, because the members failed to satisfy the council of their experimental piety.[7]

[1] Pages 8—10. [2] Pages 3—12. [3] Plain Dealing, in Mass. Hist. Col. ser. iii. vol. iii. 65. [4] Ib. 98. [5] Ib. 107. [6] Ib. ser. i. vol. ix. 148. [7] Hubbard's Hist. Mass. 273.

CHURCH, *ministers not necessary to constitute.* — Barrowe[1] shows that otherwise the existence of churches would depend on the will of ministers. But the "faithful are commanded to gather together in Christ's name; . . . for the kingdom of God consisteth not in word, but in power." Cambridge Platform declares[2] that officers are not necessary to the simple being of churches. Goodwin[3] says: "It is Christ's prerogative alone to build and erect a church, *without* the intervention of ministerial ecclesiastical power to derive that power to them. . . . Churches to be erected may and ought to have the direction and consent of neighbor churches, because a new sister is to be added to and associated with them; but they receive no power from them to become a church." "Nor[4] are ministers or their power necessary to the first gathering of a church. They may have a hand in it by directing and exhorting to it, . . . but the power is in ourselves immediately. . . . They (ministers) are to be set *in* churches, so there were churches gathered ere elders were made in them." — See Letchford's quotation from the Answer of Boston Elders to his question, mentioned in previous article, viz. CHURCH, *mode of constituting;* CHURCHES *begun without officers, &c.*

[1] Some of the Reasons of our Separation, in Han. i. 54. [2] Chap. vi. sect. 2. [3] Church Gov. 208. [4] Ib. 257.

CHURCH, *what number of members may constitute?* — Cotton,[1] Richard Mather and William Tompson,[2] and Cotton Mather,[3] all maintain that seven males are the least number that can be properly constituted into a church, because they held that number necessary to a case of discipline, as in Matt. xviii. This assumes that neither the accuser nor the witness to the second step may vote, and that the rest of the church must outnumber the accuser, the witness, and the accused. Each of these points seems, however, to need proof before it is implicitly adopted. John Robinson (see on CHURCH, *what constitutes?*) limits it only to two or three; and many of the old Congregational writers[4] supposed this to be the meaning of Matt. xviii. 20. Cambridge Platform says[5] that it "ought not to be of greater number than may ordinarily meet together conveniently in one place, nor fewer than can conveniently carry on church work." Prince[6] enumerates among the principles of Robinson's church, "A particular church should consist of no more than can conveniently watch over each other, and meet in one congregation." Eaton and Taylor[7] say, "Seven, eight, or nine may make a church." See Upham, Rat. Dis. 55, 56; Punchard, View, 47. — See CHURCHES, *distinct bodies.*

[1] Way of the Churches, 53. [2] Ans. to Herle, in Han. ii. 172. [3] Rat. Dis. 2. [4] As Goodwin, Ch. Gov. 257. [5] Chap. iii. sect. 4. [6] Chronology, 91. [7] Defence, 9.

CHURCH, *may one, have branches?* — Hooker[1] informs us that, in his time, a church sometimes sent out a colony, with part of its officers, before they were separated into a distinct church. "Mr. Wheelwright[2] was minister to a branch of Boston

Church, in a place since called Braintree, where the town had some lands." This practice was, however, generally discouraged, as it was the very thing known to have helped to diocesan and metropolitan domination over the primitive churches. — See Punchard's Hist. 20. Also CHURCH, *what number of members may constitute?*

Survey, part i. 128. [2] Eliot, Biog. Dict. 483.

CHURCH, *the majority constitute.* — John Robinson and his church in Leyden advocate this principle (in a letter to a church in London),[1] even where that majority are in error, and even heterodox. Dr. Hopkins[2] says, in matters wherein the church as a body are to decide and act, they must be determined by the voice of the major part. He shows that the minority must submit and conform, unless against their conscientious views of right; in which case no one has any right to control them. — See MAJORITIES, MINORITIES.

[1] In Han. i. 449, 450; and Works, iii. 385. [2] System, ii. 226.

CHURCH, *officers of.* — Congregationalists in all ages have agreed that pastors and deacons are church officers; that pastors and bishops are the same in Scripture language; and that the special duty of deacons is to take care of the poor, and of the temporal interests of the church. Formerly they generally maintained, that teachers and ruling elders, and, to some extent, that deaconesses or widows, were of divine appointment, rulers and helps in the churches. This opinion, however, was *never uni-*

versal among them. John Owen[1] held to essentially the same organization which prevails in New England at the present day, and confounds pastors, teachers, and elders in one and the same office. As early as 1679, this had become the *general practice* in Massachusetts. The synod of that year, however, lament[2] "that there is, in most of the churches, but one teaching officer." (See PASTOR, TEACHER, MINISTER, EVANGELIST, ELDERS, DEACONS, WIDOWS.) Many churches have of late added standing committees, which are recommended in the Congregational Manual,[3] with "special duty to institute discipline for public offences, if the same be not seasonably done by other members." This method of delegating duties is, however, questionable. Mitchell,[4] though he approves of such committees, with "a general oversight of the ordinary interests of the church," cautions lest they be invested with powers almost identical with a Presbyterian session. To commit the watch and care of a church to a permanent committee, so as to discharge the church as a body from their duties, is not Congregationalism.[5] — See POWER OF CHURCH *cannot be given away nor delegated;* OFFICERS *not to be multiplied;* OFFICERS, *what?*

[1] Catechism, quest. xxiii.; Complete Works, xix. 519. [2] White's Lamentations, in Wise's Vindication, 167. [3] Page 28. [4] Guide, 142. [5] Ib. 143.

CHURCH, *in what sense one.* — John Robinson[1] says that it is "one in nature, not one in number, as one ocean. Neither was the church at Rome, in the apostle's days, more one with the church at Corinth than was the baptism of Peter one with Paul's baptism, or than Peter and Paul were one." John Milton[2] says: "The Christian church is universal, not tied to nation, diocese, or parish, but consisting of many particular churches, *complete* in themselves." See Cambridge Platform, chap. ii. sect. 3, 4; Cotton's Way of the Churches, 10; Hooker's Survey, part i. 62, 81, 220, 253—274, part iii. 19.— See CHURCHES, *distinct bodies.*

[1] Apology, in Han. i. 374. [2] To Salmasius, in Han. iii. 373.

CHURCH, *duty of believers to join.*— Eaton and Taylor[1] say: "So long as a believer doth not join himself to some particular church, he is without, in the apostle's sense, 1 Cor. v. 12." See the duty advocated in Owen, xix. 215, and xx. 188; but especially in Ainsworth's Communion of Saints, in Han. i. 278, 279; and Cambridge Platform, ch. iv. sect. 6, which treats of the evils of not performing the duty. Dr. Emmons, v. 460—464, gives six "reasons why the subjects of special grace will choose to join the church, and enter into covenant with God."— See Punchard, View, 37, 38; Upham, Rat. Dis. 49, 50.

[1] Defence, 74.

CHURCH, *Romish, is it a true one?*— Ainsworth, in his reply to Johnson,[1] maintains that it is Antichrist; that there is as much difference between the church of Rome now and of old, as between the bishop of Rome now and the bishop then: "The antichristian church is to be esteemed in a state of damnation, though some of God's elect hidden ones are in the same." Johnson had maintained the contrary in his Treatise on the Reformed Churches.[2]

[1] In Han. i. 323. [2] Ib. 314—320.

CHURCH-MEETINGS, *by whom called.*—While ruling elders were considered a separate order of church officers, this privilege and duty was supposed to be vested in the church presbytery in the bench of elders. When there came to be but one elder in a certain church, he prevented a church meeting for fourteen years.[1] Cotton Mather[2] says: "Nor do the New England churches think that *ordinarily* a church meeting may be regularly held without the consent of their pastors." It will be evident, however, that the pastors have not usually been considered as having power to prevent church meetings, if we consult the arguments deduced under these heads, viz.:— MINISTERS, *people may do their work for them if they refuse;* OFFICERS *abdicate when they refuse to do their duties;* CHURCHES *begun without officers, and may continue despite of officers;* GOVERNMENT, *church, in the people;* POWER, *church, installed in ministry or brethren?*

[1] White's Lamentations in Wise's Vindication, 166. [2] Rat. Dis. 164.

CHURCHES, *distinct bodies, i.e. not parts of one consolidated one.*—Richard Mather, in his Apology,[1] shows from several passages of Scripture, as 1 Thes.

ii. 14 and Rev. i. 4, that they were considered distinct bodies in the days of the apostles. In his Church Government,[2] he shows that they consisted of no more than could meet in one congregation, united into one body by a holy covenant;—that those within the visible church must necessarily be members of particular churches;—that the duty of excommunicating incorrigible offenders belongs, not to a universal, but to a particular church;—and that "judging them that are within," implies that they were in particular churches. He quotes Mr. Baine,[3] that, though churches have power to govern themselves, yet, for greater edification, they confederate not to use or exercise their power, but with mutual communion, one *asking* counsel and consent of the other. And he says,[4] that "to bind churches to do no weighty matter without the counsel and consent of classes were to bind them to be imperfect." By the above assertions he seems to advocate the advisory, not the judicial power of councils. Cotton[5] shows that a church must be such a body that an offended brother can tell his case to, and with them cast the offender out of the church. He speaks[6] of "the *chimera* of a universal visible church." Burton[7] challenges the evidence of any but particular churches for the first four or five hundred years. John Robinson, in his Apology,[8] is very plain and positive on this point. T. Goodwin[9] shows that they must be distinct,—from the nature and Scripture process of discipline; from the Scripture examples of their conduct; from individual churches being addressed as whole bodies, a whole lump, whole flock, &c.; and their being so often addressed in Scripture in the plural number. The doctrine of distinct churches[10] was one of the main positions of the supplication of the exiles and others to King James I. on his accession. Henry Jacob, in his Divine Beginning and Institution of Christ's Church, says:[11] "Christ teacheth, yea requireth, in Matt. xviii. 17, that this visible and ministerial church shall be ever of one entire outward form, viz. of this special form of a particular ordinary congregation and none other, . . . and the very word *ekklesia* doth properly signify so." In his Declaration it was one of the main positions,[12] "that a true church, under the gospel, containeth no more congregations but one." Francis Johnson[13] infers, that God hath not ordained any other than particular churches, from what is recorded in the Bible of the *seven* churches of Asia generally, and particularly of those at Jerusalem, Lystra, Iconium, Antioch, Troas, Ephesus, Rome, Cenchrea, Corinth, Galatia, Philippi, Colosse, Laodicea, and Thessalonica. The distinctness of churches is urged in the Apologetical Narrative of the Independents in the Westminister Assembly.[14] So it is in Bartlett's Model.[15] John Owen says:[16] "I do not say absolutely that particular churches are not *the* parts of the catholic visible, in any sense, but that they are not *so* parts of it that it should be made up by them and of them for the order and purpose of an instituted church." He shows, in his Original of Churches, chap. iv.[17] that a church means an assembly, and therefore has reference to those who assemble in one place. And, in his Nature of Schism, chap. vii.[18] he shows that it was acknowledged by Episcopalians, that a church originally consisted of no more than could meet in one place; and their bishops were Congregational, and not diocesan. Lord King says:[19] "I find the word *church* once used by Cyprian for a collection of churches; as the church of Africa and Numidia; otherwise I cannot remember that I ever met with it in this sense in any of the writings of this or the rest of the fathers: but, whenever they would speak of the Christians in any kingdom or province, they always said, in the plural, 'the churches;' never, in the singular, 'the church' of such a kingdom or province." So much for the testimony of an impartial witness. The Boston ministers, in 1690,[20] maintain that particular church organizations are indispensable to scriptural discipline. Isaac Chauncy[21] shows that the Spirit of God always speaks of churches, in their respective places, as distinct bodies; each one entire in itself. There is not an epistle written to the catholic visible church. Each particular congregation had its proper elders, relating to *it*, and not to the catholic visible. So Hunter, in his Life of Oliver Heywood.[22] Robert Hall[23] reasons very clearly on this point. Ames[24] shows from Rev. i. 4 and 2 Cor. viii. 1, 19, that there are as many visible churches as there are congregations. "Neither[25] is this church, that is instituted by God, properly national, provincial, or diocesan; which forms were brought in by men; but is parochial, or of one congregation; the members whereof are combined among themselves, and do ordinarily meet in one place, to the public exercises of religion." Dr. Hopkins[26] says that every society of visible believers is . . . called a church; as the church at Antioch, the church at Ephesus, the churches in Judea, &c. — See CHURCH, *what constitutes? In what sense is it one? What number of members constitute?* See also Robinson's Apology, in Han. i. 372, 373; and Upham, Rat. Dis. 44—48.

[1] Pages 11, 14. [2] Pages 9—11. [3] Ib. 65. [4] Ib. [5] Way of the Churches, 1, 2. [6] Ib. 10. [7] Answer to Prynne's Full Reply, 21. [8] In Hanbury, i. 372—374; and Works, iii. 12—17. [9] Ch. Gov. 51, 52, 63, 235; and Catechism, 6. [10] Han. i. 114. [11] Ib. 229. [12] Ib. 231. [13] Reformed Churches, in ib. 314. [14] Ib. ii. 225. [15] Ib. iii. 246—248. [16] Vindication Cong. Churches, ib. 457. [17] Vol. xx. 122. [18] Vol. xix. 214. [19] Enquiry, part i. 4, 5. [20] Principles of the Protestant Religion, 129. [21] Divine Inst. Cong. Churches, 34, 35. [22] Page 58. [23] Vol. i. 332, 333. [24] Marrow of Sacred Divinity, 139. [25] Ib. 178. [26] System, ii. 224.

CHURCHES, *instituted bodies.* — Dr. Goodwin wrote the first two books of his Church Government to prove "that the order and government of the churches are established by divine institution; . . . that Christ has settled ordinances for worship and discipline, which are to continue to the end of the world; . . . that a Congregational church is thus of divine institution; . . . that Christ instituted such a church in Matt. xviii.; . . . that such Congregational churches were primitive and apostolical; . . . and that Christ hath not only instituted a Congregational church, but appointed what the extent and limits of it should be." The treatise is too extensive to admit of even an epitome in a single article. Suffice it to say, that, when the student has read and digested the whole work of four hundred and sixty-two folio pages, it will not be easy for him to conclude that Congregationalism is a nonentity. Then let him read the four Mathers, Owen, Watts, Isaac Chauncy, and a host of others, and he may begin to mistrust that there were giants in the earth even in those scouted puritanical days. Owen,[1] in his Original of Churches, chaps. i. iii., shows that God only can change the state or dispensation of his church; that the original of their church state is derived directly from Christ, as to their right and title; that whatever is required in them, by the light of nature, is of divine institution; and that, as the Scriptures require a church, it is lawful for Christians to gather into one. Samuel Mather[2] also asserts that the ecclesiastical state is a divine institution. Davenport says:[3] "Because all nations could not be joined together in one visible church, the Lord Jesus instituted a Congregational church, and calls every Congregational church his church." — See Chauncy's Divine Institution of Cong. Churches, 23, 30, 51, 52; and Upham, Rat. Dis. 34, 47. See GOVERNMENT, *church, instituted. Not lawful to alter. Not varied to suit circumstances.*

[1] Vol. xx. 65—79, 99. [2] Apology, 31. [3] Power of Congregational Churches, in Han. ii. 63.

CHURCHES, *the primitive, were Congregational.* — Goodwin argues this point at large in the sixth, seventh, eighth, and ninth chapters of his second book on Church Government, — from instances of primitive churches planted by the apostles, as that of Corinth, required to do church-work within itself, by the power of the Lord Jesus Christ, as to judge them that were within, excommunicate, and the like; — from several texts, as 1 Cor. xi. 18; Rom. xvi. 1—5; 1 Cor. iv. 17. He shows,[1] that the word *church* never means an assembly of officers, but of the people. He also argues the same from instances of the churches settled by the apostles in the lesser cities, and also from the fact that the churches of the several cities were entire churches, having government within themselves. Even Archbishop Whitgift[2] declares that the "state of the church was popular in the apostles' time." See Murdock's Mosheim, ed. 1832, i. 81—86. Neander says[3] that each individual church had a bishop and presbyter of its own, and assumed to itself the rights of a little distinct republic or commonwealth. Samuel Mather[4] maintains that every church, for the first two hundred years, was Congregational, and that churches were then always spoken of in the plural number. And[5] he quotes from Father Paul of Venice, and Cyprian, to show that the church in the beginning had altogether a democratic form, and how it was gradually changed. Isaac Chauncy[6] shows that "either a Congregational church is of divine institution, or else God hath no instituted church." — See Punchard, View, 122; also Cotton's Way of the Churches Cleared, chap. iv. 93—99. See CHURCHES, *distinct bodies.*

[1] Page 73. [2] In Han. i. 10. [3] In Hall's Puritans, 307. [4] Apology, 10—13. [5] Ib. 27, 28. [6] Divine Inst. Cong. Churches, 30.

CHURCHES *subject to no external jurisdiction.*— This has ever been a cardinal doctrine of strict Congregationalism. Bradshaw[1] says: "Christ has not subjected any church or congregation to any other superior ecclesiastical jurisdiction than that which is within itself; . . . no other churches or spiritual officers have power to censure or punish them, but only to counsel and advise them." Dr. Price says[2] of the Independents in the Westminster Assembly: "They were distinguished from the Presbyterians by maintaining the absolute independence of each church, so far as jurisdiction and discipline are concerned, and by denying the communication of spiritual power in ordination." Themselves explain, in their Apologetical Narrative:[3] "Not that they claim an entire independency with regard to other churches; for they agree, that, in all cases of offence, the offending is to submit to an open examination by other neighbor churches; and, on their persisting in their error or miscarriage, then they are to renounce all Christian communion with them till they repent; which is all the authority or ecclesiastical power which one church has over another." This they call a "middle way between Brownism and Presbytery." Davenport[4] held the power of every particular church to be chief in its own particular matters. The publisher to his Power of Congregational Churches says:[5] "There are two things which run through this whole discourse, and are legible in every line of it: First, that the power of churches is confined to their *res propria*, their own proper matters; second, that there is not any spiritual church power, to which they are, by the institution of Christ, subjected; — two grand pillar-principles of the Congregational way." The treatise on the Institution of Churches, in the Savoy Confession, says:[6] "Besides these particular churches, there is not instituted any church more extensive or catholic;" and the whole connection shows that they are subject to no jurisdiction out of themselves. Hooker[7] clearly admits the same principle, and only admits counsel "to clear the truth." In Hutchinson's History of Massachusetts[8] it is laid down as a fundamental principle of Congregationalism, "That there is no jurisdiction, to which particular churches are or ought to be subject, by way of authoritative censure." And the Congregational Union of England and Wales, in 1833, re-affirmed the same doctrine in their Declaration of Faith and Order,[9] art. iv.: "They believe that the New Testament authorizes every Christian church . . . to stand independent, and irresponsible to all authority, saving that only supreme and divine Head of the church, the Lord Jesus Christ." Letchford, in his Plain Dealing,[10] says: "No church or officers have power over another, but by advice or counsel voluntarily given or besought." Dr. Stiles says:[11] "Our churches acknowledge no jurisdiction of sister churches over them, but hold themselves to be capable, and to have the power, to determine all matters of discipline that arise in a particular church." And[12] "the moment jurisdiction enters, like creating Cæsar perpetual dictator, the beginning of the absolute loss of liberty commences. . . . The exigencies of the Christian church can never be such as to legitimate, much less to render it wise, to erect any body of men into a standing judicatory over them." Punchard[13] quotes Mosheim, Murdock's edition, i. 80—86, abundantly sustaining the same doctrines. — See COUNCIL; SYNOD; CHURCHES *distinct bodies;* POWER, *church, installed in ministry or brethren?*

[1] English Puritanism, chap. ii. art. 4, in Neal's Puritans, i. 248. [2] Ib. 462, note. [3] Ib. 492. [4] Paget, in Han. i. 541, 545. [5] Ib. ii. 61. [6] Art. vi. 26; iii. 545. [7] Survey, part iii. 40—44. [8] Vol. i. 371. [9] In Han. iii. 600. [10] In Mass. Hist. Soc. Col. series iii. vol. iii. 74. [11] Conven. Serm. 45. [12] Pages 89, 91. [13] View, 145, 146.

CHURCHES *discipline each other, but not juridically.* — Goodwin[1] says: "Churches proceed with churches not *politice*, or as armed by Christ with juridical power of giving up to Satan; but they proceed and deal with each other *modo mystico*, or with a moral declarative power only." He shows[2] that though one church has a right to call upon another to give them satisfaction, yet it may not abridge their liberty. He maintains[3] that synods have no juridical power thus to judge churches, and[4] that this power to discipline is only in a moral way, in distinction from an instituted one. Book v. chap. 12, he devotes to showing that though no church nor churches have power to excommunicate another church, yet they have power to declare non-communion with them; but that they are a church still. The apologists in the Westminister Assembly[5] hold the same doctrine. Cotton, in his Keys,[6] seems to advocate the same, yet in the next page he appears to hold that there was a kind of juridical power vested in synods, though he had just asserted that there was none. The framers of the Cambridge Platform certainly held that they had no such power; for they speak[7] of the third way of communion, by way of admonition, and of non-communion with the erring members only· and[8] they expressly deny juridical authority to synods also. In 1744 an instance of such discipline occurred in the case of the First Church in Gloucester *v.* the Second Church in Bradford.[9] The church in Bradford admitted the right thus to discipline, but denied being obnoxious in the case at issue. The defendants triumphed.[10] Samuel Mather[11] recognizes this right of disciplining and withdrawing communion from other churches, and says that it is thus that Congregational churches can be distinguished from Brownistical. (It probably cannot, however, be made to appear that either Brown or his immediate followers denied this right of disciplining by non-communion. See BROWNISTS. See also Punchard's History, 248.) Cotton Mather[12] describes the details of a method of procedure in such cases. He cites[13] *the single* instance in which the churches represented in council proceeded thus to withdraw communion. The Answer of the New England Elders to the Nine Positions[14] recognizes the power of the churches to withdraw communion from a church which should unjustly persist in deposing its minister. Burton[15] shows the manner in which this is done, and "a brotherly account required, without selling over the liberty of each church to others, so that it ceases to be a free church of Christ under his only jurisdiction." The Independents in the Westminister Assembly[16] maintain the same doctrine. Dr. Eckley[17] shows that, in case churches abuse their liberty, other churches may withdraw communion from them; which, however, should be done with great caution. In the official narrative of the proceedings of an ecclesiastical council convened in Salem in 1734, it appears[18] that the council assembled on the 20th of July, and sent a "Letter of Solemn Advice" to the church, threatening them with non-communion unless they complied; and adjourned to the 15th of October to give them time. The council, re-assembled,[19] executed their threatening, still giving a probation of three months, and wrote to the churches in the Commonwealth to sustain them. (See Felt's Annals of Salem, ii. 594, 595.) The pamphlets on this controversy fill a whole volume. Mr. Fiske the minister, and a majority of his church, did not approve of this "third way of communion;" disregarded the sentence, and outlived the storm. (See COUNCIL *expires when, &c.*) President Stiles[20] says: "No church was hereticated for not receiving the result of a synod." — See Upham, Rat. Dis. 177, 209; Punchard, View, 116, 185; both sustaining and describing the same course. — See CHURCHES *subject to no external jurisdiction;* DISCIPLINE *of one church by another.*

[1] Church. Gov. 4. [2] Ib. 149. [3] Ib. 204—211. [4] Ib. 234. [5] In Han. ii. 226, 227. [6] Page 100. [7] Chap. xv. [8] Chap. xvi. sect. 4. [9] Letters of First Church in Gloucester to the Second Church in Bradford. [10] Eliot, Biog. Dict. 41, 42. [11] Apology, 134, 141. [12] Rat. Dis. 162, 172. [13] Ib. 161. [14] In Han. ii. 38. [15] Ib. 396. [16] Ib. 509. [17] Dudlean Lect. 17. [18] Pages 66, 67. [19] Ib. 90, 92. [20] Convention Sermon, 60, 61.

CHURCHES, *objects of.* — Owen,[1] in his Original of Churches, chap. iv., lays it down as the main object of churches to subject our souls to Christ's authority, that they may be taught what he commands, and for the joint celebration of the ordinances of the gospel.

[1] Works, xx. 114, 115.

CHURCHES, *all Christians may establish.* — Goodwin argues this largely in his Church Government, showing[1] that otherwise many true Christians must ever remain out of the church of God. The same we have seen to have been the opinion of John Robinson.[2] Increase Mather, on the contrary,[3] maintains that it is indispensable to the establishment of these churches, that a consociation be formed, with power to disown all new churches not constituted by neighbor churches. This was in a work of his somewhat advanced age; and none conversant with their history and works can fail to see that the son guided the father's hand in composing this work. — See ELDERS; PRESBYTERY, *church has power over it.* See also the next article but one, viz. CHURCHES *begun without officers, &c.*

[1] Pages 256—262. [2] See CHURCH, *what constitutes?* [3] Disquisition on Ecclesiastical Councils, 34.

CHURCHES, *the seat of all power necessary to church acts.* — So declares the Savoy Confession.[1] It affirms[2] that the churches receive this power immediately from Christ himself. But Increase Mather, and some of the New England divines, who were striving for consociation and the veto power of ministers, maintained that there could not be a valid church act without the consent of the elders, as well as the brethren.[3] Dr. Mather strives to make out that this is a dividing point between Congregationalism and Brownism; but both the Savoy Conference and the Cambridge Synod maintained the reverse. Prince[4] records this among the principles of John Robinson's church, "that any competent number of saints have a right to embody into a church for mutual edification." Dr. Wisner[5] states, that those opposed to Mr. Davenport, in the First Church in Boston, who made application for a dismission, when refused, proceeded to *organize themselves* into a church, according to the advice of council. Dr. Wisner deprecates the triumph of a wrong theology in this new organization, but says that "it is to be *rejoiced* in as confirming the rights of those who had been deprived of them."

[1] Art. iv., v. in Han. iii. 545. [2] Ib. [3] Dis. Ecc. Councils, Pref. iv. [4] Chronology, 91. [5] Hist. Old South Church, Boston, 8, 10.

CHURCHES *begun without officers, and may continue without them, and act despite of them.* — John Robinson says:[1] "Whence it followeth, that both church matters, yea, and churches also, *may*, and in some cases *must*, be begun without officers; yea, even where officers are, if they fail to do their duties, *the people may enterprise matters needful*, howsoever you will have the minister the only *primum movens*, and will tie all to his fingers." Hooker[2] says: "A church, as *totum essentiale*, is and may be before the officers." He shows[3] that churches have the power of admitting new members, of the choice of officers, and, in case the officer is heretical and absolutely wicked, of rejecting him and making him no officer. A church is before its officers. He maintains, however,[4] that a church is incomplete without its officers. Owen[5] shows that a church is before its officers, and bishops are not necessary to gather it, nor ordination necessary to it; for, otherwise, "one proud sensual beast," ordained in the succession, "has more power than the most holy church on the earth." Cambridge Platform,[6] though it recognizes a power of office, yet declares that the church have power of privilege, and may designate the persons to office; and[7] it recognizes the power as vested in them; "it being natural to all bodies, and so to a church body, to be furnished with sufficient power for its own preservation and subsistence." The right of the negative vote is, however, asserted by Higginson and Hubbard, in the Postscript to their Testimony to the Order of the Gospel in the Churches of New England. But it has been rather rarely claimed by pastors or elders, and generally resisted by the people since that time. Cambridge Platform[8] also affirms, that, in cases of mal-administration, the elders are subject to the power of the church. Isaac Chauncy[9] shows that a church must be constituted before it can choose a pastor. A church is empowered from Christ to choose its own ministerial officers, "before such a church hath elders or deacons. These are plain from the nature of a body corporate." — See various documents concerning troubles in the Sou. Church in Reading, about 1846; Adams, Zabdiel, in Eliot, Biog. Dict.; Hist. of Sterling, in Worcester Mag. vol. ii. for 1826; also Zabdiel Adams, Answer to Treatise on Church Government. See also PASTORS, *have they a negative vote in the church?* CHURCH, *ministers not necessary to constitute;* POWER, *church, installed in ministry or brethren?*

[1] Reply to Bernard, in Han. i. 212; and Works, ii. 148. [2] Preface to his Survey. [3] Survey, part i. 10—93. [4] Part ii. 2. [5] Original of Churches, chap. iii.; Works, xx. 108—110. [6] Chap. v. sect. 2. [7] Chap. x. sect. 2. [8] Chap. x. sect. 7. [9] Divine Inst. Cong. Churches, 49, 50.

CHURCHES, *censures, admissions, and all ordinary matters of, in the people.* — This has been the doctrine of all Congregationalists, so far as the primary decisions of the churches are concerned. The whole doctrine of authoritative appeals to councils or to consociations places the power somewhere else. Strict Congregationalists have always placed it in the whole brotherhood. The twenty-fourth article of the Confession of the Low Country Exiles says:[1] "Christ has given the power to receive in or cast off any member to the whole body of every Christian congregation, and not to any one member or more members, . . . or any other congregation to do it for them; yet so as that each congregation ought to use the best help they can hereunto, and the most meet member they have to pronounce the same in the public assembly." The Savoy Confession says:[2] "Every church hath power in itself to exercise and execute all those censures appointed by him in the way and orde prescribed in the gospel." Cambridge Platform[3] says: "The whole church hath power to proceed to the censure of the offending member, whether by admonition or excommunication." In the Directory of Church Government of the Puritans in the reign of Elizabeth,[4] it is asserted that "for all the greater affairs of the church, as in excommunication of any, and choosing and deposing of church ministers, nothing may be concluded without the consent of the church." So of admissions, the Savoy Confession says:[5] "Nor may any person be added to the church, as a private member, but by consent of the church." So, too, of all the common affairs of the church, Congregationalists maintain that all the brotherhood are to act in them. Ainsworth[6] enumerates a list of these common affairs, in which the primitive and apostolical churches engaged. Hooker[7] also enumerates a number of such things, which churches have certainly the power to do. Samuel Mather[8] shows that the whole church have power to act, as they did in the apostolic times, in the establishment of the order of deacons, assisting in their ordination, and directing concerning the circumstances of the Gentile converts, &c. — See CHURCHES, *the seat of all power necessary to church acts.*

[1] Han. i. 95. [2] Art. xviii. of Discipline, in Han. iii. 547. [3] Chap. x. sect. 5. [4] In Neal's Puritans, ii. 440. [5] In ib. 179. [6] Communion of Churches, in Han. i. 282. [7] Survey, part. i. 193. [8] Preface to Apology.

CHURCHES, *their members have equal rights.*— This has always been the doctrine of strict Congregationalists. It was maintained by the ancient Waldenses,[1] "that none in the church ought to be greater than their brethren." The Leyden Church[2] maintained the same. The Answer (Burton's) to Prynne's Full Reply[3] declares it to be the law of nature for every one to join in such a society, where every man may have his own personal vote in every thing which concerns him. (No wonder that Prynne accused him of sentiments adverse to monarchy.) In the State of the Kingdom Stated[4] is shown the evils which obtain where this principle is discarded, and where, negative votes, with veto power in members, are admitted.

[1] In Punchard's Hist. 105. [2] Ib. 336. [3] Page 23. [4] In Han. iii. 234.

CHURCHES, *equal and independent of each other.* — Bradshaw[1] says: "Churches are in all ecclesiastical matters equal; . . . Christ has not subjected any church or congregation to any other superior ecclesiastical jurisdiction than to that which is within itself; so that, if a whole church or congregation should err in any matters of faith or worship, no churches or spiritual officers have power to censure or punish them, but are only to counsel and advise them." The Nonconformist Directory of

Elizabeth's reign[2] says: "Of all particular churches there is one and the same right, order, and form; therefore none may challenge to itself power over others." John Cook (Cromwell's principal Secretary)[3] holds "a subordination of officers in the same church, but an equality in the several congregations, which, as sisters, depend not upon one another, but are helpful to one another; . . . not excepting against consultative, persuasive, and deliberative synods, but the ruling synod that shall command any thing *imperio voluntatis.*" Mather, in his Answer to Rutherford,[4] argues that churches are all equal and independent. — See CHURCHES *discipline each other, but not juridically; subject to no external jurisdiction;* COUNCILS; CONSOCIATION.

[1] English Puritanism, chap. ii. sect. 2, 3, in Neal's Puritans, i. 248. [2] Ib. ii. 440. [3] What the Independents would Have, in Han. iii. 251. [4] Ib. ii. 184.

CHURCHES, *what ones we should not join.* — Owen[1] maintains that though the members of the ancient churches were of one mind, so far as was necessary to joint communion, yet they differed about some doctrines. He shows that Christians ought not to join any church where any fundamental article of faith is rejected or corrupted, nor where any fundamental doctrine of religious worship, church order, or the gospel ministry, is perverted. — See CREEDS; CATHOLICISM; CONFESSIONS OF FAITH; SEPARATION; SCHISM; CHURCHES, *what ones we should separate from.*

[1] Original of Churches, chap. x.; Works, xx. 202—204.

CHURCHES, *what ones we should separate from.* — Goodwin[1] lays it down as a rule, that when to the enjoying of ordinances any thing must be practised which is sinful, or where by continuing a member he must tolerate what he is bound not to tolerate, that from such a church he is bound to separate, though he might not consider them so corrupt but that he might occasionally commune with them, while he had no responsibility as to tolerating the evils which were retained in it. He evidently had his eye, in the first instance, to kneeling at the communion, which many considered as adoration of the emblems; and, in the second, to churches practising mixed communion with those who did not profess experimental religion. The twelfth chapter of his seventh book is devoted to showing, that such separation for conscience' sake ought to be allowed. The Savoy Declaration[2] maintains the same doctrine. — See CHURCHES, *what ones we should not join;* SEPARATION, SCHISM.

[1] Church Gov. 261. [2] On Discipline, art. xxviii. in Han. iii. 548.

CHURCHES, *how they should proceed towards a disorderly member of another church.* — John Cotton[1] argues that they should complain to the church of which the offender is a member. If they neglect, call a council; and, if the church still persist in obstinacy, withdraw communion from them till they acknowledge their transgression.

[1] Way of the Churches, 51.

CHURCHES, *proper proceedings when their pastors offend.* — Cambridge Platform[1] directs that the church first remove him from office (by council where it may be had), and then, if need be, deal with him, and cast him out as any other member. Cotton Mather[2] lays down the details of a proper process (with council) in such a case. — See DISCIPLINE, *mode of;* MINISTER, *how deposed;* PASTOR, *censurable by his church; a member of his church.*

[1] Chap. x. sect. 6. [2] Rat. Dis. 162—167.

CHURCHES *should assist their feeble sisters.* — Cambridge Platform[1] recognizes the duty of the more able of the churches to assist the weaker ones, founded on the Scripture example of the Gentile churches sending succor to the poor Christians at Jerusalem, and from various portions of Scripture. The Congregationalists have always been distinguished for their missionary spirit.

[1] Chap. xv. sect. 2.

CHURCHES, *early liberality of New England.* — Dr. Ware, History of Old North and New Brick Churches, Boston,[1] informs us, that in 1726 a church in Boston contributed sixty pounds for the propagation of the gospel, and that all the churches in Boston contributed ten thousand two hundred and seventy-three pounds for the sufferers by the fire in 1760. Probably more was done formerly, in proportion to the means, for the spread and support of the gospel, than at present.

[1] Page 50.

See further on the general subject of churches under the heads, DISCIPLINE, DISMISSION, MEMBERS.

COLLECTIONS, *weekly.* — These were practised by some of the churches in Cotton Mather's time,[1] who supposed them required in 2 Cor. xvi. 2. Out of these their church expenses were paid or assisted. Some moderns are beginning to revive the doctrine as applicable to charitable objects. This passage, however, is more generally considered as of special application. — See GIFTS AND OFFERINGS, *weekly.*

[1] Rat. Dis. 62.

COMMENTARIES. — John Robinson[1] says: "The simple necessity of commentaries and interpretations, which God requires for becoming an ordinary prophet, I dare not acknowledge. Of *great use* are they, but not of *simple necessity.* The prerogative of simple necessity I would challenge as peculiar to the Holy Scriptures." One of the Genevan Disputants argues[2] that "men do diversely offend, as they, on the one hand, slight God's gifts to the fathers; and, on the other, receive their comments without comparing them with the word of God."

[1] People's Plea for Prophecy, *v.* Yates, in Han. i. 355; and Works, iii. 298, 299. [2] Page 160.

COMMITTEE'S CHURCH. — See CHURCH, *officers of;* OFFICERS, *what? God's gift, and not to be multiplied at discretion*; POWER, *church, cannot be given away nor delegated;* STANDING COMMITTEES.

COMMUNION, *terms of.*—John Howe[1] says: "Suppose you judge concurrence in the use of a liturgy a sin, and the unprescribed way a duty, yet who hath empowered you to make such sins exclusive from Christian communion? . . . Hath God forbidden any to be admitted to Christian communion, but such as are absolutely perfect in knowledge and holiness?" In his preface to Carnality of Religious Contentions,[2] he says, "Whose is this table? Is it the table of this or that man, or party of men? or is it the Lord's table? Then certainly it ought to be free to his guests; and who should dare invite others, or forbid these?" In his Sermon concerning Union among Protestants, he says:[3] "To do any thing against the preponderating influence of my own judgment and conscience were great wickedness, and would unfit me for any communion whatever." This he applies against making terms of communion to which all Christians cannot conscientiously accede. In his Peace God's Blessing, he says,[4] "We are expressly required to receive one another (which cannot but mean to one another's communion), and that not to doubtful disputations." Robert Hall argues the doctrine of open communion in a most masterly manner in his Terms of Communion, and his Replies to Kinghorn and to Fuller. He sums up his arguments for the doctrine[5] as follows: "We have endeavored to show, that the practice of strict communion derives no support from the *supposed* priority of baptism to the Lord's Supper, in the order of the institution, which is exactly the reverse; that it is not countenanced by the tenor of the apostles' commission, nor by apostolic precedent, the spirit of which is in our favor; that the opposite practice is enforced by the obligations of Christian charity; that it is indubitably comprehended in the canon which enjoins forbearance towards mistaken brethren; that the system of our opponents unchurches every Pedobaptist community; that it rests on no general principle; attempts to establish an impossible medium; inflicts a punishment which is capricious and unjust; and finally, that, by fomenting prejudice and precluding the most effectual means of conviction, it defeats its own purpose." See also, for his most convincing remarks, vol. i. 403, 437; and ii. 210. His arguments for open communion are very replete, and should be studied by all who inquire what the Lord would have them to do. — See BAPTISM, *is it indispensable to communion?* CREEDS.

[1] Works, 184. [2] Ib. 457. [3] Ib. 480. Ib. 931. [5] Works, i. 359.

COMMUNION, *occasional, should be open.* — The Savoy Confession shows,[1] "That churches, consisting of persons sound in the faith, and of a good conversation, ought not to refuse communion with each other, though they walk not in all things according to the same rule of church order; and if they judge other churches to be true churches, though less pure, they may receive to occasional communion such members of these churches as are credibly testified to be godly and to live without offence."[1] Ainsworth, Answer to Paget, says:[2] "Those that are worthy to be received into the true visible church, ... with them I hold it to be lawful to have private communion." Robinson, in his Apology,[3] says: "Touching the reformed churches, we account them true churches of Jesus Christ, and both profess and practise communion with them. ... The sacraments we do administer to their members, if, by occasion, any of them be present with us." The Independents, in their Answer to the Grand Committee in the Westminster Assembly, are equally explicit on this point.[4] Cambridge Platform,[5] Hooker's Survey,[6] and Watts's Terms of Communion, quest. xi.[7] recognize the same doctrine; though Watts is less catholic than Congregationalists in general, of his day, on the question,— Whether all good Christians should be received as members of the churches? Taylor, in his Vindication of Dissenters,[8] shows that a Christian is obliged to hold "occasional communion, unless he may live like a heathen a year where he sojourns." R. Hall, in his Terms of Communion,[9] handles the argument for such open communion in an irrefutable manner.[10] He asserts that no trace of the doctrine of close communion can be found among the ancient Waldensian Baptists.— See Creeds; Catholicism *of Congregational churches.*

[1] In Neal, Puritans, ii. 179. [2] In Han. i. 338. [3] Ib. 372. [4] Ib. iii. 50. [5] Chap. xv. sect. 2. [6] Part i. 295. [7] Works, iii. 285. [8] Page 75. [9] Works, i. 292—321. [10] Ib. 354.

COMMUNION, *occasional, introduction to.*— Cotton Mather[1] says: "The pastor having first mentioned the names of the persons belonging to other churches, who request a part in the present communion, he then addresses himself, with all possible solemnity, to the celebration." The more usual method now is to invite the members in good standing of all churches, leaving it to the consciences of the strangers to decide whether they are such as the inviting church intends to fellowship as Christians.

[1] Rat. Dis. 97.

COMMUNION, *true, exists just in proportion to purity.* — Goodwin is very explicit on this point, laboring it at large in his fifth Book on Church Government.[1] Hetherington, a Presbyterian writer, says:[2] "The Independents did not, like the Brownists, condemn every other church as too corrupt and antichristian for intercommunion." Robinson, in his Apology, says:[3] "Our faith is not negative, . . . nor which consists in condemning others, and wiping their names out of the bead-roll of churches; . . . neither require we of any of ours, in the confession of their faith, that they either renounce, or in one word contest with the church of England, WHATSOEVER THE WORLD CLAMORS OF US THIS WAY." The Westminster Assembly Independents say, in their Apologetical Narrative:[4] "We always have professed that we both did and would hold communion with the churches of England as the churches of Christ. . . . It never entered our minds to judge them as antichristian." Jacob, in his Declaration, says:[5] "For my part I never was nor am separated from all public communion with the congregations of England." Robert Hall maintains the same doctrine [6] from the injunction to receive him that is weak in faith. And he says,[7] "Placing Pedobaptists, who form the great body of the faithful, on the same level with men of impure and vicious lives, is equally repugnant to reason and offensive to charity." — See CATHOLICISM.

[1] Pages 222—237. [2] Neal, Puritans, i. 489. [3] Han. i. 384; and Works, iii. 63. [4] Ib. ii. 223, 224. [5] Ib. i. 230. [6] Vol. i. 326. [7] Ib. 331.

CONFERENCE *meetings.* — T. Goodwin [1] maintains the duty of all members of churches to learn each other's spiritual state, not merely privately, but in the churches. This privilege has generally been maintained among Congregationalists, though some have endeavored to confine this work to ministers. Upham, in his Ratio Disciplinæ, says: [2] "Private meetings of Christians are kept up, as in former times; nor can it be otherwise, so long as the true Congregational spirit remains." He quotes Cotton Mather, Rat. Dis. art. x.: "It is usual among us for Christians to hold private meetings, wherein they do with various exercises edify one another." He (Cotton Mather) proceeds to describe the method in which these conference meetings were conducted. — See PROPHESYING.

Ch. Gov. 298—303. [2] Pages 252, 253.

CONFERENCES *of churches.* — Upham devotes the twenty-third chapter of his Ratio Disciplinæ [1] to a description of these, as they now exist in various portions of New England. He traces the plans for establishing them back to the synod of 1662, and even to John Cotton, who drew up a plan for such conferences near the time of his death, which may be found in Increase Mather's First Principles of New England. Upham shows at length the objects, method, and benefits of such church conferences.

[1] Pages 240—249.

CONFESSIONS OF FAITH, *their use and abuse.* The Preface to the Savoy Confession[1] says: "Confessions, when made by a company of professors of Christianity, jointly meeting to that end, . . . the most genuine and natural use of such is, that, under the form of words, they express the substance of the same common salvation. . . . And, accordingly, such a transaction is to be looked upon but as a meet or fit medium whereby to express that their common faith and salvation, and in *no way* to be made use of as an imposition upon any. Whatever is of force or constraint, in matters of this nature, causeth them to *degenerate from the name and nature of confessions, and turns them from being confessions of faith into impositions and exactions of faith;* . . . there being nothing that tends more to heighten dissensions among brethren than to determine and adopt the matter of their difference under so high a title as to be an article of our faith." Upham[2] maintains that churches "have a right to say on what conditions others, either individuals or bodies of men, shall share their fellowship;" saying,

"They can enter into fellowship with others with whose principles they more nearly agree." This reasoning seems to hold only on the supposition that churches are strictly voluntary, in distinction from divinely instituted, bodies. If churches are of divine institution, then all true Christians have a right to share in them all the privileges of the sons of God. It is their Father's table and their Father's church; and what right have their brethren to debar them? — See CREEDS.

[1] In Han. iii. 517—528. [2] Rat. Dis. 57.

CONFESSION *of secret sin.* — Increase Mather says[1] that some secret sins "ought not to be made public" by him who has committed them.

[1] Order of N. E. Churches Justified, 30.

CONFESSION *for sin.* — See REPENTANCE, *how manifested.*

CONFUSED RECORDS, *how to be interpreted.* In the Answer to the Hampshire Narrative,[1] we find that an ambiguous passage on the church records was interpreted by taking the sense of the church, when re-assembled, as to what should have been recorded.

[1] Page 43.

CONGREGATIONAL CHURCHES, *early history of.* — Congregationalists maintain that the primitive apostolical churches were all Congregational. This was admitted even by their opposers in the early days of the controversy. Archbishop Whitgift asserts[1] that "the state of the church was popular in the apostles' time." (See CHURCHES, *primitive, were Congregational;* and CORRUPTIONS *of primitive churches.*) In the early days of the reformation, Wickliffe advocated most of the essential doctrines of the Congregational polity.[2] The sufficiency of the Scriptures, the constitution of the church of visible saints, the liberty of the form of worship, and the two orders of officers, were the prime articles of his ecclesiastical creed.[3] In 1550, John Alasco, or à Lasco, a Polish nobleman, gathered a church of German refugees in London, and advocated most of the doctrines of Congregationalism. He proceeded under the great seal of King Edward VI. "out of his great desire to settle a like reformation in the English churches."[4] His church was scattered, and he banished, by the bloody Mary. He returned in the reign of Elizabeth, but could not get his former privileges confirmed, though she permitted Grindal to be the superintendent of his church, and confirmed its charter.[4] But, even in Mary's time, we are assured that there were many Congregational churches meeting secretly.[6] And "no church but such as was substantially congregational could have existed, in an organized form, during the terrible persecutions of Mary's reign;"[7] a striking indication that God designed this form of government for his churches in their state of trial. In 1554, the English exiles, with Mr. Whittingham, went to Frankfort, and established their church, July 29, on Congregational principles, making the church the *dernier resort* in all controversies, — chose their ministers and deacons, omitting many of the superstitions in the Service-book of Edward VI. Another such church was about this time set up at Embden, and another at Wessel.[8] The history of the Puritans and Nonconformists of Elizabeth's and the succeeding reigns are too well known to need a further description in this article. Those who wish to examine their history in detail will find ample material in Neal,[9] Prince,[10] Cotton Mather,[11] Winthrop,[12] Hubbard;[13] and, among the moderns, Punchard,[14] and especially Hanbury,[15] who has done a great work and a good one. Upham[16] gives a succinct account of the organization of Robinson's church. Prince[17] informs us that in 1592 a church was established in London; that fifty-four of the church were imprisoned, some of them four or five years. They were beat with cudgels, and many died; and Mr. Greenwood, their teacher, was executed, and the rest banished to Amsterdam. Their Confession, frequently referred to in this Dictionary, was first published in 1596. The present church in West Barnstable, Mass., is supposed to be the oldest Independent Congregational church in the world. It was organized in 1616 in England, and removed first to Scituate, and afterwards to Barnstable.[18] Their confession of faith was that, frequently alluded to in this work, as Jacob's Church Confession. Eliot[19] says: "The first Congregational church since the days of primitive Christianity was gathered in Geneva." — See Separation.

[1] In Han. i. 10. [2] Punchard, Hist. 159—171. [3] Ib. [4] Han. ii. 32—34. [5] Neal, Puritans, i. 83. [6] Punchard, Hist. 220—226. [7] Ib. 222. [8] Punchard's Hist. 224, 225. [9] Puritans. [10] Chronology. [11] Magnalia. [12] Journal. [13] Hist. Mass. [14] History. [15] Historical Memorials. [16] Rat. Dis. 40. [17] Chronology, 235. [18] White, Early Hist. N. Eng. 260. [19] Ecc. Hist. Mass. in Mass. Hist. Soc. Col. series i. vol. vii. 267.

CONGREGATIONALISM, *what?*—Heylyn[1] says of Goodwin, Nye, Burroughs, Bridge, and Simpson: "These men, affecting neither the severe discipline of Presbytery, nor the licentiousness incident to Brownism, embraced Robinson's model of church government in their congregations, consisting of a co-ordination of churches for their mutual comfort, and not a subordination of one to the other in the way of direction or command. Cotton, Chauncy, Hooker, and others, he alludes to, as advocating the same views in the New England churches. Punchard[2] says of their principles: "They are found in the New Testament, and their expounders are all the standard writers of the denomination, such as Johnson, Ainsworth, Robinson, and Jacob, Thos. Hooker, and John Cotton, Owen, the Mathers, the Authors of the Cambridge Platform, &c. I might go further back to Penry and Greenwood and Barrowe." Eliot[3] enumerates the principal things in which Congregationalists differ from others: 1. The subject-matter of a church,—saints by calling. 2. Constitution of the visible church,—a covenant. 3. Quantity of it,—as many as can worship in one place. 4. A denial of any jurisdiction to which churches are subject. Hon. S. Haven[4] says: "The essence of Congregationalism is, that all the power is in and proceeds from the individual church. She elects the candidate and the council, and issues the letters missive; she may arrest the proceedings in any stage of them; *and, in the very last stage, is called to signify whether she abide her determination.*" Neal says:[5] "Robinson was the first that beat out a middle track between Presbyterianism and Independency. He allowed the expediency of synods and councils for advice, but not for exercising any act of authority or jurisdiction." — See next article.

[1] In Han. ii. 40. [2] View, 27. [3] Ecc. Hist. Mass. in Mass. Hist. Soc. Col. series i. vol. ix. 13. [4] Proceedings of the First Church and Parish in Dedham, 64. [5] Hist. N. Eng. i. 73.

CONGREGATIONALISM, *epitome of principles of.* — Bartlett[1] sums these up: Matter of a visible church, saints, Rom. i. 7; 1 Cor. i. 2; xiv. 33; Phil. i. 1—7; Col. iii. 12; 1 Thess. v. 27. — Form, uniting together in one spiritual body politic, 1 Cor. x. 17; xii. 12, 20, 27; Ephes. ii. 22. — Quantity, as many as can meet together in one place, Acts ii. 1; v. 12; xiv. 27; 1 Cor. xiv. 23. — Power of government, in itself, Matt. xviii. 17—19; 1 Cor. v. 4—7, 13; Acts xv. 22, 23; Rev. ii. 20. — Office and officers, Ephes. iv. 11, 12; Rom. xii. 6, 7; 1 Cor. xii. 28. — Choosing officers, by the whole church, Acts i. 15—26; vi. 2, 3; xiv. 23. — Admission of members, the godly and their seed, Acts ii. 38, 39, &c. He goes on to give Scripture references in favor of many minor principles of Congregational order also.

I condense Mitchell's enumeration [2] as follows Church, a society of believers united together by their own consent for worship and the ordinances of the gospel. — Church power, vested in the church itself, and not in its officers. — Church officers, ministers and deacons. — Churches, in a qualified sense independent; no church or church officers have authority to interfere with the faith or discipline of another church, but an erring church is open to the reproofs of others; and, if the case requires, they may be disowned from the general communion. They do not allow the imposition of human creeds as tests of orthodoxy or terms of communion.

Punchard [3] states them thus: "The Scriptures are an infallible guide to church order and discipline. — A Christian church is a voluntary association of persons professing repentance for sin and faith in Jesus Christ, united together by a solemn covenant for the worship of God and the celebration of religious ordinances. — This company should ordinarily consist of no more than can conveniently and statedly meet together for religious purposes. — To this assembly all executive ecclesiastical or church power is intrusted by Jesus Christ, the great Head of the Church." To this he adds a summary of their doctrines, viz.: — But two orders of church officers, bishops and deacons; equality of all bishops; councils have no juridical authority; churches, though independent in worship and discipline, should hold themselves ready to give account to sister-churches of their faith and religious practices. He gives a similar epitome in his View.[4]

Rev. J. Allyn, in his Plymouth Anniversary Sermon;[5] Mr. Thacher, in his History of Plymouth[6] (from Dr. Belknap); Prince, in his Chronology;[7] and Upham, in his Ratio Disciplinæ,[8] give the principles of Robinson's church, corresponding with the above summaries.— See GOVERNMENT, *Congregational.*

[1] Model in Han. iii. 246. [2] Guide, 37, 38. [3] Hist. 13, 14. [4] Page 29. [5] Pages 13, 14. [6] Page 261. [7] Pages 91—93. [8] Page 37.

CONGREGATIONALISM *by divine right.* — Neal[1] says that the "Independents in the Westminster Assembly opposed the proposition of the divine right of Presbytery by advancing a counter divine right of their own scheme. . . . They maintained that the church at Jerusalem was no larger than could meet in one place, Acts ii. 46; v. 12, 14; that, even when they were grown very large, the whole multitude came together to choose deacons, Acts vi. 2—5; and that, even after the general dispersion, they all met in one place, Acts xv. 4, 22." This they advanced in opposition to the argument that there was a Presbyterial church there, consisting of several separate assemblies. Samuel Mather[2] maintains that the rejecting of Congregationalism is the rejecting of the kingly authority of Christ, and giving the inheritance of our fathers to others. Increase Mather[3] maintains that Congregational discipline is *jure divino.* Henry Jacob[4] says: "Every particular ordinary congregation of faithful people in England is a true and proper visible church, *jure divino*,—by right from God." His Church Confession[5] shows that there is no other way in which they can obey the divine command, "Tell it to the church." Cambridge Platform[6] says: "A Congregational church is, by the institution of Christ, a part of the militant visible church."

[1] Puritans, vol. ii. 9. [2] Apology, 143. [3] Preface to Disquisition on Ecclesiastical Councils, iii. [4] Reasons for Reforming the Churches in England, in Han. i. 222. [5] Art. xxviii. in Han. i. 303. [6] Chap. ii. sect. 6.

CONGREGATIONALISM *adopted by those who had no personal interest to serve.*—The Independents in the Westminister Assembly say,[1] that it was in their expatriation that they commenced inquiring, "What were the first apostolic directions, pattern, and examples of those primitive churches recorded in the New Testament? We had, of all men, the greatest reason to be true to our own consciences in what we should embrace, seeing it was for our consciences we were deprived of whatsoever was dear to us." A notable instance occurred in the case of Mr. Higginson and his church in Salem. They, on their way to New England, set about establishing the most scriptural form of church government, now that they were under no necessity of conformity. They adopted a Congregational form, while they had great prejudices against their Plymouth neighbors, growing out of the current misrepresentations of their tenets, till Dr. Fuller made the surprising discovery that the two churches, looking to the Scripture alone for a directory, were essentially on the same basis of church order and discipline.[2] The exiles at Frankfort, and Mr. Robinson, with his church, also adopted essentially the same plan, without concert.[3]

In Han. ii. 222. [2] Hall's Puritans, 220—223. [3] Ib. 74, 147.

CONGREGATIONALISM *has power to prevent and redress error.* — It has been a standing accusation that it has no such power; but the charge is not admitted. Simpson, in his answer to Forbes, or Anatomist Anatomized,[1] asks: "What flaming sword is there in a classical Presbytery to keep men out of errors, which may not be in a Congregation?" And says: "If the counsel and advice of other neighbor-churches be required, a congregation may have that as well, and perhaps sooner than a classis can. There have been as great defections, both of ministers and people, unto errors under Presbyterial government as under any other, as is clear in the Low Countries, where many ministers and people turned Arminians, Papists, Socinians, . . . and in other countries too." T. Welde, in his Reply to Rathband,[2] says: "But we have had 'divisions' amongst us. These 'divisions' were not caused by our church discipline, but by certain vile opinions brought us from England. When these opinions did *fall*, our discipline *stood;* which shows that our discipline bred them not, but destroyed them." Burroughs, in his Irenicum,[3] says: "There is no church government that holds forth more means to reduce from error than this doth. . . . If men will not conscientiously regard what is done to reduce them from evil, there is no help within the church but an appeal to Christ." Punchard[4] shows at length, "that it presents the most efficacious barrier to the inroads of heresy, false doctrine, and general corruption." — See APPEALS; CONGREGATIONALISM, *its prospects realized.*

In Han. ii. 245. [2] Ib. 297. [3] Ib. iii. 118. [4] View, 248—255.

CONGREGATIONALISM *fitted to all circumstances of the church.* — Goodwin devotes the tenth chapter of his second book on Church Government to establish this point. His arguments may be thus epitomized. In answer to the theory, that, when whole nations turn Christian, the church government should be conformed to the national, he shows "that God designed to redeem his church *out of* every nation;" that, if he had intended that there should have been national Christian churches, he would have given rules answerable, as he did to the Jewish church. He shows that Congregational churches are so constituted that they will suit all circumstances, in the beginning of the gospel, and the continuance of the gospel; all places, whether villages or cities; all conditions, whether of persecution or peace, whether pure or corrupt, whether reforming or to be reformed. He clearly shows, that there are many circumstances in which no other form of church government can be practised, as of outward persecution or isolated churches, churches deprived of officers, &c. — See CONGREGATIONAL CHURCHES, *early history of;* CONGREGATIONALISM *has power to prevent error.*

CONGREGATIONALISM, *whence its greatest danger.* — Higginson and Hubbard, in their Testimony appended to Cambridge Platform, say:[1] "Concerning all sinful attempts to overturn the order of the gospel hitherto upheld in New England, and to spoil the glorious work of God, which we have seen him doing, with a series of remarkable providences, in erecting such Congregational churches in these ends of the earth, — they are doubtless displeasing to the Lord Jesus Christ, who walks in the midst of these golden candlesticks, and will prove bitterness in the latter end. . . . And *one great point* in the decay of the power of vital godliness is men's growing weary of the Congregational discipline, which is evidently calculated to maintain it." Punchard[2] mentions several causes of the decline of Congregationalism; among which are the impression "that no efforts are required to protect and promote our excellent system of church government; . . . the dearth of modern books upon Congregationalism; . . . a prevalent impression that Congregationalists have no well-defined and settled principles of church polity." He says: "Have these principles made New England an intellectual and moral garden, and shall we be told that they will not answer for the South and West?" Whether with definite aim or drawing a bow at venture, he says:[3] "But if the professors in any of our theological seminaries are even *apparently* indifferent to our church polity, we need not be surprised to find their pupils *really* so."

Page 68. [2] View, 23—25. [3] Page 25.

CONGREGATIONALISM, *duty to abide by.*— Lobb, in his True Dissenter, says:[1] "What can the breaking down of the Congregational bonds, changing the congregational offices, deposing their officers, and setting up new ones after the diocesan model, and governing by other laws and rules, be but a rejecting of Christ, a destroying of his government, and an open breach of our allegiance to him?" Upham[2] says: "And we may safely aver of such an edifice, erected with great labor and sanctified by prayer, and now rendered venerable by age, that it is not to be lightly esteemed, still less wantonly abandoned. But it becomes us, as in the days of Jeremiah, to stand in the way, and see and ask for the old paths, where is the good way, and walk therein, and we shall find rest for our souls."

[1] Page 129. [2] Rat. Dis. 33.

CONGREGATIONALISM, *its prospects foreseen.* John Robinson, in his Justification of Separation, in answer to Bernard,[1] says, in reply to his taunts concerning the "fewness of their numbers:" "Religion is not always sown and reaped in one age. One soweth, and another reapeth. The many that are already gathered, by the mercy of God, into the kingdom of his Son Jesus Christ, and the nearness of many more through the whole land,—for the regions are white unto the harvest,—do promise, in less than a hundred years, if our sins and theirs make not us and them unworthy of this mercy, a very plentiful harvest." A foresight by no means discouraging to those who, on forbidden "ground," now labor to establish the discipline which Christ has instituted.

[1] In Han. i. 209; and Works, ii. 66.

CONGREGATIONALISM, *its prospects realized.* Hutchinson, in his History of Massachusetts, says:[1] "But, however this constitution may appear in theory, we shall seldom meet with an instance in which there has been so steady and so general an adherence to the principles on which it was founded, and so much harmony subsisting, not only in particular churches, but also between one church and another, for fifty years together."

[1] Vol. i. 374. — See further on the general subject of Congregationalism under the head INDEPENDENCY.

CONSCIENCE. — Lord Brooke, in his Disquisition on Episcopacy,[1] says: "No power on earth ought to force my practice any more than my judgment." He admits church power to expel him, but no farther. The conforming prelates required uniformity in all things, without respect to conscience: hence the conscientious suffered, and the unprincipled escaped. Burton, in his Rejoinder to Prynne, maintained[2] that it is the greatest hypocrisy in the world to pretend to follow what authority commands, and yet man's own conscience thinks ought not to be done. Again:[3] "If I am bound to believe what they say who are in authority, then my conscience is subject to error." S. Mather shows[4] that decisions of councils should be accepted when they are reasonable and scriptura. only. R. Williams and his followers had carried the doctrine of liberty of conscience to such an extreme as to assert that no man should be censured for any thing when he *pleaded* conscience. By this they found that they had stultified themselves, when one Verrin pleaded conscience for preventing his wife from meeting with them.[5] John Cook[6] says he (an Independent) thinks it better that Protestants, who are in a parish, if they are of three different opinions, should have three several meeting-places, than fight and live in perpetual jars with one another. Isaac Chauncy shows[7] that Christians ought not to subject their consciences to human will or laws. John Howe, in his Union among Protestants,[8] appeals to those who most severely blame any for dissent,—if they (Dissenters) should declare, "It is truly against our consciences to communicate with you on your terms, yet, to please you, and avoid temporal inconvenience, we will do it,"—whether we should not thereby make ourselves incapable of any communion, either with you or any others? John Corbett[9] says: "When men's commands contradict the commands of God, it is God, and not man, that must have the preeminence. With us it is no controversy whether the king or conscience be the supreme governor." The Savoy Confession[10] says: "God alone is Lord of conscience, and hath left it free from doctrines and commandments of men, which are in any thing contrary to his word, or not contained in it: so that to believe such doctrines or to obey such commands, out of conscience, is to betray true liberty of conscience; and the requiring of an implicit faith, and an absolute and blind obedience, is to destroy liberty of conscience, and reason also."

[1] In Han. ii. 122. [2] Page 19. [3] Page 48. [4] Apology, 5, 6. [5] Winthrop's Journal, i. 283. [6] In Han. iii. 258. [7] Divine Inst. Cong. Churches, Preface, vi. [8] Works, 480. [9] Princip. and Pract. of Several Nonconformists, 9. [10] Chap. xxi. in Upham's Rat. Dis. 288, 289.

CONSECRATIONS *discarded.*—Consecrations of churches, vestments, and implements, were among the things objected to by the Separation against the church of England. Neal[1] speaks of these as one great objection to Archbishop Laud's administration; he proceeding even to consecrated knives to cut the sacramental bread. The Bishop of Norwich is represented[2] as instituting the inquiry, in his *primary* articles of visitation, "whether the churchyards were consecrated?" This was a question stoutly disputed on Archbishop Laud's trial.[3] The managers objected to the consecrating of chapels, churchyards, altars, furniture, &c., as popish innovations. The archbishop maintained the necessity of the same, in order to render them holy things. The managers asserted, that "we have no credible authority for consecrating churches for the first three hundred years."[1] Barrowe[4] inveighs against the "hallowed church and churchyard, and hallowed fonts, hallowed bells, organs, and musics." Ainsworth[5] is out upon such consecrations, saying that none of Jeroboam's priests could turn their hands to such powerful works as the advocates of "consecrated churches, chapels, ministers, bells, fonts, and churchyards, the relics of the idolatry of Rome, practised even by those who hate the whore and eat her flesh." Robinson, in his Apology,[6] condemns "a holy place, as it is counted by most, consecrated either to God himself or to some saint." He does not object to a meeting-house, "provided the opinion of holiness be removed." In his Posthumous Treatise,[7] he says, in answer to an objector to worshipping in a consecrated church: "I have no more religious use for the place in which I hear publicly, than in which I pray privately in my house or chamber." It appears from the Magnalia,[8] that Congregationalists had no consecrated meeting-houses, and that houses for public worship might be used for secular purposes, provided it were done in such a manner that no implicit affront was thereby offered to Him who was worshipped there. Of late, however, there seems to be a lamentable degeneracy among the descendants of the Puritans in this particular. We often hear expressions in dedicatory prayers of meeting-houses, which imply a complete consecration, even to denouncing any who shall henceforth put the building to any secular use. We have also consecrating prayers at ordinations and forming of churches; and even Mr. Mitchell, in his Guide,[9] though he disclaims all reverence for mere wood and stone, treats of the inconsistency of dedicating a house to God, and then using it for secular purposes; quoting the words which were applied to the consecrated temple, "Ye shall reverence my sanctuary." One of the Genevan Disputants[10] says of the consecration of the emblems of the Lord's Supper: "They are to be condemned who attribute some holiness to the signs; and as for those who worship them, these we utterly detest as open idolaters." — See DEDICATIONS, CEREMONIES.

[1] Puritans, i. 304. [2] Ib. 325. [3] Ib. 509, 510. [4] In Han. i. 60. [5] Ib. 237, 238. [6] Ib. 382, 383; and Works, iii. 59. [7] Han. i. 457; and Works, iii. 374. [8] Vol. ii. 226. [9] Pages 216, 217. [10] Page 164.

CONSOCIATIONS, *origin of.* — Trumbull informs us,[1] that in 1659 the General Court of Connecticut ordered a council, the decision whereof should be final. The General Court of Massachusetts endeavored to establish the same thing, and so called the synod of 1662. These synods embraced not only all the ministers of the colony whose legislature called them, but also certain specified individuals of the other colonies, to ensure majorities. But they failed of such a majority in Connecticut, through this over-management. The Boston Synod was more successful, and recommended a consociation, having first, however, premised that it should be shorn of its locks, by being stripped of juridical power. (See CONSOCIATIONS, *power of.*) The General Courts having attained their main ends in the decisions for the half-way covenant, and the churches generally and some of the principal ministers opposing, the matter of consociations slumbered till about the beginning of the eighteenth century, when Cotton Mather, having converted his father in his dotage, led in a strenuous effort to establish a virtual consociation. Proposals were introduced into the Boston Association, and through them to the Massachusetts Convention; but they were successfully opposed by John Wise of Ipswich and others.[2] The proposals, which may be seen in Wise's Quarrel of the Churches Espoused,[3] were rejected in Massachusetts, but were soon received in Connecticut, and from that time have formed the basis of their consociations. Trumbull[4] gives a particular account of the introduction of the Saybrook Platform, and of the opposition which was made to it by some of the churches. President Stiles informs us,[5] that in 1662 Mr. Shepard drew up proposals for a consociation to hear and give judgment in ecclesiastical controversies, but it was rejected; that it was ripened into a formal plan in 1700, and renewed in 1705, but the opposition in the associations, and from the unassociated pastors, prevented its being recommended to the churches, "where it would have met with still greater opposition, through the spirit of liberty." Serious attempts have since been made to revive the subject, but without success.

[1] Hist. Conn. chap. xiii. [2] See Wise's Quarrel of the Churches Espoused, a work recommended by Samuel Moody, Peter Thacher, Joseph Sewall, Thomas Prince, John Webb, William Cooper, and Thomas Foxcroft. [3] Ib. 77—80. [4] Hist. Conn. 507—514. [5] Conv. Sermon, 68, 69.

CONSOCIATIONS, *power of.* — The Boston Synod of 1662[1] say: "Every church . . . has received from the Lord Jesus Christ full power and authority, ecclesiastical within itself, regularly to administer all the ordinances of Christ, and is not under any other ecclesiastical jurisdiction whatever: . . . hence it follows, that consociations are not to hinder the exercise of his power, but by counsel from the word of God to direct and strengthen the same upon all just occasions." They go on to define the objects of consociations, and to recommend them to the churches. Samuel Mather shows[2] that a consociation of churches was acknowledged by the early New England Congregationalists, in the sense of *asking light not of government.* What is the authoriry of the consociations in Connecticut, it seems, is still as ever an open question; and Mitchell, following Stiles,[3] maintains that it was designedly left ambiguous whether they should be juridical or merely advisory, because in that way only could they succeed in establishing it in the beginning. Dr. Stiles[4] shows that the first principles and the (evident) interlining of the Saybrook Platform clash; the one giving unlimited power to the churches, and the other vesting controlling power in consociations. He argues that it is to be interpreted in a sense subordinate to the first great declared general principle; as that is, doubtless, the sense in which the adopting churches received it. He shows that the history of consociations, for the first forty years, proves that they were then only meant and received as advisory. He, however, clearly shows that there was a design in a part, and only a part, of the framers of the Saybrook Platform to make consociations juridical. It seems that that which is crooked cannot yet be made straight; some men are still wearying themselves to learn how the Saybrook Convention meant to define the power of consociations, which this sermon proves conclusively that they did not mean to define at all. — See SAYBROOK PLATFORM.

[1] Ans. 1 to Quest. 2. [2] Apology, 21. [3] Guide, 229, note. [4] Conv. Sermon, 72—80.

CONSOCIATIONS, *reasons urged for.* — Increase Mather, in his Disquisition on Ecclesiastical Councils, says:[1] "That there should be such a consociation, agreeing among themselves that no new churches shall be owned by them, or pastor ordained or deposed without them, . . . is not only lawful, but absolutely necessary for the establishment of these churches." Yet he says:[2] All "Congregationalists, of which Mr. Cotton is not the least, deny that synods have any authority of rule or jurisdiction." He quotes Norton, asserting that the power of synods is decisive, not authoritative. Mitchell[3] enumerates six advantages of consociations, one of which is, they have, as he affirms, entirely (?) done away with the evil they were originally designed to remedy, — the calling of council against council. The Historical Account of Saybrook Platform[4] represents them as — "1. The promotion of order and harmony among ministers and churches. 2. The regular introduction of candidates into the ministry. 3. And especially the establishment of a board of appeal." Dr. Dwight[5] is loud in the praise of consociations, or courts of judicature, and only laments that there is not "a still superior tribunal to receive appeals in cases where they are absolutely necessary." In a word, the arguments for consociations are, like those for Presbytery and Hierarchy, all founded on the supposed benefits of unity and concert in all action, and would be unanswerable were the tribunal itself proved to be infallible.

[1] Page 34. [2] Pages 28, 29. [3] Guide, 231, note. In Congregational Order, 37. [5] Works, Serm. clxii.

CONSOCIATIONS, *objections to.* — Congregationalists, strictly so called, have uniformly objected to these with juridical powers. The framers of Saybrook Platform did not, at first, claim to be strict Congregationalists.[1] Richard Mather and William Tompson[2] assert, — and quote Dr. Ames's Cases of Conscience, book iv. chap. xxiv. sect. 17, — "That if the power to reprove scandals, and cast out the wicked, belongs to churches that have no neighbors, then it belongs to those who have them; so consociation, or 'neighborhood of churches,' does not abridge the power of individual churches." Goodwin[3] shows that the consociation principle was not practised by the church at Corinth, because they did not call in the neighboring church of Cenchrea in their case of difficulty, but excommunicated and restored, as having entire jurisdiction within themselves. Hooker is claimed as the great patron and projector of consociations; but he argues[4] that none of us deny a consociation by way of *advice*, but it is a very different thing from a church of churches. John Wise says of the Proposals,[5] that such a proposition out-bishops all the bishops, and out-popes the pope himself. Trumbull[6] frequently speaks of Consociationists in distinction from the strict Congregationalists. So does the Appeal of Eastern Association of Windham County, Conn.;[7] as also President Stiles. He says, in his Convention Sermon:[8] "If a consociated church is excommunicated (for denial of jurisdiction), it reverts to the state of a Congregational one, and has communion with Congregational churches." In his Election Sermon,[9] he speaks of the *Congregational*, the *Consociated*, and the *Presbyterian* churches. Davenport[10] recommends a consociation for mutual advice *only*. Burton says:[11] We hold communion or consociation of churches for counsel in doubts and comfort in distress, but deny any such combination of churches as whereby the liberty of any particular church is taken away. President Stiles has another objection to Connecticut consociationism:[12] it makes "a majority of the pastors, as well as of the consociation, necessary to pass a valid act," so that "the legs of the lame are not equal." Increase Mather, in his Disquisition on Ecclesiastical Councils (Preface), deprecates such a monopoly of power. Gov. Wolcott also wrote an Answer to Mr. Hobert, in which he compared the Cambridge and Saybrook Platforms, and argues the latter to be inconsistent with the principles of toleration and religious freedom.[13] Cotton Mather, though the *primum mobile* of the original movement, retracts his zeal for the necessity of consociations in his Ratio Disciplinæ,[14] saying: "It may be the prudent servants of God had it (the confusion which was feared for want of consociation) more in fear than there was any real need of. . . . The churches have not, in fact, seen much of this confusion." A frank and very important confession from such a man, vanquished as he had been twenty-one years before. — See COUNCILS, SYNODS, POWER. See Punchard's View, 103—113, Upham's Rat. Dis. 191—195.

[1] Trumbull's Hist. Conn. i. 486, 487. [2] Ans. to Herle, in Han. ii. 172, 173. [3] Church Gov. 71, 72. [4] Survey, part i. 87. [5] Page 148. [6] Hist. Conn. chap. xiii. xix. [7] Page 19. [8] Page 88. [9] Page 57. [10] Apologetical Reply, 230. [11] Ans. to Prynne, in Han. ii. 394. [12] Convention Serm. 71. [13] Eliot, Biog. Dict. 510. [14] Page 183, 184.

CONTUMACY. — Cotton Mather says:[1] "If the person do out of contempt refuse to make his appearance, the pastor moves the church to concur (after some further exercise of forbearance, if in their lenity they think necessary) in his excommunication." This is believed to be the universal sentiment on this point; the delinquent refuses to hear the church. Care should, however, be taken to be sure that the absence is not providential, involuntary, or necessary.

[1] Rat. Dis. 14C.

COUNCILS, *early*. — Increase Mather informs us[1] that the first, after the apostolic, assembled A.D. 180, and condemned the heresy of Montanus. Also, that the second Ephesian synod, A.D. 450, *compelled their members by torture* to submit to the decrees of the majority. T. Hooker[2] declares that there was no *general* council after our Saviour by the space of three hundred years. In the view of Congregationalists, it had been well if such councils had never assembled again. Owen, in his Nature of Schism,[3] says: "I do not know of any thing, which is extant, bearing clearer witness of the degeneracy of the Christian religion, . . . than the stories of the acts and laws of councils and synods." He shows that there neither has been nor can be any proper general council representing the whole church, since the apostles. Punchard[4] alludes to some of the steps by which these general councils corrupted the early churches.

[1] Disquisition on Ecc. Councils, 3, 4. [2] Survey, part i. 238. [3] In Han. iii. 440. [4] Hist. Cong. 21.

COUNCILS, *proper objects of.*—Thomas Goodwin says[1] of the church at Antioch: "They did not, . . . as wanting power, appeal . . . as to a court of judicature, . . . but only sent for advice and counsel in a difficult case." Richard Mather[2] represents the objects of councils to be "to communicate light, not for the imperious binding of the church to rest in their dictates, but by propounding their grounds from the Scriptures." He shows[3] that churches are independent, but "confederate, not to use or exercise their power, but with mutual communion one asking counsel of the other. . . . To bind them to do no weighty thing without counsel . . . were to bind them to be imperfect. . . . THE DECREE OF A

COUNCIL HATH SO MUCH FORCE AS THERE IS FORCE IN THE REASON OF IT." Punchard [4] shows that these were also the opinions of John Robinson. Rapin [5] affirms that the Independents in the Westminster Assembly differed from the other reformed churches only about the jurisdiction of classes, synods, and convocations, and the point of liberty of conscience. Ainsworth, in his reply to Paget,[6] shows that, as many godly Christians are not able to perform the work of examining candidates for church officers, they call in the council of other churches; but he denies the necessity of such councils to ordination. Davenport, in his Power of Congregational Churches,[7] says: "Where a church wants light, she should send for counsel, but preserve the power entirely in her own hands, where Christ has placed it." Welde, in his reply to Rathband, says:[8] "If the sufficiency of such men as they intend to call into office be not *well known*, then they are to call in the help and assistance of the elders of other churches, to survey their abilities, and inform them thereon." Rathband having insinuated that they arrogated to ordain without the concurrent authority of other churches or church officers, Welde replies:[9] "Authority is either coercive or from rule: the former we use not, for want of Scripture ground; the latter we improve upon all occasions, by calling in other churches, and hold ourselves bound to follow their counsel, *so far as it is founded on the word of God.*" Bartlett [10] embraces, in his Compendium, "craving help and assistance of neighbor churches, in difficult cases, by way of advice and counsel." John Cotton[11] shows that churches do not choose officers nor depose them without the approbation of other churches, because in the multitude of counsellors there is safety. He shows[12] that where a case is doubtful, and a minority dissent, they call for light from other churches. Hubbard[13] gives an instance of such a council in Dorchester, in 1640, and its happy results. Mr. Haven[14] says: "The power of councils is merely advisory, nor can they volunteer that service. They cannot come till they are asked, nor extend their inquiries beyond the point submitted; and their advice may be regarded or not, as may seem best to the party asking."

The Petitioners of the Church and Town of Woburn to the General Court[15] "do not deny counsel in difficult cases," but maintain that it is not always difficult to determine whether a man may preach. "A council can bind no farther than they can make it fasten by convicting demonstration." Dr. Osgood[16] says, the decree at Antioch, "passed in the name of the Holy Ghost, was written by men confessedly inspired, and did but confirm what inspired men had taught before." He is astonished that this should be made the foundation of so many councils and canons.

Ch. Gov. 85. [2] Ch. Gov. 62. [3] Ib. 65, 66. [4] Hist. 359, 360. [5] In Neal, Puritans, i. 493. [6] In Han. i. 346. [7] Ib. ii. 65. [8] Ib. 316. [9] Ib. 317. [10] Ib. iii. 246. [11] Way of the Churches, 45. [12] Ib. 96. [13] Hist. Mass. 278. [14] Dedham Con. 55. [15] In Mass. Hist. Soc. Col. Serm. iii. vol. i. page 40. [16] Dudlean Lect. 14.

COUNCILS, *have they authority to ordain and depose?* — Richard Mather[1] affirms that it is "the practice to call in the aid of other churches; but it is not lawful nor convenient to call in such assistance by way of authority or power of ministers, or of other churches." Cotton[2] maintains that "ordination is a work of church power," and that "the power of the keys is a liberty purchased to the church by the blood of Christ," and *should* not be parted with at a less price. He inquires also, On what ground shall presbyters censure a brother that is a member of another church? Clemens Romanus[3] complains of the unworthy course of the Corinthian church, but never of their having exercised their power without a council. Goodwin[4] shows that the bringing in new ministers should be with the privity and knowledge of neighbor ministers and churches; "but that will not arise to this, that the neighbor ministers have the power of ordination, the power of deposition, or that they have a negative vote, by way of jurisdiction, to which the church must, by virtue of an institution, submit. . . . It must be remembered, that giving the right hand of fellowship is not giving the right hand of AUTHORITY, to choose them elders or to lay hands upon them." Dr. H. Ainsworth[5] acknowledges the advice of councils good and lawful, but not to do those actions which are peculiar to any church to do for itself. The General Court of Massachusetts undertook to interfere and make councils necessary to ordination in 1651, but never succeeded.[6] Prince[7] informs us that the church in Salem sent to that in Plymouth to attend Mr. F. Higginson's ordination, "that they might have the approbation and concurrence, if not the direction and assistance, of the other." Rev. C. W. Upham, in his Appendix to Dedication Sermon,[8] says: "They expressly declared that the church in Plymouth should not claim any jurisdiction over the church in Salem; and, further, that the authority of ordination should not exist in the clergy, but should depend on the free election of the members of the church." The same is corroborated in Eliot's Biog. Dict. p. 252, art. "F. Higginson," and elsewhere. Dr. Emmons[9] shows that a council can neither put a pastor into his office, nor put him out of it, without the consent of the church.

[1] Ch. Gov. 41. [2] Way of the Churches, 50. [3] Epistle to the Corinthians, 24, 25. [4] Ch. Gov. 229. [5] Answer to Paget, in Han. i. 344. [6] Hubbard's Hist. Mass. 550. [7] Chronology, 190. [8] Page 52. [9] Vol. v. 448—451.

COUNCILS, *have they authority to reverse decisions?* — Richard Mather[1] says: "No ecclesiastical power on earth can reverse or disannul church censure." And,[2] "Councils are to give light, *not by imperious binding of the church to rest in their dictates*, but by propounding their grounds from the Scriptures. And,[3] "The sentence of a council is of itself, *only advice*, . . . not, of itself, *authority* nor *necessity*." The Leyden church believed[4] that no church or church officers have any power whatever over other churches or church officers. T. Goodwin maintains the same: he says,[5] "The church at Corinth had an entire judicature within itself, not depending upon the advice of any for sentence." Dr. Emmons[6] says: "Councils, presbyteries, synods, and general assemblies, are of mere human device, and have no authority over individual churches. It is at their option whether they will ask counsel; and, if they do ask it, their advice is only advisory, and they have a right to accept or reject."

[1] Ch. Gov. 47. [2] Ib. 62. [3] Ib. 66. [4] Punchard, Hist. 362. [5] Ch. Gov. 71. [6] Vol. v. 450.

COUNCILS, *have they any juridical power?*—The Independents in the Westminster Assembly maintain[1] that even the appeal of the church at Antioch was only for advice, and not for a judicial determination. Samuel Mather[2] says that the churches are not obliged to acknowledge the authority of councils for their direction. He shows[3] that synods have no juridical power; that they are persuasive, and not compulsive; and "the churches are still free to accept or reject their advice." He moreover informs us,[4] that some, in his day, wanted a juridical power; but he argues at length to show that the power which Christ has given to his churches is sacred; and concludes[5] that churches ought to call councils, when they want light or peace, and, *if they see meet*, conform to the same. John Wise, in his Vindication,[6] and through his whole book, shows that a council has only consultative and not juridical power. He wrote the book expressly to meet the proposals to establish such a power. In John White's Lamentations,[7] he censures a council which tried to induce the parties to agree to acquiesce in their decisions before they heard the case, — thus ensnaring their consciences. He censures[8] also the councils which usurped the power of judgment, and also of admonition. Trumbull[9] asserts that it was the opinion of the principal divines, who settled New England and Connecticut, that determinations of councils were to be received with reverence, but that they had no juridical power. Hooker[10] concludes his argument on this point by saying: The juridical power of councils is, "I fear, an invention of man." In Norton's Catechism, question — "What is the power of a council?" the answer is — "To declare truth, not to exercise authority." Dr. Osgood[11] says: "No number of churches assembled by their representatives, have, from Christ or his apostles, the least authority to decide any matters of controversy, either of faith or discipline." From the Answer to the Hampshire Narrative,[12] it seems that the association argued that "to ask advice is to ask to be directed." The council reply that "it is not then asking to be advised, but to be commanded." Dr. Stiles[13] says: "Churches reserve to themselves to refuse or accept the advice of council: . . . Congregational churches *universally* hold a negative on the result of council. . . . The decision of council is of no force, till received and ratified by the inviting church, nor does it render that church obnoxious to community if she recedes from advice of council." He maintains that Congregational councils are advisory only, and our churches are absolutely free from foreign jurisdiction. He shows that juridical power in councils clashes with the complete power of the churches, and that the synod of 1662 declared that a particular church is not under any other ecclesiastical jurisdiction whatever; that[14] the "notions" of the framers of the Cambridge Platform were, "that, in cases of difficulty, councils assembled on invitation, *not to decide and determine authoritatively*, but to advise the church how to decide and determine it; and,[15] "however fond they were of the power of presbyteries *in* the church, they were very opposite to the power of classes, councils, and synods, *out of* the church;" that Cotton and Davenport wrote largely against these in their Answer to Paget; and that churches only, and not the advisory synods, could perfect the sentence of non-communion. He says[16] that "no church was hereticated for not receiving the result of synod." That "councils are to *advise* what is to be done, and churches to *do* what is to be done," was the opinion of Hooker, Chauncy, Davenport, and Oakes. He quotes especially from Hooker's Survey, part iv. page 47,* "The council's determination takes place, not because they concluded so, but because the churches approve of what they determined." Neal[17] says, Robinson allowed of councils for advice, but "not for exercising authority or jurisdiction." Bliss, in his History of Rehoboth,[18] shows that the parties bound themselves beforehand to abide the result of council relative to the dismission of Mr. Carnes in 1763. This is the earliest instance which I have noticed, save the cases to which John

* Some falsely ascribe the fourth part of this work to Cotton.

White alludes in his Lamentations in Wise's Quarrel, page 165. — See LAWS OF NEW ENGLAND; CHURCHES *discipline each other, but not juridically;* COUNCILS, *proper objects of;* CONSOCIATIONS; SYNODS.

[1] In Neal's Puritans, ii. 9. [2] Apology, 6. [3] Ib. 118. Ib. 122—129. [5] Page 133. [6] Page 45. [7] Page 165. [8] Page 167. [9] Hist. Conn. i. 297. [10] Survey, part i. 121. [11] Dudlean Lect. 15. [12] Pages 27—35. [13] Convention Sermon, 46—48. [14] Ib. 59. [15] Ib. 60. [16] Ib. 62. [17] N. Eng. i. 73. [18] Page 209.

COUNCILS, *of whom composed.* — John Robinson[1] maintained, "that it was not orderly that the bodies of churches should be sent to for counsel, but some chief persons. Power and authority is in the body for election and censures, but counsel for direction in all difficult cases in some few." Ainsworth, in his Answer to Clyfton,[2] replies to an objection to sending to the church in Leyden, because "they were in the same case," by saying, "The same objection could have been brought by the church in Antioch against the church in Jerusalem." The Independents in the Westminster Assembly[3] argued that a council should not be selected by location, but by agreement of the troubled church or opposing parties. Increase Mather[4] says: "For councils to take it upon them to determine, without elders and messengers from the churches, is prelatical, even though the church declares that they will not send them." And[5] he asserts that it belongs not to ministers to direct to whom or to what churches aggrieved persons shall send for counsel. He shows[6] that ministers sit in council only by virtue of delegation from their churches. In his Order of the Churches of New England,[7] he shows, at length, that the brethren as well as pastors have a right to sit in councils. Samuel Mather[8] informs us, that, in the synod of 1679, certain pastors were not allowed to sit till they had lay delegates to sit with them. John Wise[9] maintains that ministers may be left out of the choice of delegates to councils, if so their churches will. From Balch's Vindication of the Second Church in Bradford, it appears[10] that the church, about 1746, sent to the ministers of one association with their churches to constitute a council. The letter of the Boston ministers to the distressed churches in Connecticut, at the time of the Episcopal defection, recommends a council, impartial, and *not confined to the vicinity.* Mr. Davenport[11] was invited to sit with the synod at Cambridge. Upham, in his Ratio Disciplinæ,[12] affirms that "there does not appear to be any Congregational authority whatever for the particular church that assembles the council to invite individuals to sit and act in the same, in their own persons and right, and not as the representatives of sister-churches." If this is so, and I find nothing either in principle or ancient precedent to contradict it (unless the case of Mr. Davenport above be taken as an exception),* then, if the services of ex-pastors or others are specially needed on councils, applications should be made to the churches of which they are members. It may be asked, If councils are merely advisory, why not

* See references to Trumbull, in art. CONSOCIATIONS, *origin of.*

leave the parties to counsel with whom they choose? It is answered, they have a right to counsel with whom they choose for *mere* advice; but, if it be concerning a matter involving church fellowship and mutual church help, then there are certain points of propriety to be regarded in choosing a council which is truly ecclesiastical. Increase Mather[13] strenuously maintains that it is not necessary or proper to confine the parties to the nearest churches, but that this is an infringement of their liberty. Mitchell, in his Guide,[14] says they are usually from the same neighborhood, but sometimes from places more remote. Cotton Mather[15] shows that, in his time, there was usually more than one delegate sent from a church, — the pastor nominating one or more, and the church adding to them at their election. From one to six delegates[16] were chosen from each church to a council in Dorchester about 1794. Rev. Dr. Fiske, of New Braintree, informs the compiler, that in his early days the churches resented being limited in the number of delegates they were requested to send to a council. The Boston Synod of 1662 say[17] that they should be called "with special reference to those churches which by providence are planted in a convenient vicinity, though with *liberty*, reserved *without offence*, to make use of others, as the nature of the case, or the advantage of opportunity, may lead thereunto." — See COUNCILS, *pastors sit in, by virtue of their delegation;* DELEGATES.

[1] In Punchard's Hist. 360; and Han. i. 448; and Works, iii. 382. [2] Han. i. 254. [3] Ib. ii. 508. [4] Dis. on Ecc. Councils, Preface.

[5] Ib. 33. [6] Ib. 13—26. [7] Pages 83—90. [8] Apology, 117. [9] Quar. of the Churches Esp. 144. [10] Page 22. [11] Eliot, Biog. Dict. 149. [12] Pages 126, 127. [13] Disquisition, 31. [14] Page 226. [15] Rat. Dis. 159, 160. [16] Votes of the Church and Ecc. Council in Dorchester, 21, 22. [17] Page 116.

COUNCILS, *how chosen.* — In the work entitled Congregationalism as contained in the Scriptures and explained by the Platform, it is asserted that a council should be chosen, one half by each party separate, and not in meeting of the whole body, which would give the minority no voice in the selection. The answer to the Hampshire Narrative[1] says: "It is a universal custom for the church to agree with the candidate what churches shall constitute the council." So Upham.[2]

[1] Page 39. [2] Rat. Dis. 189.

COUNCILS, *how convened?*—Mitchell[1] describes the method now practised, by letters missive, asking for a pastor and delegate; a point too well understood to need a particular illustration. C. Mather[2] also describes the usual method in his time, varying from the present practice only in the number of delegates and the mode of their nomination. — See COUNCILS, *of whom composed?*

[1] Guide, 227. [2] Rat. Dis. 159, 160.

COUNCILS, *occasions of.* — Mitchell[1] enumerates these as follows, viz.: Ordination, dismission, and deposition of ministers; troublesome cases of discipline; dissensions or other difficulties in a church, which the church itself is unable or indisposed to settle; and, in general, all those occasions which require the advice or concurrent action of more churches than one. The ancient writers usually described the occasions of councils in such general terms as these, — Where a church wants either light or peace. See Upham, Rat. Dis. 188, 189; and Punchard's View, 114. — See COUNCILS, *proper objects of.*

[1] Guide, 226.

COUNCILS, *have pastors a negative vote in?* — This question is discussed at length in Increase Mather's Disquisition;[1] and, though he had then gone over to favor Consociationism, he was still "vehement in the negative." — See CONSOCIATIONS, *objections to.*

[1] Pages 7—13.

COUNCILS, *pastors sit in, by virtue of their delegation, and not as pastors.* — Increase Mather[1] strenuously maintains this ground, and hence argues that they have no negative voice, but are only equal with other delegates of the churches. He argues the point at length, showing that, as their power is only consultative, there is no good reason why judicious laymen should not have as great a voice as pastors. The opposite of this doctrine had been set up about this time by the authors of the proposals for a consociation.[2] In his Order of the Gospel Justified,[3] Dr. Mather says: "Not their office, but their delegation, gives them power to be members of synods; . . . none ought to be admitted to such assemblies but those whom the churches shall send. . . . So, in ecclesiastical councils, not only the officers but others may receive a commission from the churches, and then have equal power with the pastor." Upham[4] says there does not appear to be any congregational authority for inviting persons to sit in council by their own right, and not as delegates of councils. — See DELEGATES.

[1] Disquisition, 13—26. [2] Wise's Quarrel of the Churches Espoused, 159. [3] Page 86. [4] Rat. Dis. sect. 84.

COUNCILS, *ex parte.* — Cotton Mather says:[1] "The churches of New England have a remedy for oppression, that is to say, a council. If the church refuse to call a council, the aggrieved may do it without them, only informing them what he does." He describes the mode of procedure of such a council,[2] and says: "If they find the person to have suffered palpable injury, they endeavor to convince the church. If the church refuse, they order that the person be admitted to some other church in the neighborhood, and so to communion with them all." He says[3] that churches thus persisting run a risk of a withdrawal of fellowship, by a ratification by the churches which sent their delegates to the council. He asserts, moreover,[4] that a council may be called by a neighbor-church, applied to by the aggrieved party. S. Mather[5] informs us that this calling a council by another church, on application of the aggrieved, was the only way known in his day in which testimony might be borne against mal-administration in any particular church. See Upham's Rat. Dis. 197—204; Punchard's View, 112, 266; Bacon's Church Manual, 143—145.

[1] Rat. Dis. 158. [2] Pages 159—162. Page 161. [4] Page 162. [5] Apology, 139.

COUNCILS, *are they beneficial?* — Whoever wishes to see the full arguments for the affirmative of this question, should consult Increase Mather's Disquisition on Ecclesiastical Councils, throughout.

COUNCILS *have no power to enforce creeds.* — This is demonstrated in Watts's Christian Church, in his Complete Works, vol. iii.

COUNCILS *expire when they have given the advice for which they were called.* — Hon. S. Haven, Proceedings of First Church and Parish in Dedham, 52. See the Fiske case in Salem, under the head CHURCHES *discipline each other*, for an early innovation on this important Congregational rule. Upham, in his Rat. Dis. sect. 157, represents re-assembling, or doing other business than that for which they were called, as "at variance with Congregational principles." — For the whole subject of councils, see APPEALS, SYNODS.

COVENANT, *what?* — This was held by the early Congregational writers to be that which constitutes a church, and a person a member of a Christian church. They held that it ought to be explicit, but might be implied. (See CHURCH, *what constitutes?*) The advocates both of a national and a catholic visible church accused the Congregationalists of unwarrantable strictness on this point. Thomas Goodwin, in his Letters to John Goodwin, says:[1] "The church covenant is no more with us than this, — an agreement and resolution, professed with promise to walk in all those ways pertaining to this fellowship, so far as they shall be revealed to them in the gospel. Thus briefly and indefinitely and implicitly, and in such like words and no other, do we apply ourselves to men's consciences, not obtruding upon them the mention of any one particular before or in admission, . . . leaving their spirits free to the entertainment of the light that shines or shall shine on them and us out of the word." Daniel Buck, a member of the church organized in London in 1592, declared,[2] on his arraignment before three magistrates, that when he came into the congregation "he made this protestation, that he would walk with the rest of the congregation, so long as they would walk in the way of the Lord, and as far as might be warranted by the word of God." Burton, in his Rejoinder to Prynne's Answer concerning the Twelve Considerable Questions,[3] maintains that it is enough that there be a covenant either expressed or implied. Cotton[4] shows that a covenant may be "by silent consent, Gen. xvii. 2; by express words, Ex. xix. 8; or by writing and sealing, Neh. ix. 38." Cotton Mather says,[5] that, in an Apology of Justin Martyr, we find Christians, who were admitted into church fellowship, agreeing in a resolution to conform in all things to the word of God; which seems to be as truly a church covenant as any in the churches of New England. In the organization of the Salem Church, Mr. Higginson drew up a covenant* and confession of faith; and those who were afterward admitted were required "to enter into a like covenant-engagement as to the *substance*, but the *manner* was to be so ordered by the elders as to be most conducive to the end, *respect being always had by them to the* LIBERTY and *ability* of the person."[6] Congregationalism as contained in the Scriptures, &c.[7] quotes from Hooker's Survey, part. i. 46: "This covenant may be either explicit or implicit; explicit where there is a formal covenant, implicit where they practise without a verbal written formal covenant." This covenant, he maintains, is for life as essentially as is the marriage-covenant. Prince[8] quotes Gov. Bradford: "Upon which these people shake off their antichristian bondage, and, as the Lord's free people, join themselves by covenant in a church state, to walk in all his ways, made known or *to be made known to them*, according to their best endeavors, whatever it cost them." Thus it seems that covenants were originally the basis of Congregational church organizations, and that with regard to the *substance*, and not the words of them. Many of the old writers, particularly Goodwin, show that a covenant, expressed or implied, is absolutely necessary to the establishment of any society whatever. Formulas

* It is given in Neal's Puritans, i. 300.

of doctrine, as a test of admission, were of much later origin, as will appear under the next article. A laconic covenant of the ancient Independent Church in Wattesfield, Suffolk, may be found in Neal's Puritans, ii. 179, note.—Further illustrations of the general subject may also be found in Hanbury, i. 85; ii. 309—314; iii. 76.

[1] Page 44. [2] In Punchard's Hist. 277, 278. [3] Page 25. [4] Way of the Churches, 3. [5] Rat. Dis. 12. [6] Hubbard's Hist. Mass. 119, 120. [7] Pages 7, 8. [8] Chronology, 4.

CREEDS, *should they be a binding rule of faith and practice, and a test for admission to the churches?* Richard Mather[1] says: "They may have a platform by way of profession of their faith, but not a binding rule of faith and practice. . . . If so, then they ensnare men attending more to the form of doctrine delivered from the authority of the church . . . than to the examining thereof according to the Scriptures." Required subscription was the parent of English Independency. Burton, in his Rejoinder to Prynne's Reply to his Answer to Twelve Considerable Questions, says:[2] "It is the greatest possible tyranny over men's souls to make other men's judgments the rule of my conscience." Thomas Goodwin, in his letter to John Goodwin,[3] is equally explicit on this point:* so is Hubbard, in his History of Massachusetts.[4]† Neal, in his Puritans,[5] represents the chief error of the Brownists to be their unchurching all other churches. Gibbon, in his Decline and Fall,[6] says the churches of the

* See extract from this letter in the preceding article. † See ib.

Roman empire "were united only by the ties of faith and charity." Hanbury[7] says of the Confession of the Low Country Exiles, it was transmitted to the authorities at home, not with "any expectation that it should be erected into a standard. If they entertained, however, any such modes of fixing religious belief, time has shown their utter futility for that purpose. . . . The unadulterated word of God shall stand for ever." J. Cotton, in his Answer to Ball, says:[8] "When a church is suspected and slandered with corrupt and unsound doctrine, they have a call from God to set forth a public confession of their faith; but to *prescribe* the same as *the* confession of faith of that church to their posterity, or the prescribed confession of faith of one church to be a form and pattern unto others, sad experience has showed what a snare it has been to both." Even Herle, in his controversy with Mather and Tompson,[9] disclaims "such a fan to purge the religious floor with, and SETTING THE SUN BY THE DIAL." The Apologetical Narrative of the Independents in the Westminster Assembly[10] asserts that their rules of admission were such "as would take in any member of Christ. We took measure of no man's holiness by his opinions, whether concurring with us or adverse from us." Baillie, in his Letters to Spang, says:[11] "Thomas Goodwin, at that meeting, declared that he cannot refuse to be members, nor censure when members, any for Anabaptism, Lutheranism, or any errors which are not fundamental and maintained against knowledge." The same principles are advanced by Cotton, in his Holiness of Church Members;[12] in the preface to the Savoy Confession;[13] and by the Congregational Union of England and Wales,[14] as late as the year 1833. Lord King[15] gives various forms of ancient creeds, and says they were handed down from father to son, not in the precise words, but varying, and never repeated in the same words, even by the same father. John Owen[16] says: "We will never deny the communion to any person whose duty it is to desire it." Samuel Mather shows[17] that all Christians ought to be admitted to any of Christ's churches. Cotton Mather says:[18] "The churches of New England make only vital piety the terms of communion among them; and they all, with delight, see godly Congregationalists, Presbyterians, Episcopalians, Anti-pedobaptists, and Lutherans, *all members of the same churches*, and sitting together without offence in the same holy mountain, at the same holy table." Speaking of the use then made of creeds, he says[19] of candidates for admission: "To the relation of his religious experience is added either a confession of faith of the person's own composing, or a briefer intimation of what publicly-received confession he chooses to adhere to." He says:[20] "It is the design of these churches to make the terms of communion run as parallel as may be with the terms of salvation. A charitable consideration of nothing but true piety, in admitting to evangelical privileges, is a glory which the churches of New England would lay claim to." Dr. Watts, in his Terms of Christian Communion,[21] shows that the churches may not appoint new rules of admission; as a general rule should admit all who make a *credible* profession of religion; exclude no sheep of the fold, and admit no unclean beast; take heed not to make the door of admission larger or straiter than Christ made it; and that nothing be in their covenant but what is essential to common Christianity. He has a list[22] of substantial articles, all very fundamental, save that of the mode and subjects of baptism, which he argues (whether consistently or no) is fundamental to the peace of the church. And he shows[23] that the Christian church flourished more than a hundred years without any set creeds, and argues their utter insufficiency, because they often have the assent neither of the head nor the heart. So late as 1801, Dr. Worcester's church in Fitchburg say, in defence of their creed,[24] if the candidate dissented from any article, and it did not appear to result from enmity to the truth, he was admitted; "FOR IT WAS NEVER DESIGNED TO EXCLUDE ANY FROM COMMUNION WHO APPEAR TO BE REAL SUBJECTS OF EXPERIMENTAL RELIGION." Thomas Goodwin[25] shows that we are to bear with Christians for the sake of Christ that is in them, and therefore tolerate them as Christians, but contend earnestly for the faith. Dr. Kippis, in his Vindication of Dissenting Ministers, says:[26] "We dissent because we deny the right of any body of men, whether civil or ecclesiastical, to impose human creeds, tests, or articles; and because we think it our duty not to submit to any such imposition, but to protest against it as a violation of our essential liberty to judge and act for ourselves in matters of religion." He adds:[27] "They will not subscribe to human forms, which themselves believe, when such formularies are pressed upon them by an incompetent and usurped authority." He shows[28] that ministers, believers in the doctrine of the Trinity, voted that no human composition or interpretation of that doctrine should be made a part of the Articles of Advice in 1719. Plymouth Church[29] covenanted "to walk in a church state, in all God's ways made known or *to be made known to them.* They reserved an entire perpetual liberty of searching the inspired records, and forming both their principles and practices from those discoveries they should make therein, without imposing them on others." This appears from their original covenant in 1602.[30] Milford Church, Conn., founded in 1640, had a covenant; but no mention is made of any confession of faith. New Haven and Guilford had a doctrine of faith, short, comprehensive, and highly Calvinistical.[31] The original covenant of the First Church in Boston, after the preamble, is simply this:[32] "Do solemnly and deliberately, as in Christ's holy presence, bind ourselves to walk, in all our ways, according to the rule of the gospel, in all sincere conformity to his holy ordinances, and in mutual love and respect to each other, so far as God shall give us grace." Every member wrote his own confession in his own way, and to the satisfaction of those who received him into their fellowship. At first the churches of New England were usually constituted with no other form than a covenant. The author of Seasonable Thoughts on Creeds and Articles of Faith as Religious Tests, asks:[33] "Do not the framers and advocates of creeds, as tests of orthodoxy and Christian communion, seem to confess that they are not satisfied with the Bible on this subject? . . . If creeds are necessary to guard against heretics, the Bible is not a sufficient rule. . . . *Do* they operate, *have* they operated, or are they likely *ever* to operate, as an effectual preventive to unprincipled and heretical men gaining admission into a Christian church?" He seems, in the sequel, to misapply these just sentiments, to advocate receiving such as build not on the Christian foundation. Dr. Eckley shows[34] that if creeds could be made perfect, then nothing would be necessary but to learn the creed. Foxcroft, in his Century Sermon,[35] says: "The Congregationalists were for having the rule of Christianity be the rule of conformity." Morton, in his New England Memorial, says:[36] "Higginson's Confession of Faith and Covenant was acknowledged *only* as a direction pointing to that faith and covenant contained in the Holy Scriptures; and therefore *no man was confined to that form of words*, but only to the substance and scope of the matter contained therein; and, for the circumstantial manner of joining the church, it was ordered according to the wisdom and faithfulness of the elders, together with the liberty and ability of any person. Hence it was that *some* were admitted by expressing their consent to that written confession of faith and covenant; *others* did answer questions about the principles of religion, that were publicly propounded to them; *some* did present their confession in writing, which was read for them; and *some*, that were able and willing, did make their own confession, in their own words and way." Letchford, in his Plain Dealing,[37] shows very minutely that profession of faith was made either by question and answer or else by solemn speech, as to the sum and tenor of the Christian faith laid down in the Scriptures, the officers in the church, and their duties. Such is the evidence of one who complained of their too great strictness, because they required evidence of experimental religion. He spoke that which he knew, and testified that he had seen. Such testimonies, it would seem, ought to set for ever at rest the notion that Higginson's Confession of Faith was used as a constitution of the church and a test of admission. John Corbett says:[38] "We need no human addition to sacred things, nor any mutable circumstances to be terms of fellowship." Cotton Mather, in his Letter to Lord Barrington,[39] says: "No church on earth so notably makes the terms of communion run parallel with the terms of salvation. The *only* declared basis of union among them is that vital piety in which all good men, of different names, are united." Robinson reminds the Plymouth immigrants, on parting,[40] that it is an article of their church covenant "to be ready to receive whatever of truth shall be made known to them from the written word of God." The Rev. C. Upham shows[41] that it is a fundamental principle of Congregationalism not to impose a test, which may not be complied with by all sincere Christians. In a similar manner argue Dr. West (Anniversary Plymouth Sermon, 58, 59), President Stiles (Convention Sermon, 45), John Howe (Works, 459, 931), and Mauduit (Case of Dissenting Ministers, 34, 35). It is not, however, the use of creeds, but making them separate acknowledged Christians, which our fathers condemned. Their confessions were orthodox explicit manifestoes, not tests of admission. Some churches at this day have similar creeds, but require assent only to the substance of them; while others, making tests of their creeds, have frittered them down to the standard of those weakest in the faith. Few churches have too high a standard of admission, but it should consist only in true faith and vital godliness. Mr. Mitchell says:[42] "Congregationalists object to creeds being used as tests, or set up as standards to enforce uniformity. . . . As articles of peace and bonds of union, we fear they create divisions as often as they prevent them;" and, speaking of some "who think that heaven and earth should pass, rather than one jot or tittle of the exact wording of the prescribed creed... be not fulfilled," he says: "Any brother that offends in one point they hold to be guilty of all, and obnoxious to ecclesiastical censure. They put their strait-jacket upon the limbs of Charity, who loves freedom as she loves truth, and make their narrow views the jail-limits, within which she walks afflicted and confined."

Upham, in his Ratio Disciplinæ, says:[43] "None of these various sects [among which he has enumerated Congregationalists], so far as known, is destitute of an authorized and settled constitution; each of them embodying what it conceives to be the sense of Scripture in certain articles of faith, . . . which the individual members are in general not at liberty to disregard." And the Congregational Manual[44] says: "The *instrument* by which individual believers are constituted one body in a church is a *Confession of Faith.*" (See CHURCH, *what constitutes?*) Bellamy, in his Letters to Scripturista,[45] maintains the right of test-creeds, because it is matter what people believe. If men change their views, they should honestly declare it. True; but should we test and reject men who appear to be Christians, because they agree not to our expositions of portions of the Holy Scriptures? Andrew Fuller, in his Ecclesiastical Polity,[46] argues for test-creeds, on the ground that individuals and society have a right to form their own connections with those with whom they agree in views. But the premise is denied in this case, because Christ has given the injunction,—"Him that is weak in the faith *receive* ye." Professor Pond, in his Treatise on the Church,[47] argues in the same strain as do Bellamy and Fuller.—See Dr. Bacon's Church Manual, 22—28. See FUNDAMENTALS, MEMBERS.

[1] Church Gov. 64. [2] Page 19. [3] Pages 44, 45. [4] Pages 119, 120. [5] Vol. i. 150. [6] In Han. i. 7. [7] Ib. 98. [8] Ib. ii. 162. [9] Ib. 166, 167. [10] Ib. 225. [11] Ib. 558. [12] Ib. iii. 401. [13] Ib. 521. [14] Ib. 598. [15] Enquiry, part ii. 57—67. [16] In Hall's Puritans and their Principles, 295. [17] Apology, 34, and elsewhere. [18] Rat. Dis. Introduct. 4. [19] Page 88. [20] Page 90. [21] Works, iii. 235—250. [22] Pages 258—262. [23] Page 265. [24] Facts and Documents, 8.

[25] Ch. Gov. book vii. chap. 12. [26] Page 29. [27] Page 30. [28] Pages 34, 57. [29] Prince's Chronology, 4. [30] Ib. 89. [31] Lambert's Hist. New Haven, 101, 164. [32] Art. John Cotton, in N. Englander, Aug. 1850, p. 412. [33] Pages 8, 9. [34] Dudlean Lect. 23. [35] Page 9. [36] Page 146. [37] In Hist. Soc. Col. series iii. vol. iii. 68. [38] Princip. and Pract. of Several Nonconformists, 2. [39] Hist. Soc. Col. series i. vol. i. 19. [40] Upham's Dedicat. Serm. 29. [41] Century Serm. 56. [42] Guide, 53, 54. [43] Page 35. [44] Page 26. [45] Works, i. 371—390; and Doctrinal Tract Society's edition, i. 597—613. [46] Works, ii. 629, 630. [47] Pages 23—27, and Appendix, note C.

DANCING. — Neal [1] notes, among the anti-puritan movements after the Restoration, that "interludes, masquerades and *promiscuous dancing*, profane swearing, drunkenness, and a universal dissolution of manners, were connived at, and the very name of godliness became a reproach. — See AMUSEMENTS.

[1] Hist. of the Puritans, ii. 247.

D. D. — Dr. Owen [1] declares that he did not use the title, save out of respect to the university which conferred it, nor till some were offended because he left it off; and it is found that most who have received it since, feel the same great respect for the good judgment and just discrimination of those who confer it; while the class of expectants are very mute, and the rest are perplexed with the meaning of *Rabbi* in Matt. xxiii. 8, finding no Rabbi to expound it to their mind. They are, therefore, reminded of the fable of the Fox and the Grapes. R. Williams [2] is violent against them, as vain titles, and calling men Father and Rabbi.

[1] In Han. iii. 473. [2] Hireling Ministry none of Christ's, 15.

DEACONS, *their office.* — Goodwin, in his Catechism,[1] shows at length that this is to take care of the temporal affairs of the church, particularly receiving and distributing of alms; and not without a separate appointment to preach the word, as Philip did after God called him to be an evangelist. Hooker, in his Survey,[2] demonstrates the same doctrine, and shows also that it is appropriate to their office to provide the elements for the Lord's table, and also to see that each member of the church contribute his due share, and bring delinquents to censure. John Owen, in his Catechism,[3] asserts their duties to be to take care of the poor, receive collections, and distribute alms. Cotton Mather says[4] that it is "to relieve the pastors of all the temporal affairs of the church." Mitchell[5] describes their duties to be to receive and distribute the alms of the church; to distribute the bread and wine at the Lord's Supper; to act, in some respects, as assistants and substitutes to the pastor. He says: "In the pastor's absence, they preside at the meetings of the church; and, when there is no preacher, they conduct its worship." These last duties were, in earlier times, held appropriate to ruling elders. Punchard[6] makes it the duty of the senior deacon to preside in the absence of the pastor. Owen, in his Nature of a Gospel Church, chap. ix.,[7] says that a deacon has no authority to rule, i.e. preside in a church. Cambridge Platform[8] defines their office and work to be "to receive the offerings of the church, gifts given to the church, and to keep the treasury of the church, and therewith to serve the tables, which the church is to provide for; as the Lord's table, the table of the ministers, and of such as are in necessity, to whom they are to distribute in simplicity." The king's book, drawn up by bishops and divines in the latter part of the reign of Henry VIII. admits "that their office, in the *primitive church*, was partly to administer meat and other necessaries to the poor, and partly to minister to the bishops and priests." Foxcroft, in his sermon at the ordination of a deacon, says[9] the design of deacons is to provide for the Lord's table, the minister's support, and the poor saints. Churches should furnish them with the means of distributing to the necessity of saints; otherwise the choice of them is solemn mockery. John Webb, in his Sermon at the Ordination of a Deacon, maintains[10] that they are to provide for the table of the Lord, of the ministers, and the poor. It is no part of their work either to preach or baptize. Dr. Dwight[11] maintains that they are to be assistants to the ministers, which he argues from Paul's directions, the nature of their office, and ecclesiastical history; moderators of the church in the absence of the minister; to distribute the sacramental emblems (anciently they also carried them to those that were absent), and to distribute the alms of the church. Isaac Chauncy, in his Divine Institution of Congregational Churches, says:[12] "He that ministers to the external concerns of the church is a deacon. . . . There may be one or more, as the concerns of the church are." — See Punchard's View, 92—102; Upham's Rat. Dis. 74—78.

[1] Pages 25—27. [2] Part ii. 37, 38. [3] Works, xix. 538. [4] Rat. Dis. 128. [5] Guide, 171. [6] View, 170. [7] Works, xx. 524. [8] Chap. vii. sect. ii. [9] Pages 14, 37. [10] Pages 3—5. [11] Works, Serm. clv. [12] Page 62.

DEACONS, *their qualifications and induction.* — John Owen, Nature of a Gospel Church, chap. iv.[1] shows that they are an institution of apostolical power from Christ; that they are to be chosen by the people: and their necessary qualifications are to be of honest report, and full of the Holy Ghost and of wisdom. John Webb, in his Sermon at the Ordination of a Deacon,[2] maintains that they are to be introduced to their office by the suffrage of the brethren and prayer. T. Foxcroft, in his Sermon at such an ordination, says[3] that the practice was then (1731) almost extinct. Dr. Dwight[4] discusses the subject at length, maintaining that they are to be chosen by a vote of the church, and ordained by the imposition of hands. They must be grave, sincere, temperate, free from avarice, acquainted with and heartily attached to the doctrines of the gospel; of a fair Christian reputation, the husbands of one wife, and ruling their families well. See Punchard, View, 92—101, 167; Upham, Rat. Dis. 74—79; Owen, Works, xix. 538.

[1] Works, xx. 412. [2] Page 13. [3] Page 3. [4] Works, Serm. clv.

DEACONS, *what they "purchase" in a "good degree."* — Owen, in his Nature of a Gospel Church,[1] shows that it does not mean that they may preach, unless by virtue of a new office, as that of a deacon is defined. (See PREACH, *who may?*) Watts, in his Foundation of a Christian Church,[2] says: "They obtain a good degree of honor and respect, knowledge and graces, and a good step towards the office of ruling or teaching elder." T. Hooker[3] says that one of the first inlets to the Man of Sin was to lift up a deacon above his place. He shows that a "good degree" means a good standing in the church, and that a deaconship is no necessary preparation for the ministry. Foxcroft, in his Sermon at the Ordination of a Deacon,[4] says, if bishops and deacons are two orders of ministers, why are we able to produce a divine commission for but one of them? Cotton Mather[5] supposes that the passage, 1 Tim. iii. 13, means (as he says some critics read) seats of eminence in the church. Hence, probably, was the origin of the deacons' seats in the old meeting-houses. They were seats of honor.

[1] Works, xx. 529. [2] Works, iii. 315. [3] Survey, part ii. 35, 36. [4] Page 9. [5] Rat. Dis. 130.

DEACONS' WIVES. — Cotton Mather says:[1] "'Tis often inquired, when deacons are chosen, whether their wives are such as directed; but there is a mistake about the meaning of the text in 1 Tim. iii. 11. It is *gunaikes*, women, i. e. the deaconesses or widows; and there is not there one word about deacons' wives any more than the pastors'.

[1] Rat. Dis. 131.

DEDICATIONS. — The Waldenses, in one of their early confessions,[1] say: "So many superstitious dedications of churches . . . are diabolical inventions." Goodwin[2] says Christ gives many directions about the public prayers of the church, — not in places dedicated as holy, with difference from others, as the temple was, — but "I will that prayers be made everywhere." Lord King[3] says of the primitive churches, that they did not imagine any such sanctity or holiness to be in their places of worship as to recommend, or make more acceptable, the services that were discharged therein, than if they had been performed elsewhere. He quotes Clemens Alexandrinus, Justin Martyr, and Dionysius (Bishop of Alexandria), to sustain him: "So that the primitive practice and opinion, with respect to this circumstance of place, was that, if the state of their affairs would permit them, they had fixed places for public worship, which they set apart to that use for conveniency and decency's sake, but not attributing to them any such holiness as thereby to sanctify those services that were performed in them." Cotton Mather,[4] speaking of private devotions on coming into a place of public worship, says: "And so far as holiness of places is the ground therein gone upon, the principle is discarded." Dr. Emmons[5] says: "How many have argued in favor of dedicating new meeting-houses, because the temple was dedicated!" He shows that the Christian dispensation superseded the Mosaic, and so that the conclusion does not follow. Rev. C. Upham, in his address at the laying of the corner-stone of the new meeting-house in Salem,[6] speaks of their disappointment at not finding some plate or memento under the old one. He might, with equal probability of success, have looked there for a papal crucifix or the identical one which Endicot cut out of the king's colors. Dr. Ware, in his History of the Old North and New Brick Churches,[7] speaks of the dedication of a meeting-house as early as 1721. — See CONSECRATIONS.

[1] In Punchard's Hist. 108. [2] Ch. Gov. 13. [3] Enquiry, part ii. 118, 119. [4] Rat. Dis. 63. [5] Vol. v. 439. [6] In Appendix to Ded Serm. 59. [7] Page 26.

DELEGATES, *are pastors*, ex officio, *in councils?* Cotton Mather shows[1] that it has been strongly pleaded that no church officers sit as delegates as such, but only by being sent by their churches; yet that practically the churches act as though their pastors were *ex officio* members, though they do not admit pastors without delegates; and once a synod sent immediately to a church for delegates who had only sent their pastors. — See COUNCILS, *of whom composed; pastors sit in, by virtue of their delegation.*

[1] Rat. Dis. 175.

DELEGATION OF RIGHTS *condemned.*—Owen, in his Nature of a Gospel Church, chap. v.[1] shows that no part of essential church power can be delegated; as admitting members, choosing officers, and the like. See Han. i. 273. — See POWER, *church, cannot be given away, nor taken from them, nor delegated.*

[1] In Works, xx. 440.

DELEGATION, *power of churches to send, and call to account.*— Samuel Mather[1] argues this point at length, maintaining it from the delegation from Antioch to Jerusalem. He shows that the same right was afterwards exercised in sending Clement's epistle from Rome to the Corinthians; also that it is fit in itself, and that there is a parallel to such calling to account, in the case of Peter, by the church at Jerusalem, after his eating with Cornelius, which Peter satisfactorily explained to them.

[1] Apology, 73—75.

DEMOCRACY *in church government.* — John Wise, in his Vindication,[1] takes a great stride (seventy years) in advance of the times, and boldly advocates the legitimacy of democracy and republics, both in civil and ecclesiastical government. He shows that it is agreeable to the law of nature, and that nothing but ill-nature is ever necessary to transform a monarch into a tyrant. He shows, both by theory and examples, how it may be made both a just and efficient government, and how the cause of true piety has always flourished most where this divinely constituted ecclesiastical government has been maintained, besides instancing many cases where God has blessed it in a civil government. Previous to this time, Congregationalists had met with some terrible posers from their antagonists, who pleaded that their principles tended to foster republicanism and democracy. Prynne, for instance, pressed this point in his Twelve Considerable Questions; while the Congregationalists wearied themselves to find the door of truth, — not having abandoned the notion of the divine right of kings. They therefore urged special powers in the ministry and elders to make a mixed government. (See PASTOR, *has he a negative vote ?*) This is one of the few points in which the modern Congregationalists seem to have made advances in favor of liberty, and to see the light clearer than did their fathers. — See INDEPENDENCY *endangers monarchy.*

[1] Pages 40—42, 60—66.

DEVOTION, *private, in public assemblies.* — Cotton Mather says:[1] "It is in these churches neither preached nor approved. So far as it openly proclaims a secret and singular devotion, it is condemned as a pharisaical ostentation; so far as the holiness of places is the ground gone upon, the principle is discarded."

[1] Rat. Dis. 63.

DISCIPLINE, *for what required?* — Owen, in his Catechism,[1] enumerates the causes of discipline to be — moral evils, false fundamental doctrines, and blasphemy. He[2] raises the question whether the church should discipline a flagrant offender, who at once declares his penitence openly, before the church commence their process with him; and answers in the negative, unless they may reject whom Christ reeeives; for the end of discipline is attained in the recovery of the sinner. Cotton Mather[3] says: "The churches of New England have no agreed catalogue of crimes, that shall expose to church censure, except what is in the Bible itself. . . . It belongs to such plain trespasses as a person with our measure of illumination cannot obstinately persist in, without forfeiting an interest in the kingdom of God." Mitchell[4] says: "No matter can be a subject for discipline at all (though it may be for private reproof), for which the offender could not be scripturally excommunicated, in case of his persisting in it. A question closely connected with this is, "Should a member be disciplined and excluded who has already withdrawn from the church?" For an answer, see WITHDRAWING.

[1] In Works, xix. 560. [2] Ib. xx. 558—560. [3] Rat. Dis. 142. [4] Guide, 115.

DISCIPLINE, *proper, a privilege.* — It is often, if not generally, treated as a warfare among brethren; but, rightly conducted, it is a divinely instituted privilege of every erring Christian to be reclaimed from his faults. See this matter wisely handled in Samuel Mather's Apology, 94—96. Dr. Ames[1] says it is not the proper end of reproof, that there may be an entrance made to excommunication, but that the necessity of excommunication, if it can be, might be prevented.

[1] Marrow of Sacred Divinity, 168.

DISCIPLINE, *mode of procedure in.* — The rule for all private offences, it is unanimously conceded by Congregationalists, is that laid down in Matt. xviii. See Samuel Mather's Apology, 74; Dr.

Dwight, Works, Serm. clxii.; Cotton's Way of the Churches, 92, and Keys of Heaven, 85; Cambridge Platform, chap. xiv.; Mitchell's Guide, 84—96; and John Robinson, in Punchard's History, 339. The True Description of the Visible Church says:[1] "If the fault be private, holy and loving admonition and reproof are to be used, with an inward desire and earnest care to win their brother; but if he will not hear, yet to take two or three brethren with him, whom he knoweth most meet for that purpose, that by the mouth of two or three witnesses every word may be confirmed; and if he refuse to hear them, then to declare the matter to the church." In the same points agree all the writers above cited. Cotton Mather[2] says: "A scandalous transgression, known to one or two," should be proceeded with as is a private offence. Letchford, in his Plain Dealing,[3] says: "Ordinarily, matter of offence is to be brought before the elders in private." But, where the offence is public, most Congregational writers argue that there is no need of these private steps. Letchford also adds:[4] "Public offences are heard before the whole church, and strangers too, in Boston." For this course argue John Robinson,[5] Thomas Goodwin,[6] John Cotton,[7] Cambridge Platform,[8] Mitchell,[9] and Samuel Mather.[10] These, and the other advocates for a more summary process, in cases of public notoriety, claim to deduce their conclusions from such passages as 1 Tim. v. 20, and 1 Cor. v. Many are, however, unable to perceive how these, or any other directions, concerning the treatment of transgressors, limit the application of the rule laid down in Matt. xviii. If, for instance, an offended brother proceeded against the incestuous Corinthian just as though his had been a private offence, why was not Paul's injunction fulfilled to the letter, just as much as it was, provided the whole church proceeded in a more summary way? But, as a faithful lexicographer, I am constrained to admit that most Congregational writers argue the contrary. The universal application of the rule in Matt. xviii. would prevent ten thousand disputes, whether offences come under the head of public or private. Dr. Dwight,[11] though he denies the necessity, yet advocates the expediency, of universal private dealing in public offences, "because the persuasion that it is necessary is so universal, that it is necessary for the satisfaction of all." Dr. Hopkins[12] argues very conclusively, from the nature and ends of discipline, that it should always be according to Matt. xviii., even for public offences. He shows that, when the offence is known only to one person, he cannot proceed in discipline, for want of witnesses. Mitchell[13] says,— Charges against an offending brother should be distinctly specified, and seasonably communicated to him, commonly in writing. They should be sustained by evidence. The two or three witnesses are to be called to judge of the crime, fault, or offence, and not to proceed, unless the offence is against some express rule of the gospel, nor unless there be evidence of the fact. In default of these, they should endeavor to convince the brother offended. If it be told to the church, and the delinquent refuse to hear, then it is agreed that he should be cut off from the church. (See Upham's Rat. Dis. 139—143.) Punchard, in his View,[14] says: "The regular course of procedure . . . is substantially this: A brother, who is acquainted with the circumstances of the case, immediately, and without conference with any one, seeks a private interview with the trespasser; he tells him plainly, but with gentleness and kindness, what he has seen or known offensive or unchristian in his conduct. . . . If the offence be strictly private, . . . a private acknowledgment . . . and promise of reformation would be deemed satisfactory. . . . If known only to few, confession to these might be deemed sufficient. But if the cause of complaint be extensively known, the confession must be public. . . . Confession and satisfaction should be as public as the offence. So said John Robinson, so say we. If the offender refuses to give satisfaction, the complainant selects one or two . . . brethren to assist him in his efforts to convince and reclaim the erring brother. If these efforts prove unavailing, a regular complaint is laid before the church, generally . . . in writing, specifying the particular charges, . . . and the persons by whom, and the means by which, it can be proved, and the attempts that have been made to adjust the difficulty privately. It is . . . out of order for a church to receive a complaint till assured that the private steps have been taken. The church then vote to examine the charges. Evidence of the truth of these is then called for. Witnesses may be introduced who are not professors of religion. If the church are convinced of the guilt of the accused, they . . . labor to convince him of his sin, and to induce him to make Christian satisfaction. If unsuccessful, the church, after suitable delay, proceed to admonish him, suspend him from their communion (see SUSPENSION), or to excommunicate and cut him off from all relation to or connection with the church; . . . to cast him out as a heathen man and a publican. The decision of the church should be announced to the offender by the pastor, and thus solemnly pronouncing his excision from the visible body of Christ, . . . or by a letter of the same general import, written in the name of the church." In a note[15] he says: "Many churches make an exception" to the rule of private labors in case of public offences; but he prefers the private course, "for one prominent reason, if for no more, viz., that it is better adapted to secure one great end of all church discipline, — *the reformation of the offender.*" See RIGHTS *of accused.*

[1] In Punchard's Hist. 370, 371. [2] Rat. Dis. 148. [3] In Hist. Soc. Col. series iii. vol. iii. 72. [4] Ib. [5] In Punchard's Hist. 339; Han. i. 263; and Works, iii. 134, 135. [6] Church Gov. 130, 131. [7] Keys, 85. [8] Chap. xiv. [9] Guide, 105, 108, 109. [10] Apology, 97. [11] Works, Serm. clxii. [12] Vol. ii. 355, 358. [13] Guide, 102, 103. [14] Pages 178—180. [15] Ib. 180.

DISCIPLINE, *every member is bound to proceed in.* — The obligation to this is clearly stated in Cotton's Keys, 35.

DISCIPLINE, *churches should assist in, with advice and council.* — Thomas Goodwin[1] demonstrates this from the nature of the case, and the example of the church at Jerusalem in the dispute at Antioch.

[1] Catechism, 21.

DISCIPLINE *of one church by another.* — Neal[1] shows that even the Brownists held that one church might thus advise, counsel, and, if need be, withdraw fellowship from another. The Independents, in their Apologetical Narrative,[2] say: "The offending church is to submit to an open examination by the neighbor churches; and on their persisting in their error or miscarriage, then they are to renounce all Christian communion with them." John White[3] and Cambridge Platform[4] lay down the same rule under the title of the Third Way of Communion of Churches. So does Thomas Goodwin.[5] — See CHURCHES *discipline each other, &c.*

[1] Puritans, i. 150. [2] Ib. 492. [3] Lamentations, in Wise's Vindication, 170, 171. [4] Chap. xv. sect. 2. [5] Catechism, 21.

DISCIPLINE, *Congregational, efficient.* — That it is the reverse has been the stereotyped complaint of those who are unacquainted with it, and of some who are. N. Whitaker[1] complains of the almost total destitution of discipline here, and says: "The purity of the New England churches is boasted of, but not to be found." He ascribes the cause to the democratic element contained in their constitution. He discards Clement's Epistle to the Corinthians; mistaking it for the work of Clemens Alexandrinus in the middle of the third century, instead of Clemens Romanus who died A.D. 100. Some of his conclusions appear about as correct as is this premise. Many communions have been more strict in disciplining for departures from their sectarian Shibboleth; but, with all our culpable remissness, we challenge the production of more strict and efficient discipline with respect to moral character and Christian deportment. The appellation "Puritan" was applied to our fathers by way of reproach, and was retained by those who were the chief advocates of Congregational doctrines.

[1] Confutation of Wise, 38, 87.

DISCIPLINE, *how affected by decisions of civil courts.* — Cotton Mather[1] argues that church discipline should not be brought into dependence on the decisions of civil magistrates, as that may be evidence to a church (?) which is not admissible in a civil court, and vice versâ. Also, that, when the session of a court is near, the church may forbear to try a cause, "lest they prejudice that court, of which they should be very careful at all times."

[1] Magnalia, ii. 230.

DISMISSION, *are churches bound to give, to all not under discipline who ask it?* — The Answer of the New England Elders to this question,[1] speaking of one who wishes to remove, contrary to the minds of the church, says: The churches dissuade from the evil, and show the sin, and do not consent if it seem wrong, but suspend their vote against him, not willing to make our churches places of imprisonment. Welde, in his reply to Rathband, says:[2] "If any man be desirous and steadfastly bent to depart, the church never holds him against his will, though she sees little or no weight in his reasons. What would he have them do, when they cannot be satisfied with the grounds of his departure? Must they say they are satisfied, when they are not? All they can do is, through indulgence, to suspend their vote, and leave him at liberty." He goes on to show that the church can testify to all his good conversation; and on this testimony he can be received, and so need not be left like a heathen. True, these remarks were made with special reference to changing of residence, in the feeble days of the colonies, and specially of the frontier towns; but the principle will apply to all removals from one church to another. Were it understood and acted upon, it would save nearly half the present bickerings between churches and their disaffected members, and half the "delivering up to councils." Here is a system of perfect liberty on both sides. Cotton Mather[3] says: "When one judges that he can, with more edification, enjoy the blessings of the new covenant in another society, except the society have any just exception against his judging so, he does well to ask a dismission, . . . and they ought to give it. If they refuse, a council may order it." Isaac Chauncy[4] says: "A letter of dismission may be either with or without recommendation, as the case may require, or the carriage of the member hath been, *though he hath not been under dealing* of the church for any censurable action." — See AFFINITY; MEMBERS, *improperly detained*, — *remove with consent*, — *received without dismission;* SEPARATION; SCHISM.

[1] Page 74. [2] In Han. ii. 324, 325. [3] Rat. Dis. 138, 139 Divine Institution of Cong. Churches, 119.

DISMISSION *should be denied to one under dealing, or when asked either to the world or to a false church.* — So argues Isaac Chauncy.[1] The church in Boston thus refused to dismiss F. Hutchinson to no church.[2] — See AFFINITY; MEMBERS, *may they be received from other churches without dismission and recommendation?*

[1] Divine Inst. Cong. Churches, 120. [2] J. Cotton's Letter to F. Hutchinson, in Hist. Soc. Col. series ii. vol. x. 185, 186.

DOCTRINES *of Congregationalism.* — Punchard[1] enumerates the most important of these to be, " The Scriptures recognize but two orders of church officers. . . . There should be an entire ecclesiastical equality among all Christian elders. . . . Councils . . . have no juridical authority, being simply advisory bodies. . . . Churches, though independent of each other, . . . yet should hold themselves ready to give account to sister-churches of their faith and religious practices." He shows[2] that these were among the doctrines of the Ærians, and of the Reformers in the reign of Edward VI.

[1] Hist. 14. [2] Ib. 75, 210, 211.

ECCLESIASTICAL POWER, *what.* — T. Goodwin defines this to be " an investiture with the authority of Christ, merely out of his will, whereby men are authorized and enabled, by commission from Christ and in his name, to do what others cannot do; and, by virtue of which, that which they do hath a special efficacy in it, from the power of Christ seconding and accompanying it, which also the conscience acknowledging, submits itself to, as unto the power of Christ, for the sake of his will or institution." By this he evidently means things of divine institution, in distinction from what synods, councils, churches, or church officers, decree of their own wills, without an express institution of Christ. It is evident, too, that Goodwin held a special power given to the church to deliver to Satan.— See EXCOMMUNICATION.

[1] Church Gov. 17.

ELDERS, *ruling*.—This was formerly one of the most vexing subjects in the Congregational churches. In the beginning of the separation, they were in somewhat general use, but are now almost universally discarded. Ainsworth, in his Answer to Smith,[1] maintains that they were of divers sorts, from the use of different words to designate them in 1 Tim. v. 17; Phil. i. 1; and Acts xx. Smith had advocated their diversity in his Book of Principles, but now retracted, and considered them all one and the same. Simpson, in his Anatomist Anatomized,[2] declares that he believes in their diversity, but asserts that even some Presbyterians believed in their identity with pastors. John White[3] argues the divine right of ruling elders from Rom.

xii. 8; 1 Tim. v. 17; and 1 Cor. xii. 28: maintaining that "governments" here means church governors distinct from teachers. Cotton Mather[4] advocated ruling elders, but tells us that they were almost extinct in his day; and that it was argued that 1 Tim. v. 18 was the only Scripture that asserted that office, and that those there referred to might be only differently employed ministers. He quotes a Scotch writer to prove their necessity, who still concedes that he can find no express mention of them for the first three centuries, but argues their use from analogy as necessary to guard the rights of the people. Mather also says:[5] "There are some who cannot see any such officer as ruling elder appointed in the word of God. Our churches are now (1697) generally destitute of such helps." But,[6] in the Heads of Agreement, it is agreed that the question of ruling elders shall make no break among them. Owen, in his Nature of a Gospel Church, chap. vii.[7] says: "Some begin to maintain that there is no need of but one pastor, bishop, or elder" (see ib. chap. viii.). Baillie[8] says: "The Independents (i. e. in the Westminster Assembly) were flat against the institution of any such office by divine right, though they were willing to admit them in a prudential way." See Punchard's View, 78—84. See next article.

[1] In Han. i. 183. [2] Ib. ii. 245. [3] Lamentations in Wise, 168. [4] Rat. Dis. 122—128. [5] Magnalia, ii. 206. [6] Ib. 236. [7] Works, xx. 481. [8] In Han. ii. 218.

ELDERS, *same as bishops.* — One of the charges

against Barrow and Greenwood before the High Commission was, that they maintained that every elder, though no doctor or pastor, is a bishop.[1] Lord King[2] maintains, and shows conclusively from the fathers, that the same identity was recognized in the primitive churches. T. Goodwin, notwithstanding he was for a distinctive order of ruling elders, shows conclusively[3] that there are but two orders of church officers, bishops and deacons; that elders and bishops are the same, the bishops being those whom God had made overseers of the flock (See Baillie in the preceding article.) Isaac Chauncy[4] maintains that Christ appointed elders to care for the internal concerns of the church, and deacons for the external. "Elder, bishop, and presbyter we may find taken in the Scriptures for one and the same thing: they are taken indifferently for any ruling or teaching minister." Elder means an old man: applied to an officer, an alderman is elderman. He shows that the pastoral office comprehends the whole ministry; but, if the pastor is unable to do the whole work, he may have "helps, a teacher to aid in preaching, and ruling elder to assist in governing."

[1] Punchard's Hist. 253. [2] Enquiry, part i. 65. [3] Catechism, 14, 20. [4] Divine Inst. Cong. Churches, 59—62.

ELDERS, *ruling, when out of date.* — President Stiles[1] informs us that several churches, in compliance with the sentiments of their pastors, had ruling elders and teaching elders, yet they at length ceased to use the ruling elder; and the teaching elder, as distinct from pastor, is now dropped. Mr. Felt[2] says: "The office of elders continued to be esteemed in the churches till the middle of the last century." Dr. Bentley[3] says: "The office of elder never existed in Salem but in name, and did not survive the first generation; they were chosen, but never possessed the shadow of power." Dr. Ware[4] says ruling elders were obsolete in 1735; and, though the church then chose two, they could induce but one only to accept, which ended the matter. Dr. Stiles[5] says: "Neither lay nor teaching elders ever obtained in many of the churches of the first (New England) generation." Neal[6] affirms that they were obsolete in his day.— See two next preceding articles; also, Neander, Church Hist. i. 101.

[1] Convention Sermon, 64. [2] Annals of Salem, 29. [3] Description of Salem, in Mass. Hist. Soc. Col. series i. vol. vi. 243. [4] Hist. Old North and New Brick Churches, 29. [5] Con. Serm. 67. [6] Hist. New England, i. 273—275.

ELDERS, *was there a plurality of, in ancient churches?*— Goodwin[1] argues the affirmative, from their being mentioned in the plural, especially in Acts xiv. and Titus i. Hopkins[2] maintains the negative, from there being but one angel of each church addressed in the Revelation. Perhaps both were right.— See close of last preceding article but one.

[1] Ch. Gov. book vi. chap. 6. [2] System, ii. 232.

ELDERS, *their office.*— T. Goodwin[1] says: "It is the elder's office to see that no drone or unprofitable servant be in the church, which may live on other men's labors, 2 Thess. iii. 10, 11." Cambridge Platform maintains the same.[2] It makes it the duty of ruling elders to open and shut the doors of God's house (officially) by admission, ordination, excommunication, and restoring; to call the church together; to prepare matters in private for public church meetings; to moderate church meetings; to be leaders and guides in church actions; to see that none of the church live without a calling, or idly in their calling; to prevent and heal offences in life or doctrine; to feed the flock, visit the sick, and pray with them when sent for and at other times. Prince[3] mentions among the principles of the Robinson church, "Ruling elders should teach but occasionally, through necessity, or in their pastor's absence or illness." — See Hooker's Survey, part ii. 9—19; Hutchinson's Hist. Mass. 376.

[1] Catechism, 20. [2] Chap. vii. sect. 2. [3] Chronology, 92.

ELDERS, *rule of, what?* — Cotton, in his Keys,[1] makes it consist in authority so binding that nothing can be done without them, and nothing esteemed validly done unless they are present. Cambridge Platform[2] holds the same doctrine of a mixed administration, so that no church act can be consummated or perfected without the consent of both elders and people. By giving the people power to depose their elders, they, however, virtually limited their power to that of mere moderators, subject to appeal to the church. Robinson, in his Apology,[3] says: "It behoves the elders to govern the people in voting, in just liberty given by Christ whatsoever. Let the elders publicly propound and order things in the church, and so give their sentence on them. Let them reprove them that sin, convince the gainsayers, comfort the repentant, and so administer all things according to the prescript of God's word," though the people are freely to vote in the elections and judgments of the church. In this way he makes the elders only moderators, though he is endeavoring to prove a mixed government. — See ELDERS, *ruling*, *when out of date; their office; rule as stewards; servants of the church; rule as moderators;* NEGATIVE VOTE.

[1] Page 14. [2] Chap. x. sect. 11. [3] In Punchard's Hist. 349; and Works, iii. 43.

ELDERS *rule as stewards.* — This is maintained by Richard Mather[1] and Clemens Romanus.[2] John Robinson, in his Apology,[3] says, as we willingly leave these things (admitting, reproving, &c.) to the elders alone, so we deny, that, in the settled and well-ordered state of the church, they can be rightly or orderly done, without the people's privity and consent. It belongs to the people primarily to rule and govern the church. In his Justification,[4] he says: "The people's obedience stands, not in making these elders their lords, sovereigns, and judges, but in listening to their godly counsels and following their wise directions; . . . so neither stands the elders' government in erecting any tribunal . . . over the people, but in instructing, comforting, and improving them by the word of God." He shows that the elder is set over the church as the physician over the patient, the lawyer over his client, and the steward over the family, or the watchman over the city. Goodwin[5] says: "The government of the church is not lordly, but stewardly and ministerial." Welde, in his Answer to Rathband,[6] shows that elders are both servants and governors, and that to them it pertains to be the mouth in the execution of the sentences of the church. Cotton[7] advances essentially the same arguments, and uses some of the same words. Cambridge Platform says:[8] "Church government or rule is placed by Christ in the officers of the church, who are therefore called rulers, while they rule with God; yet, in case of mal-administration, they are subject to the power of the church." John Robinson shows the same in his Apology.[9] — See MINISTERS, *authority of.*

[1] Ch. Gov. 59. [2] Epist. to Cor. 28, 30. [3] In Punchard's Hist. 346, 349; and Works, iii. 34. [4] Ib. 329; and Works, ii. 144. [5] Catechism, 19. [6] In Han. ii. 318. [7] Keys, 54. [8] Chap. x. sect. 7. [9] In Han. i. 379.

ELDERS, *servants of the church.* — Robinson, in his Justification of Separation,[1] says: "We profess the bishops or elders to be the only ordinary governors in the church, . . . only we may not acknowledge them for lords over God's heritage; but we hold eldership as other ordinances given to the church for her service, and so the elders or officers servants and ministers of the church." Ainsworth, in his Answer to Johnson and Clyfton,[2] says: "Neither should the elders be minded, like Ahithophel, to take it ill if their counsel be not followed." Barrowe, in his reply to Giffard, asserts[3] that, in default of elders, the church have power not only to choose, but also to ordain them; for the eldership doth not add more power, but more help and service, to the church in this action." Owen, in his Catechism, Ans. 42,[4] says: Discipline, by authority, is admitted to the elders; trial, judgment, and consent, to the brethren. But he before asserts,[5] Ans. 28, that the elders guide the worship by authority, not from the church, but from Christ. — See Neander's Church History, i. 109. See OFFICERS, *servants of the church.*

[1] In Han. i. 205. [2] Ib. 250. [3] Ib. 58. [4] Works, xix. 547. [5] Ib. 529.

ELDERS *rule as moderators.* — So taught John Robinson,[1] in his Apology[2] and in his Answer to Helwisse.[3] He says of prophesying, that the officers were to moderate and determine the whole exercise. Ainsworth, in his Answer to Clyfton,[4] says: "The elders are to teach, direct, and govern the church in the election of officers. They are to do the like in judging and excommunicating, . . . and other public affairs." He had just asserted "that to give voices, in the decision of controversies and judging of sinners, is not a part of *government*, but of power, which saints out of office have." To this agrees Cotton.[5] Cartwright, in his reply to Whitgift,[6] says that Paul and Barnabas acted as moderators, while the churches elected pastors. Hopkins says:[7] "To rule over the churches means only to take the lead or preside in the churches;" yet he seems to hold to the necessity of their acting in concurrence with the church. — See MINISTERS, *authority of.*

[1] In Punchard's Hist. 349; Han. i. 380; and Works, iii. 43. [2] Ib. 369. [3] In Han. i. 261, 262. [4] Ib. 249. [5] Keys, chap. v. [6] Page 44. [7] System, ii. 238.

ELDERS, *how invested with rule.* — Cotton[1] says: "The brethren of the church invest him with rule; partly by choosing him to the office which God hath invested with rule, partly by professing their own subjection to him in the Lord." He argues that those can thus invest others with rule who have themselves no power to rule. So Owen, in his True Nature of a Gospel Church, chap. vii.[2] says: "Rule, or the execution of authority, is in the hands of the elders." — See POWER, *church may give, &c.*

[1] Keys, 73. [2] Works, xx. 472.

ELDERS, *is their office perpetual?* — The exiles in Amsterdam, in their reply to Junius,[1] object to the Dutch churches that their elders change yearly, and do not continue in their office, according to the doctrine of the apostles and practice of the primitive churches, Rom. xii. 4; Acts xx. 27, 28; 1 Pet. v. 1—4. Robinson makes the same objection in his Apology.[2]

[1] In Han. i. 144. [2] Ib. 378.

ELDERS *to be chosen by the people.* — Goodwin in his Church Government,[1] argues that because God has appointed elders and deacons to be set up by choice, and the people did choose their deacons, therefore we infer that they may choose their elders. See PASTOR, *power to elect, in the church.*

[1] Page 20.

ELDERS, *does their power extend beyond their own church?* — The Independents in the Westminster Assembly[1] maintain the negative: from Scripture, which limits their power to a particular flock, Acts xx. 28; 1 Pet. v. 2; Coloss. i. 7; and from a pastor's office, in which preaching and ruling are joined. They enumerate a host of incongruities in their being elders to other flocks. Goodwin shows this, at great length, in various parts of his Church Government.[2] He shows[3] that the elders were ordained city by city or church by church, as Titus i. 5 should be rendered; and[4] that nothing can deprive a church of the right to have elders of their own to preside over them. Tompson and Mather, in their Answer to Herle,[5] say: "Ordinary elders are not, like the apostles, to feed *all* flocks, but *that* flock over which the Holy Ghost hath made them overseers." They show that, by consequence, elders cannot ordain elders of other flocks, unless invited so to do.

[1] In Han. ii. 462—472. [2] Particularly 53—191. [3] Page 82. [4] Page 138. [5] In Han. ii. 176.

ELDERS, *is one or more, necessary to the power of the church to act?* — Goodwin[1] maintains that they are necessary to any further action than to supply themselves with such an eldership. Query, Do they not thus supply themselves, *pro tem.*, when they choose a moderator from among themselves? Wise[2] says, that when the pastors will not convene a church, they may consider themselves without a ruler, and may convene, as when they have no minister to choose one.— See GOVERNMENT, *church, power of, in the people;* PASTOR, *has he a negative vote?* MINISTERS, *people may do their work if they neglect it;* POWER, *installed in the ministry or the people?*

[1] Ch. Gov. 138. [2] Quar. of the Churches, 168.

ELDERS, *have they exclusive government?*— This was claimed by Francis Johnson, on the ground that otherwise the people would rule both the minister and the elders.[1] Studley maintained the same, when some of his people wished to dismiss him for his misconduct. He says:[2] "Here was a beginning to tread the path of popular government, the bane of all good order, both in church and commonwealth." Ainsworth, in his Answer to Clyfton,[3] shows that, on this ground, there never were any true churches which were constituted before there were any elders to govern them.

[1] Han. i. 217. [2] Ib. 245. [3] Ib. 247.

In taking leave of this once important — now obsolete — subject of ruling elders, it may be remarked that the opponents of our fathers continually alarmed them with the bugbear of democracy. They had never dared question the divine right of kings, and seem to have been often appalled by the sight of their own likeness. They little dreamed that the truths which they demonstrated would be followed with such democratic consequences and results. Being sincere monarchists, they tried to make out a mixed government in Congregationalism; Christ being the King, the ruling elders the aristocracy, and the churches the people. But, as their principles obliged them to make their elders amenable to the people, they in fact reduced them to mere presidents of democratic assemblies under the great divine constitution. Thus their democratic church notions and the growing spirit of democratic civil liberty mutually strengthened each other, till, long before the American Revolution, the advocates for tory rule and aristocratical eldership became comparatively few. The same spirit of democratic liberty is now making vast inroads into the Hierarchal and Presbyterial communions; and causing revolutions, based more or less on Congregational principles, by those who as yet only see men as trees walking. May they soon see every man clearly! Every new triumph of civil and religious liberty adds to the growth of that stone which is destined to become a great mountain, and fill the whole earth. — See INDEPENDENCY *endangers monarchy.* For the whole subject of elders, see OFFICERS, MINISTERS, PASTOR, PRESBYTERY.

ELECTION *gives power, but does not transmit it.* Owen, in his Nature of a Gospel Church, chap. iv.[1] shows that election to office only gives the power of that office, as Christ directs, but does not transmit power from one to another. The power of office is not in the electors. And, under the head of ORDINATION, it will appear that it is not in the ordainer, but is directly from Christ to those whom the people elect.

[1] Works, xx. 426.

EVANGELISTS, *what.* — Thomas Goodwin[1] asserts that they were extraordinary ministers, to cease. And he attempts to prove it[2] from 1 Tim. i. 3, and Tit. i. 5. He says their business was "to perfect the work which was begun, and to settle the churches." John Cotton[3] says: "But, for the continuance of this office of an evangelist in the church, there is no direction in the Scriptures." — See Punchard's View, 76, 77.

[1] Ch. Gov. 129. [2] Ib. 312. [3] Keys, 78.

EVANGELISTS *not to be ordained for the conversion of infidels.* — Owen, in his Nature of a Gospel Church, chap. v.[1] maintains that no church has power to ordain men for the conversion of infidels, unless by designation of divine Providence; that the primitive churches ordained none but to office in a particular church. He asserts that such ordinations were forbidden in the ancient churches, and that the Council of Chalcedon* declared them null. "Such ordination wants a constituted cause," viz. election by the people. On this principle all our ordinations of missionaries, evangelists, &c. are uncongregational. When there is a church to need

* A.D. 451.

a pastor, they are competent to ordain him. And, as for the necessity for it to their administering occasional communion to destitute churches, it should be borne in mind that this was formerly considered as out of order. (See MINISTERS, *may they administer seals in another church?*) But suppose Richard Mather's and Dr. Watts's theory the true one, viz. that the church may lawfully employ any of their own number to administer them, — (see SEALS, *can a church authorize? &c.*) — then there is no need of any special unction, by ordination, either in a broken or an unbroken succession, to give this power. I. Chauncy [2] says that an evangelist "needs no other ordination than the approbation of the church of which he is a member, accompanied with solemn prayer for a blessing on his ministry." There was an ordination of several evangelists for the Society for promoting Christian Knowledge, in Boston, in 1733.[3] See Neander's Planting and Training of the Church, book iii. chap. 5. The arguments for, and the mode of procedure in, the ordination of evangelists and missionaries, are given at length in Upham's Rat. Dis. sect. 86—94. Suffice it to recommend the careful investigation of this question. — See ORDINATION *of missionaries.*

[1] In Works, xx. 456. [2] Divine Inst. Cong. Churches, 83
[3] Rev. Dr. Sewall's Sermon at their Ordination.

EXCOMMUNICATION, *what.* — A question much agitated among the old Congregational writers and some others. The True Description out of the Word of God of the Visible Church[1] holds that "it is a casting out of their congregation and fellowship, covenant, and protection of the Lord, and delivering to Satan," &c. Goodwin[2] maintains the same doctrine of an official spiritual punishment, from which there is no appeal on earth. He heads his sixth chapter, book I.: "That by excommunication more is meant than a mere casting out of the church; that it is an ordinance of Christ to deliver the excommunicate person to Satan, in his name and power." And fully does he sustain his caption, in his positions, if not by his arguments. He makes the execution of the sentence the *anathema maranatha*, and maintains that Satan is ever ready to visit with special terrors such as are cast out. His arguments are specious and terse. Lord King[3] shows that it was thus viewed by the ancients, as, for instance, from Tertullian: "That the delinquent was banished from communion of prayers, assemblies, and all holy converse; being looked upon as unworthy of human society, cast out of the church of God, and, impenitently dying in that state, as certainly excluded from the kingdom of God hereafter." John Owen, in his Nature of a Gospel Church, chap. x.[4] defines it "a giving up to the state of the heathen and the kingdom of Satan, and declaring him liable to everlasting punishment without repentance."

Others, however, advocated a different theory. Burroughs, in his Irenicum,[5] says: "It is a great question among our brethren, whether this *traditio Satanæ* were not apostolical, peculiar to the apostles, so as ordinary elders had it not." Bartlett, in his Model,[6] asserts that the same was a great question among the Presbyterians in the Westminster Assembly. Hetherington[7] says: "The Independents practically admitted no church censure but admonition; for that cannot properly be called excommunication, which consisted, not in expelling an obstinate offender, but in withdrawing themselves from him." We see, however, that this was not Goodwin's opinion, nor can I find that Burroughs denied the power of expulsion from a church. The Declaration of Discipline, published anonymously (of necessity) in 1574 (probably Udal's), says:[8] Excommunication is a cutting off from the communion and fellowship of the faithful; but declares it to be "foully abused." It[9] reprobates execration as a medium in excommunication. Cotton Mather[10] says: The difference between the greater and the lesser excommunication seems so little, that "the suspension laid upon an offender, at the time of his admonition, is often stopped at." And[11] "formerly they pretended to a formal giving to Satan; the pastors of some churches have now espoused another notion of this passage, — a prerogative apostolical and extraordinary." S. Mather[12] is out upon the doctrine with a vengeance. He says: "As to a power fastened to the keys, . . . by which men can deliver up a person to the devil, in the name and authority of Jesus Christ, we pretend to no such power, . . . nay, we detest it." Beginning thus, he goes on to do justice to his position, and wonders that churches advanced in the doctrines of the Reformation should adopt a theory which so props the doctrine of the infallibility of the church, and about which there are no charges and special directions in the word of God. He says that these churches pretend to no more power over their members than a society of grave philosophers over theirs, viz. "to censure and exclude from their society, when they have forfeited its privileges." And he says that all such as are thoroughly Congregational will be content with this power. Isaac Chauncy[13] says: "Excommunication puts a person but into the condition of publicans and sinners, with respect to ordinances." Professor Knowles, in his Memoir of Roger Williams, says:[14] The churches of Plymouth were in advance of those in Massachusetts, because they held ecclesiastical censures to be wholly spiritual. John Milton, in his Treatise on Christian Doctrine, says:[15] Deliver to Satan, i.e. "give him over to the world, which, as being out of the pale of the church, is the kingdom of Satan." Punchard, in his View,[16] seems to recognize the doctrine of sometimes giving up to Satan, in the distinction which he makes between excommunication and withdrawment of fellowship; the latter affecting the church standing, but not the Christian standing, of the disorderly brother: but he acknowledges his lack of Congregational authorities for the distinction.

[1] In Punchard's Hist. 371; and Han. i. 33. [2] Ch. Gov. 3, 35, 39, *et al.* [3] Enquiry, part i. 123—125. [4] Works, xx. 540—544. [5] In Han. iii. 111. [6] Ib. 240. [7] Note in Neal s Puritans, i. 489. [8] Page 168. [9] Ib. 176. [10] Rat. Dis. 149. [11] Ib. 155. [12] Apology,

106—109. [13] Div. Inst. Cong. Churches, 122. [14] Page 39. [15] Vol. ii. 208. [16] Pages 181, 281—286.

EXCOMMUNICATION *by vote of the church.* — The Answer of the New England Elders[1] says: "The power of excommunication is in the church." Robinson, in his Answer to Helwisse,[2] says: One of the elders pronounces it, upon the people's assent; . . . the men manifesting their assent by some convenient word or sign, and the women by silence. The Robinson Church, in their True Description, &c.[3] advocate the same course. So all Congregationalists agree. Their views may be found in Goodwin, Ch. Gov. 109, 112, 146, 209; Han. i. 254; ii. 482, 493; iii. 41, 246, 248; Cotton's Keys, 31, 88—91; Hooker's Survey, part i. 62, 197; part iii. 45, 46; Watts's Complete Works, iii. 200; Confession of Low Country Exiles, in Han. i. 95; Ainsworth, in his Controversy with Johnson, ib. 248; and Allin and Shepard, in their Defence of the Answer to the Nine Positions, in ib. iii. 41.

[1] Page 72. [2] In Punchard's Hist. 339; and Works, iii. 136. [3] Ib. 371.

EXCOMMUNICATION *through the officers, by the power of the church.* — Ainsworth, in his Answer to Broughton,[1] says: "Myself alone never excommunicated any, but together with the church, whereof I am, in the name and power of Christ." The Congregational Union of England and Wales say:[2] "The power of rejection from a Christian church we believe to be vested in the church itself, through its own officers." Owen, in his Nature of a Gospel Church, chap. x.[3] says: The church have power to put away an offender without an officer; though judicial power is properly in the church, and executive in its officers.

[1] In Han. i. 152. [2] Ib. iii. 600. [3] Works, xx. 547.

EXCOMMUNICATION, *is improper, valid?* — Owen, in his Nature of a Gospel Church,[1] says that "this depends on the person's own conscience. . . . If he knows himself to be guilty, it is not void because wrongfully performed. If he knows that he is innocent, their wrong course cannot injure him before God." And I am so sadducaical as to suspect, that his own conscience, and the frightful bugbear doctrine, have much more to do with his terrors than any satanical influence, which it is now in the power of churches, by their vote and their elders' anathemas, to raise against him.

[1] Works, xx. 567.

EXCOMMUNICATION *should be only for great sins.* — The Independents, in their Apologetical Narrative,[1] say: "They apprehend that excommunication should be only for crimes of the last importance." * Robinson, in his Answer to Bernard,[2] says: "The church of England is in a heavy case, that plays with excommunications as children do with rattles." Hooker[3] shows that toleration must be granted to corrupt members till the evil be examined, the parties convened, and censures applied

* They evidently refer to what they termed the greater excommunication, or delivering to Satan.

for reformation. Cutting off is only used when things come to an extremity. (See RIGHTS *of the accused.*) He maintains[4] that gross sins "only deserve excommunication by the law of Christ." Owen, in his Nature of a Gospel Church, chap. x.[5] shows that excommunication should be only of scandalous offenders for known sin. The fact must be confessed or clearly proved, a previous process had, and the case determined by the whole church. "*Haste is the bane of church rule.*"

[1] In Neal's Puritans, i. 492. [2] In Han. i. 209; and Works, ii. 60. [3] Part i. 27, 28. [4] Ib. part iii. 39, 40. [5] In Works, xx. 549—551.

EXCOMMUNICATION *in difficult cases; churches may have counsel previous to.* — So says Cotton Mather, in his Ratio Disciplinæ.[1] T. Goodwin, in his Church Government,[2] seems to lay down principles which go against this conclusion, though he is arguing against a previous consultation of a classical Presbytery.

[1] Page 155. [2] Pages 144—150.

EXCOMMUNICATION *should be made public.* — There is such a relation of churches that such an act should be made public. Thus the church in Salem apprised the church in Dorchester of their dealings with Roger Williams.[1] The reason is obvious, that there should be sufficient publicity for the community to be informed in what relation the individual stands to the church. In whatever way this is made public, it is sufficient.

[1] Hutchinson's Hist. Mass. i. 371.

EXCOMMUNICATION *may take place in the absence of the offender.* — Thus the church excluded Mr. Eaton, first teacher of the school in Cambridge.[1] If it be asked, How is this consistent with the rule in Matt. xviii.? it is answered, in the language of one of the old Puritan writers, "Whatever is the dictate of the law of nature is the law of God." Otherwise, the delinquent might claim to be in good standing in the church, so long as he kept out of the way.

[1] Winthrop's Journal, i. 313.

EXCOMMUNICATION, *one church has not power of, over another.* — Ainsworth, in his Communion of Saints,[1] says: "For although we may advise, exhort, warn, reprove, &c. so far as Christian love and power extend, yet we find no authority committed to one congregation over another for excommunicating. . . . Christ reserveth this power in his own hand." Burton, though he seems in words[2] to maintain the contrary, yet evidently refers to a mere withdrawal of fellowship. — See CHURCHES *discipline each other, but not juridically.*

[1] In Han. i. 285. [2] Ib. ii. 77.

EXCOMMUNICATED, *how to be treated.* — The views of Congregationalists differ on this point, correspondingly to their views of the nature of excommunication. Should he be treated as the Jews treated publicans and sinners, or as Christ treated them? John Cotton says:[1] "With a publican the Jews would not eat; . . . no more should we with excommunicate persons." Cotton Mather says:[2] "They are not excluded from civil privileges, but from familiarity; thus acting according to the apostle's rule to avoid them." The Robinson Church, in their True Description, &c.,[3] say: "They (the church) are to warn the whole congregation, and all other faithful, to hold him as a heathen and a publican, and to abstain themselves from his society, as not to eat or drink with him, &c.; unless it be such as of necessity must needs, as his wife, his children, and family. Yet these, if they be members of the church, are not to join with him in any spiritual exercise." This was written either by Clyfton or Smith, Robinson's predecessors. Robinson says[4] that "excommunication should be wholly spiritual, a *mere* rejecting the scandalous from the communion of the church, in the holy sacraments and those other spiritual privileges which are peculiar to the faithful." John Cotton[5] argues that they were to walk towards them as the Jews walk towards heathen and publicans, withholding from them familiar civil communion; for so the Jews said to Christ's disciples, "Why eateth your Master with publicans and sinners?" A most unfortunate quotation for his argument, unless the example of the Pharisees is to be followed rather than that of the Lord Jesus Christ. Cambridge Platform,[6] Hooker's Survey,[7] and Owen's Catechism, Ans. 46,[8] teach the doctrine of non-intercourse. But Samuel Mather[9] advocates the contrary; the church, as he argues, having gone to the extent of their commission when they have cast the offender out of their communion. Mitchell[10] supposes the injunction "no, not to eat," to refer to persons guilty of gross iniquities; "with *such* a one not to company;" though he advocates a distinction in the conduct to be observed towards excommunicates and other impenitent persons. Dwight[11] holds the same view of the interpretation of the passage. Ames, in his Marrow of Sacred Divinity,[12] says: "They who are lawfully excommunicated are to be avoided of all communicants, not in respect of duties simply moral, or otherwise necessary, but in respect to those parts of conversation which are wont to accompany approbation." Letchford, in his Plain Dealing,[13] says: "The excommunicated is held as a heathen man and a publican, yet children may eat with their parents. The excommunicated may come, and hear the word and prayer. But at New Haven, where Mr. Davenport presides, he is held out of the meeting in frost and snow, if he will hear." Perhaps this is an old edition of blue-law fictions. But sure it is that even some of our Puritan fathers retained so much dread of what the popes invented, that they supposed excommunication the most dreadful of evils, and helped to make it so. In John Cotton's Letter (in behalf of his church) to Francis Hutchinson,[14] it is admitted that he should sit at table with his mother, though they deny that others than near connections may thus eat. Who gave the dispensation for connections not to esteem the excommunicate as a heathen and a publican? — See Excommunication, *what;* Excommunicated, *may they set up churches?*

Way of the Churches, 93. [2] Rat. Dis. 155, 156. [3] In Punchard's Hist. 371. [4] Ib. 363. [5] Keys, 81. [6] Chap. xiv. sect. 5. [7] Part iii. 39. [8] Works, xix. 559. [9] Apology, 93—109. [10] Guide, 130. [11] Works, Serm. clxii. [12] Page 169. [13] In Hist. Soc. Col. series iii, vol. iii. 73. [14] Ib. series ii. vol. x. 186.

EXCOMMUNICATED, *his sentence to be treated as right, till the matter is examined and judged by others.* — Goodwin[1] shows that this is right in itself, and was practised by the primitive churches. Mitchell[2] clearly advocates the same doctrine, which has been ever practised. By the advice of council, however, those deemed to have been unjustly cast out are received into other churches.[3] — See DISMISSION; MEMBERS *received without dismission.* — See also the last preceding article.

[1] Ch. Gov. 204, 227. [2] Guide, 118. [3] Hubbard's Hist. Mass. 419

EXCOMMUNICATED, *may they set up churches?* Goodwin[1] strenuously maintains the negative, on the ground of his hobby doctrine, — their being judicially delivered to Satan. Here he at one blow unchurches all the churches of the Reformation. They were again and again excommunicated under the most awful execrations. Besides, he here loses sight of his own exception, — that unjust excommunication is null and void in the sight of God. Admit this exception, and his proposition amounts to no more than the doctrine of all orthodox Congregationalists, viz. that none but penitent believers have a right to church membership.

[1] Ch. Gov. 207.

FAITH, *particular, i.e. assurance of having the thing prayed for.* — Thomas Goodwin held the doctrine of a particular faith, and prayed not for Cromwell's recovery, of which he was assured; but his assurance proved unfounded presumption.[1] John Howe held the contrary doctrine.

[1] Eliot's Ecc. Hist. Mass., in Hist. Soc. Col. series i. vol. ix. 9.

FELLOWSHIP, *all Christians have a right to it.* Goodwin[1] shows that every godly man has a right to the sacraments and to church fellowship; yet to the sacraments only in virtue of his church relation, as every freeman has a right to the comforts of the marriage state, but is entitled to them only through marriage itself. Samuel Mather[2] represents Cotton as having declared to his congregation, that, if even "a poor Indian should step forth and say, I love the Lord Jesus Christ in sincerity and truth, and should testify his willingness to walk according to the gospel, though his defects were great for ignorance and the like, he should be for admitting him to the Lord's table." — See Creeds.

[1] Ch. Gov. 259. [2] Apology, 86, note.

FELLOWSHIP *of various kinds and degrees.* — Goodwin[1] shows that fellowship is of three kinds; Personal, in secret duties; mystical, common to all the saints; and in a communion in an instituted church.

[1] Ch. Gov. 255.

FELLOWSHIP, *rules of.* — Owen, in his Eshcol,

or Duty of Walking in Fellowship,[1] says the rule of walking in fellowship is "cheerfully to undergo the lot of the whole church in prosperity and affliction, and not to draw back under any pretence whatever." That which leads to shrink from one duty will lead to shrink from other duties, till the member becomes a backslider. Another rule which he lays down[2] is, Watching over and admonishing every brother, and telling the church if he be not reclaimed. He shows[3] that telling the elders is not telling the church.

[1] In Works, xix. 98. [2] Ib. 103. [3] Ib. 106.

FLIGHT *in persecution is admissible.* — So argued John Robinson, in his Answer to Helwisse,[1] and applied the *argumentum ad hominem* (i.e. applied it personally).

[1] In Han. i. 265; and Works, iii. 159.

FORMS, *needless in ordinances.* — Cotton Mather, in his Ratio Disciplinæ,[1] speaking of ordination, says: "For these things the churches of New England have no forms. They are instructed and united in the substance, and their not being tied to forms does but give them the delight of the more variety in expressions and in circumstances."

[1] Pages 40, 41.

FUNDAMENTALS *of Christianity.* — As the Congregational rule is, Union with all who embrace the fundamentals of Christianity, there will still be a want of agreement just so far as they disagree as to what the fundamentals of Christianity are. The Independents presented to Parliament sixteen articles, which they deemed fundamental. These embrace the usual orthodox views of God, the Scripture, the atonement, total depravity, justification by faith, the damnableness of continuing in known sin, worshipping God according to his will, the resurrection, and the final judgment and retribution. They are plain and simple, and contain nothing objectionable to any evangelical Christian. They may be seen at length in Neal's Puritans.[1] Watts, in his Foundation of a Christian Church,[2] says that the fundamentals required to be professed will be different, according to the different degrees of light of the professor. They should include such knowledge as is essential to Christianity. He gives a list[3] of substantial articles, all very fundamental save the one on infant baptism, which he pleads is fundamental to the peace of the church, though not of Christianity. He maintains,[4] that confessions of faith made to the church should be confined to no set form of expression, and declaims against those set confessions which exclude for nonconformity to one little point or word. Letchford, in his Plain Dealing,[5] says: Mr. Cotton lately preached a sermon, showing that there are twelve, which tried by, any church may receive them in. They are substantially these:— The Trinity; God's universal government; God only to be worshipped; his worship is instituted in the Scriptures; the fallen state of man; inability to save ourselves; incarnation for the work of redemption; salvation offered only to believers; no man can come to Christ, except the Father draw him by his word and Spirit; justifying grace; the justified regenerated and sanctified; imperfect sanctification in this life. Ignorance concerning the foundation of the church, as baptism, imposition of hands, &c., he argues, should not hinder from admission. — See CONFESSIONS OF FAITH; CREEDS.

[1] Vol. ii. 143. [2] Vol. iii. 256. [3] Ib. 258—262. [4] Ib. 262, 263. [5] In Hist. Soc. Col. series iii. vol. iii. 69, 70.

FUNERALS. — Our Puritan fathers saw so much superstition connected with the burial service, consecrated graveyards, and the like, that they, for a time, almost wholly discarded all funerals. The First Independent Church in England say, in their Confession, art. xxiii.:[1] "Concerning making marriage, and burying the dead, we believe that they are no actions of a church minister, neither are ministers called to any such business; neither is there so much as one example of any such practice in the whole Book of God, either under the law or under the gospel; without which warrant we believe it unlawful, whatsoever any minister doth, at any time and place, especially as a part of his ministerial office and function." Cotton Mather, in his Ratio Disciplinæ,[2] says of the New England practice: "In many towns, the ministers make agreeable prayers with the people, come together at the house to attend the funeral of the dead, and in some they make a short speech at the grave: in other places, both these things are wholly omitted.

However, they are not forbidden, as in the French churches, where the prohibition runs, 'There shall be no prayer or sermon at funerals, to shun superstition.'" The Apology of the Overseers, &c., of the English Church at Amsterdam, says[3] ministers should not be burdened with civil affairs, as marriages, burials, &c. Letchford, in his Plain Dealing,[4] shows that they have funerals without reading or sermons, but in silence. Dr. Ware, in his History of the Old North and New Brick Churches,[5] says: "Dr. Samuel Mather, at his own request, received a private funeral in 1785." (How?)

[1] In Han. i. 300. [2] Page 117. [3] Pages 37—61. [4] In Hist. Soc. Col. series iii. vol. iii. 94. [5] Page 23.

GIFTS, *weekly.* — Jacob's Church say, in their Confession, art. xxv.[1] of gifts and offerings: "Though they be free and voluntary in the givers, touching the particular quantity, yet that they do thus give and offer every Lord's day is a very commandment of God, and a point of necessary obedience in man." See COLLECTIONS, *weekly.*

[1] In Han. i. 300.

GIFTS *which God gave to men.* — Goodwin[1] shows that these are pastors, teachers, and church officers.

[1] Ch. Gov. 263.

GOVERNMENT, *church, instituted in the Scriptures.* — John Milton, in his Treatise against Prelacy,[1] says and demonstrates "that such government is set down in the Scriptures, and that to teach otherwise is *unsound* and *untrue*." J. Burroughs, in his Sermon before Parliament,[2] says: "Ecclesiastical government, being of divine institution, must be the same where churches are complete." Prince, in his Chronology,[3] says of the founders of Plymouth church and colony: "They observed God's institutions as their *only rule* in church order, discipline, and worship." J. Corbett, in his Principles and Practice of Several Nonconformists, says:[4] "We believe that it is Christ's high prerogative, transcending all human authority, to institute spiritual officers." Goodwin taught the same doctrine abundantly in his Church Government. — See CHURCHES, *instituted bodies*.

[1] Works, i. 84. [2] Page 33. [3] Page 5. [4] Page 4.

GOVERNMENT, *church, not lawful to alter.* — Pierce, in his Vindication of Dissenters,[1] quotes from Wickliffe: "'Tis not lawful for a Christian, after the full publication of the law of Christ, to devise to himself any other laws for the government of the church." Eaton and Taylor, in their Defence,[2] say: "The way of discipline is one and essentially unchangeable." 1 Tim. vi. 13, 14.

[1] In Punchard's Hist. 161. [2] Page 107.

GOVERNMENT, *church, should it be varied to suit circumstances?* — Answer: When God thus alters it. Goodwin shows[1] that, under the patriarchal dispensation, it was in the head of the family; under the Mosaic, it was hierarchal; and under the

Christian, when the church was to be dispersed among all the nations, it was made congregational. Burton, in his Vindication of Independent Churches, in answer to Prynne's Twelve Considerable Questions,[2] shows that, in case it might be varied without his direction, it might be obliged to conform to that which is unscriptural; and that the gospel might just as well be varied, and sent to different countries garbled to suit the wishes of the rulers and the people.

[1] Ch. Gov. 175. [2] In Han. ii. 389—393.

GOVERNMENT, *church, in the people.* — Robinson[1] says: "It should seem, then, that it appertains to the people, . . . unto the people primarily, under Christ, to rule and govern the church." Goodwin, in his Church Government,[2] maintains the same doctrine, and discusses it at large. The Puritan ministers of England, in their Letter to the General Assembly of Scotland in 1641,[3] assert that "the whole power of government, and all acts thereto pertaining, are, by divine ordinance, *in foro externo,* to be determined by the most voices in and of every particular congregation. They moreover plainly intimate that their acts ought to be determined "without any authoritative — though not without a consultatory — interposition." Mitchell, in his Guide,[4] says: "The church, though destitute of a minister, is still competent to discipline, though the presence and aid of a pastor is very desirable." — See ELDER, *is one, or more, necessary to the church's power to act?* MINISTERS, *authority of what?* PAS-

TOR, *has he a negative vote?* POWER, *installed in ministry or brethren?* MINISTERS, *people may do their work for them, if they neglect it.* — See also the next article.

[1] In his Apology, in Punchard's Hist. 347; and Works, iii. 34. [2] Page 44—49. [3] In Han. ii. 98. [4] Page 94.

GOVERNMENT, *church; is it mixed?* — Notwithstanding the old Congregationalists so strenuously maintained that the government was in the people, yet they took pains to argue that it was a mixed one. This they did to avoid the imputation of democratic sentiments and practices. Jacob, in his Divine Beginning and Institution of Christ's Visible Churches,[1] maintains that it is democratical as to the necessity of the free consent of the people; aristocratical so far as the direction of the elders and pastors is concerned; and also partly monarchical, alluding doubtless to Christ's rule over it, which is acknowledged by all. Hooker, in his Survey,[2] and Cambridge Platform,[3] assert the same thing in similar language; yet they are careful to put an effectual check on the aristocratical power of the elders, in making them amenable to the church for mal-administration. The language of the Platform[4] is: "Church government or rule is placed by Christ in the officers of the church, who are therefore called rulers, while they rule with God. Yet, in case of mal-administration, they are subject to the power of the church." This explanation puts an end to the idea of an irresponsible vetoing aristocracy; a sentiment not likely to prevail among

Americans of this age.— See the cross-references under the last preceding article.

[1] In Han. i. 228. [2] Part i. 206. [3] Chap. x. [4] Pages 39, 40.

GOVERNMENT, *Congregational, how distinguished.* — Hooker, in his Survey,[1] among other distinguishing points, notices these: The power of judgment is not the power of office. The people are superior to their elders in point of censure, and do not give away the power of judgment when they choose an officer. The officers may call them together, enjoin them to hear, enjoin silence, and dissolve (?) the meeting when they act disorderly. The power of judgment is in the church *formaliter*, in the rulers *directive.* Mitchell says:[2] "The things which distinguish the Congregational plan from others are two: the importance it gives to the brotherhood, in matters of discipline and government; and the independence of the churches of foreign control or supervision. . . . The powers of government are vested in the church as a body with its officers; the latter acting in their official capacity, as the guides and the executive of the church." — See CONGREGATIONALISM, *epitome of principles of.*

[1] Part i. 191—196. [2] Guide, 57.

GOVERNMENT, *civil, what obedience do we owe it?*— I quote several old writers on this point, observing the order only of the pages of the books quoted. Bridge, in his Wounded Conscience Cured,[1] quotes several German, French Protestant, Genevan, Dutch, Scotch, and English divines, maintaining that if the prince turn traitor, and the people resist, they are not rebels. He says:[2] "The power (of government) abstractly is from God; ... the designation of the person that is to work ... under this power is of man.... We leave this power where we found it. But, if the person entrusted with that power shall not discharge his trust, it falls to the people to see to it; which they do as an act of self-defence, not of jurisdiction over their prince." He shows[3] that "there is a difference between disposing of a thing by way of DONATION, and by way of TRUST:" the one may, and the other may not, be resumed. The power of the prince he holds to be only a trust-power. But "if the conqueror conquer the whole kingdom, and keep them under by conquest only, why may not the subjects rise, and take up arms, and deliver themselves from slavery?" J. Burroughs, in his Glorious Name of the Lord of Hosts,[4] notes several things which the spirit of a Christian should not bear; viz. "A natural slavery in these three things: his property, which God and nature hath given him, to be wholly at the will of another ...; subjection to a government that he has in no way yielded assent unto ...; and to be in such a situation, that, whatsoever he does, he shall receive nothing for it by way of justice, but merely of favor. This is slavery, which an ingenuous spirit cannot bear." In his Answer to Fearne,[5] he says: The apostle does not say, Whosoever resists the highest man resists the ordinance of God, but Whosoever shall resist *exousia* (the authority, not *dunamis*, mere force). He infers[6] that we are subject to the king's power, i.e. what the laws give him, but not to his will. The apostle requires us not to resist the *exousia*, but does not require us not to resist tyranny. The power is of God, but designing the person to exercise that power is *anthropine ktisis*, a human creature, 1 Pet. ii. 13. The right to govern comes not from conquering, but from some agreement antecedent or consequent. He maintains that acting without law is not an abuse of any lawful power, but only usurpation and tyranny. Hannah Adams, in her History of New England,[7] says: The influential characters in New England maintained that "birth is no necessary cause of subjection;" and that, when they removed, they owed no subjection but a voluntary one, founded on their compact with the king. Cotton pleaded that "government is a theocracy," and that none but the pious should be chosen rulers, and that magistrates should have coercive power over churches![8] Withers, in his History of Resistance,[9] says: The late Lord Chief Justice (Holt), at the time of the abdication of James II., decided that "he who hath a trust, acting contrary, is a disclaimer of the trust." Baynes, in his Diocesan's Trial,[10] says: "If kings be not absolute monarchs, it was never deemed absurd to say that their people had power, in some cases, to depose them." Dr. William Ames the younger, in his Legislative Power is Christ's Prerogative, maintains that all legislative power is from him, and that men are bound to obey all laws which are right and proper, and not those which come of the ten horns of the beast. Philip Nye, in his Oath of Supremacy Lawful, and the Power of the King in Civil Affairs, says:[11] "ALL MEN ARE BY NATURE EQUAL," and yet lamely argues the divine right of kings. He asserts[12] that no power, civil or ecclesiastical, can enforce the soul. He argues[13] that the civil magistrate, and not classes, ought to have a power of jurisdiction over the several congregations in his dominions. Pierce, in his Vindication of Dissenters,[14] says: The Puritans admit that the power of magistrates is from God, but the power to designate the magistrate is in the people. In the High Church Politics,[15] it is asserted that, in 1683, twenty-seven propositions were condemned by the University of Oxford, among which are, — "All civil authority is derived originally from the people. There is a mutual compact, tacit or express, between a prince and his subjects; and, if he perform not his duty, they are discharged from theirs. If lawful governors become tyrants, and govern otherwise than by the laws of God and man they ought to do, they forfeit the right they had to their government. . . . The doctrine of the patient suffering of injuries is not inconsistent with the violent resisting of the higher powers, in case of persecution for religion. There lies no obligation upon Christians to passive obedience, when the prince commands any thing against the laws of our country; and the primitive Christians chose rather to die than to resist, because Christianity was not yet established as the laws of the empire." We are told,[16] that Dr. Sacheverell, in his Fifth of November Sermon, 1709, before the Lord Mayor and Aldermen of London, said: "The grand security of our government, and the very pillar on which it is founded, is a steady belief of the subject's obligation to an *absolute* and unconditional obedience to the supreme power in all things lawful, and the illegality of resistance *under any pretence whatever*." And we are also informed, that these passages made the groundwork of his impeachment.[17] He defended himself on the ground that it was "the doctrine of the church." — See Goldsmith's History of England, iii. 111—115; and Abridgment, 200, 201, on reign of Queen Anne. See RESISTANCE.

[1] Pages 6, 7. [2] Ib. 20. [3] Ib. 41, 42. [4] Page 94. [5] Page 2. [6] Ib. 7—14. [7] Page 32. [8] Ib. 34. [9] Page 19. [10] Page 88. [11] Page 17. [12] Ib. 32. [13] Ib. 41—43. [14] Page 319. [15] Page 88. [16] Ib. 96. [17] Ib. 99.

GRAVES, *their position.* — In the reign of superstition under Elizabeth, one of the primary ones of Bishop Wren's ridiculous articles of visitation was, Are your churchyards duly consecrated? and "Are the graves due east and west, and their bodies buried with their heads to the west?"[1] Men who despised the law of conformity to such idle ceremonies, when they came to this wilderness took evident pains to disregard this rule, as may be still seen in some of our old graveyards, particularly in Seekonk, Mass.* Mr. Newman, the pastor there, had been seven times obliged to flee his parish in England, on account of his nonconformity. The studied

* I have it from good authority that the same is true of the old graveyard in Plymouth.

irregularity of these graves speaks a language like the round cap of the Puritan divines, not very beautiful in itself; but, when the law required an oath of the necessity of a square one, it spoke like Daniel's open window, when he prayed to the God of heaven in defiance of the decree of the king. — See CEREMONIES, HABITS, NONCONFORMITY.

[1] Neal's Puritans, i. 324, 325.

HABITS, *Popish, rejected.* — This was done because the common people then held them sacred on account of their consecration. One of the first considerable moves towards nonconformity was on the occasion of Bishop Hooper's refusing to be made a bishop in these habits.[1] Here rose up, or rather greatly increased, the Puritans, who held that things indifferent in themselves ought not to be required by law, to the ensnaring of men's consciences;[2] and multitudes lost their livings by the act of uniformity.[3] Bucer and Peter Martyr both inveighed against the habits. Bucer would not wear the square cap, "because his head was not square."[4] The foreign divines, when consulted, all decided against these habits; yet they were pressed, and multitudes of the best ministers in the land lost their places rather than conform. The question was not about the mere trifle, whether they should wear a cap or surplice, but whether they should wear such a one as would ensnare weak consciences, and lead them to idolatry. Whoever would understand this controversy should study Neal's History of the Puritans, i. 51—107, and much else in this valuable work. Wearing these habits, they considered, would be understood as approving of many Popish superstitions. (See Bradshaw's Treatise on Worship, pages 1, 16.) Neal, in his History of New England,[5] says: The first set of Protestant bishops under Elizabeth were opposed to the habits. "Grindal calls God to witness, that it did not lie at their door that they were not quite taken away." Pierce, in his Vindication of Dissenters, says:[6] "Burnett tells us, that Cranmer and Ridley designed to have procured an act to abolish the Popish garments;" and[7] that "John Rogers positively refused to wear the habits, unless the Popish priests were enjoined to wear upon their sleeves a chalice with a host." When they pulled off Latimer's garments at his degradation, he said: "Now I can make no more holy water." He and Bucer were both opposed to the habits. And[8] he shows that the habits have always been offensive to good men, churchmen as well as dissenters. R. Parker, in his book Against Symbolizing with Antichrist, especially in the Sign of the Cross, says:[9] They say the cross and surplice "being consecrate to his service, they begin to be the things of God, yea, parts of God, whose worship is a worship of God, as the purple is wont to be worshipped with the king: . . . images and crosses must be adored, like holy vessels, holy books, holy vestments, with the like." He asserts[10] that the cross, surplice, &c., are "incurable and irrecouerable idolothites," and proceeds to prove it, showing that things ill consecrate necessarily become unholy. Prince, in his Chronology,[11] informs us that Fuller says that John Rogers and Bishop Hooper were the heads of the reformers called Puritans. Hooper refused to comply with the habits; and the matter progressed till Archbishop Cranmer, Bishop Ridley, Bishop Latimer, Dr. Taylor, Mr. Philpot, Mr. Bradford, and other glorious martyrs, came into the same sentiments. The whole case is described in sect. ii. part ii. — See Ceremonies.

[1] Hist. Puritans, i. pref. ix. 51, 52. [2] Ib. 79. Ib. 77. [4] Ib. 92. [5] Neal's N. Eng. i. 48. [6] Page 11. [7] Ib. 32. [8] Ib. 476. [9] Page 8. [10] Ib. 9. [11] Pages 212—216.

HALF-WAY COVENANT. — This was a doctrine which, having previously taken root, prevailed to a considerable extent in the last half of the seventeenth and first half of the eighteenth centuries. To give an adequate analysis of the controversies on the subject would be to compose quite a volume. Dr. Harris, a seeming advocate for the doctrine in the present century,[1] calls on such as have taken this covenant to fulfil their vows, maintaining[2] that it is just as binding as the covenant of full communion. Stoddard, in his Instituted Churches, carried the doctrine so far, that he asserts[3] that infants descended from parents under church censure are not to be denied baptism; and[4] that the baptized are not to be debarred the communion for the want of the exercise of faith. Increase Mather was one of the great champions of this doctrine, having been brought over in a dispute with Mitchell of Cambridge. He tells us plainly, in the epistle to the reader, in his First Principles of New England concerning Baptism, that he had changed his mind on this point. He argues from authority, asserting that the members of the Synod of 1662 had greater facilities for understanding the truth on this subject than others. He maintains[5] that it is not an innovation, as some suppose, but was the doctrine of the first fathers of New England. (See BAPTISM, *who are subjects of?*) The great scope of the book is an attempt to prove, that the doctrine of the Synod of 1662 was no innovation. Eliot, in his Ecclesiastical History of Massachusetts,[6] says: "It was a very great innovation;" and he tells us that "Mr. Allin of Dedham replied to the Anti-synodalia of Chauncy; R. Mather to Davenport (who wrote against the result of synod); and Mitchell to Increase Mather. Some say that Mr. Davenport overthrew the arguments of the synod, though they do not like his reasoning on the whole." President Edwards, in his Treatise on Full Communion,[7] shows that "they who pretend to own the covenant, and do not profess piety, do rather reject it." The preface to this essay, by Prince, Webb, Foxcroft, and Byles, asserts that its doctrines were maintained by the fathers of this country, above threescore years, without dissension. Hemmenway, in his Remarks on Dr. Emmons's Dissertation, takes the ground that baptized children are all in covenant with God. Dr. Emmons, in his Dissertation, maintains the contrary. President Chauncy, in his Anti-synodalia, maintains that his doctrine had "been the judgment and the practice in the Bay Patent (some few inconsiderable excepted) for the space of thirty years. He says[8] that "it is a palpable untruth for an unbeliever to engage himself to keep the Lord's covenant." He maintains everywhere, that the baptized are under church watch, personally to warn them, but they are not in covenant.

For the origin of the movement in favor of the half-way covenant, it appears that the General Court of Connecticut called a council, which decreed it in 1657; but that the churches generally considered it an innovation on the principles of Congregationalism, and were so warmly opposed to it, that it could not be effected without a synod.[9] In 1662, the Synod in Boston decided in favor of it, but against considerable opposition. The General Court of Connecticut then[10] "required the ministers and churches to inquire whether they should not receive all who have a competency of knowledge to their communion." Trumbull further asserts,[11] that few churches admitted the half-way covenant for many years, and some never did. He says:[12] "It does not appear, that in 1667 so much as one church in the colony" had assented to the half-way covenant. In this year a synod met by order of the General Court, consisting of all the preaching elders in the colony, and certain selected ones in Massachusetts (evidently to carry a point); but they still failed, and found that the clergy and people would not give up their private opinions to the decisions of councils. Whoever reads the thirteenth and eighteenth chapters of Trumbull's History will see that the churches and ministers nobly withstood the encroachments of state authority, and only yielded to virtual force and power. Since the days of President Edwards, the practice has gone into disuse in the orthodox churches.—See Upham's Rat. Dis. 224—231; Punchard's View, 251. See BAPTISM, *does it admit to the church? Does it make infants members? Subjects of;* VOTERS.

[1] Sermon on Covenant Engagements, 20. [2] Ib. 12. [3] Page 18. [4] Ib. 20. [5] Pages 1, 2. [6] In Hist. Soc. Col. series ii. vol. i. 201—205. [7] Page 32. [8] Page 30. [9] Trumbull's Hist. Conn. 318. [10] Ib. 326. [11] Ib. 327. [12] Ib. 482.

HERESY.—The popular notion of a heretic is a believer in doctrines fundamentally false. But the true idea of one, according to Congregational principles, is, in the language of Mitchell,[1] "a leader of a faction, raised commonly on the ground of his peculiar doctrinal opinions, but applicable to any factious leader, whether the division be for doctrines, measures, or men." On this ground, the appellation "heretic" often falls, like any curse causeless, on the head of him who opprobriously utters it. John Cook, in his pamphlet, What the Independents Would Have,[2] says: "He (i.e. an Independent) believes that a heretic is but to be rejected, and, as Luther said, to be burned with the fire of charity."

[1] Guide, 98. [2] In Han. iii. 256.

HOLY DAYS, *extra, unlawful.*—Jacob's Church, in their Confession,[1] say (art. xxii.): "We believe that under the gospel there is not any holy day besides the Lord's day." John Robinson, in his Apology,[2] speaks of them as "reared up by the side of divine institutions, much more holy than the Lord's day." He condemns the making other days, to commemorate the resurrection, &c., than the one which is consecrated by Christ himself and his apostles. Isaac Chauncy says:[3] "It is not in the power of the church to set apart stated times, yearly or monthly, to be observed, for that would be superstition and will-worship (Gal. iv. 10; Col. ii. 16, 17); but days of fasting and humiliation may be appointed by any church, according as weighty reasons lead thereto" (Acts xiv. 23). Pierce, in his Vindication of Dissenters,[4] shows that the Scriptures make certain the identity of but two of the extra days observed as holy; that two of them are Sundays, and it is absurd to try to make these more holy. It is uncertain on what day Christ was born, or the purification of the Blessed Virgin occurred, and impious to thank God that such things took place on such and such days. The articles of the Leyden Church say:[5] "The Sabbath is the only day which is set apart, as holy and to be kept sacred, in the Scriptures; but churches and congregations are at liberty to set apart days of fasting, thanksgiving, and prayer."

[1] In Han. i. 300. [2] Ib. i. 381. [3] Divine Inst. Cong. Churches, 91. [4] Page 502. [5] Upham's Rat. Dis. 39, 249.

IDLENESS *a disciplinable offence.* — This has ever been a doctrine of Congregationalism, founded on 2 Thess. iii. 11—14 and 1 Tim. v. 13. — See ELDERS, *their office*.

IDOLATRY, *remnants of, discarded.* — Robinson, in his answer to Hall,[1] more than intimates that it is idolatry to kneel at the consecrated bread; so of kneeling to the ordinary, when we take the oath at his hands. Ainsworth, in his Arrow against Idolatry,[2] reckons the consecrated places, implements, and even ministers, with many other ceremonies, derived from idolatrous Rome, among the idolatries practised by the English church. — See Ceremonies; Habits; Kneeling.

[1] In Han. i. 194; and Works, iii. 411. [2] In Han. i. 238.

IMPOSITION OF HANDS *in ordination; is it necessary?* — This is a subject concerning which there has been some diversity of opinion, both among Congregationalists and other reformed churches. Goodwin[1] maintains that it is one of the first principles of the Christian religion. Welde, in his Reply to Rathband,[2] quotes the Answer to the Thirty-two Questions, page 67: "Though the essence of a minister's call consists in his election, yet we look upon ordination, by imposition of hands, as necessary, by a divine institution." Others, as Dr. Watts,[3] suppose that "the imposition of hands was the means of conveying miraculous powers." With this view,[4] it was not practised in the Dutch nor the French churches; nor has it ever been used in the Scotch churches at all. This is recorded as a fact bearing on the controversy between Clyfton, Johnson, and Ainsworth. It is asserted that in the Scriptures we find that some officers were admitted with it, and some without it. The Independents in the Westminster Assembly[5] consented to the cere mony, "*provided it was attended with an open declaration, that it was not intended as a conveyance of office power.*" The Savoy Synod[6] say: "The way of ordaining officers . . . is, after their election by the suffrage of the church, to set them apart with fasting and prayer, and imposition of the hands of the eldership of the church, though, if there be no imposition of hands, they are rightly constituted ministers of Christ." But they do not allow, that ordination to the work of the ministry, though it be by persons rightly ordained, conveys office-power without a previous election of the church. Mr. Pemberton[7] argues, from the Scripture instances of ordination, that imposition of hands may not be neglected without sin. Isaac Chauncy[8] says that there is not the least mention of imposition of hands in the New Testament, where the translators use the word *ordination* in its proper sense, i. e. installing a person into office, though the word signifies uplifting of the hands, by way of suffrage, in the election of officers. He maintains[9] that laying on of hands conferred extraordinary gifts, and many think it obsolete. He concludes[10] that it is an obsolete ceremony, which has ceased, and assigns sixteen reasons for his conclusion, among which are the following: — The end and signification of the rite have ceased; it never was appropriate to the ordination of ministers; most of the apostles were ordained without it, and no ordinary pastor (that we read of) ordained with it; the church's solemn and public election is ordination, Acts xiv. 23; there is no more ground for the continuance of this rite than for the washing of feet, or the anointing with oil; it has been abused by Papists, and idolized by Protestants. Increase Mather, in his Order of the New England Churches,[11] shows at length that imposition of hands is indifferent, while election is indispensable to a pastor. Notwithstanding all this, our forefathers, I believe universally, practised imposition of hands in ordination, and usually repeated it in installations. The latter they did to do away the impression of a peculiar unction and an indelible character made by ordination. — See Neander's Planting and Training of the Church, 97, 98; Upham's Rat. Dis., 120; Punchard's View, 96, and Bacon's Church Manual, 60; Coleman's Primitive Church, 139, 141. — See CALLING; ORDINATION, *none besides election necessary*; TRANSLATION.

[1] Ch. Gov. 262. [2] In Han. ii. 330. [3] Serm. at the Ordin. of Deacons, Works, iii. 312. [4] Han. i. 242, 243. [5] Neal's Puritans, ii. 8. [6] Ib. 179. [7] Ordin. Serm. of Rev. J. Sewall, 6. [8] Divine Inst. Cong. Churches, 68. [9] Page 74. [10] Pages 78—83. [11] Pages 90—100.

IMPOSITION OF HANDS, *by whom?* — Richard Mather, in his reply to Rutherford,[1] maintains that, because the Presbytery laid hands on Timothy, it does not follow that no others may engage in this ceremony. Trumbull, in his History of Connecticut,[2] informs us that Mr. Fitch was ordained at Saybrook in 1646 by two lay brethren, though Mr. Hooker, his theological instructor, was present; and that they did the same in 1660, at the ordination of Mr. Buckingham, though a council was present.

The council considered it an innovation; but the brethren were tenacious of what they esteemed their right, and it could not be prevented without inconvenience. The same year, Mr. Newton was installed at Milford by a ruling elder and two brethren. Isaac Chauncy[3] inquires: "Who should ordain when there is no elder? Answer,— Who should do it but the church that called him?... The power is in the church to lay on hands, if necessary, by some brother delegated and appointed thereto; for foreign ministers cannot do an authoritative act in that church." — See ORDINATION *by the people.*

[1] In Han. ii. 188. [2] Vol. i. 299. [3] Divine Inst. Cong. Churches, 70.

IMPROVIDENCE *disciplinable.* — Mitchell[1] says that this is "an offence against nature, justice, and religion." He asserts that it is disciplinable, according to 1 Tim. v. 8.— See IDLENESS.

[1] Guide, 99.

INDEPENDENCY, *what; wherein owned, and wherein denied.* — This word has two technical significations, as used by different writers, both ancient and modern. Hence, of those who held the same sentiments, we often find one lauding and the other condemning Independency. In one of these significations it implies merely the independency of the churches from all juridical power out of themselves; in the other, that one church has no right to call another to account, and pass sentence of non-communion against it. Congregationalists admit the first, and deny the second. Hence the authors of the Cambridge Platform[1] say: "The term Independent we approve not," while their brethren in England, then, and to this time, call themselves Independents. It was on account of the extravagancies of some, who in most things copied the intolerance of Brown, that Robinson and our New England forefathers thought best to avoid the name. Lord Say, in his speech in Parliament,[2] says: "The bishops do know that those to whom they usually do apply the term Separatists are Brownists. The Brownists differ from us in no fundamental point of doctrine or saving truth. Their failing is this: They hold that there is no true church in England, no true ministry, no true worship, which depend one upon another. They distinguish not between the purity of a church and the being of it." Welde, in his reply to Rathband,[3] shows that we admit representative councils, and can pass sentence of non-communion, but cannot cast churches out of Christendom. Burton, in his Answer to Prynne,[4] says of the word Independent: "We are not so ashamed of it as absolutely to disclaim it, for two reasons, — first, for distinction; second, because the word Independent is to signify, that we hold all particular churches of Christ to be of equal authority, and none to have or exercise jurisdiction over another:" but he rejects the nickname, as implying that they denied "subjection to civil government, or good correspondence with sister-churches, by way of help." Burroughs, in his Irenicum,[5] shows that we admit the ways of reproving churches held by the

Presbyterians, till we come to delivering them to Satan, where, he says, "lies the knot of the controversy." "They are not independent as respects giving account to the churches about them, but of being bound, on penalty of being unchurched, to obey their decisions." Bartlett, in his Model,[6] denies that it can be shown of any Congregationalists, in Old England or New, that they exclude the advice of other churches, or refuse to be accountable to those who in a fair and orderly way desire them. The Propositions to Parliament for Gathering Churches,[7] will give a pretty good view of the "desires" of those "commonly but falsely called Independents." "Falsely" doubtless refers to the first definition, as given at the commencement of this article. — See Upham's Rat. Dis. 41—43; Punchard's View, 185.

[1] Chap. ii. sect. 5. [2] In Han. ii. 136. [3] Ib. 337—341. [4] Ib. 403, 404. [5] Ib. iii. 110, 111. [6] Ib. 238. [7] Ib. 247—249.

INDEPENDENCY *of churches to exercise government within themselves.* — Gibbon, in his Decline and Fall, says:[1] Independence and equality formed the basis of the internal constitution of the primitive churches in the Roman empire. Goodwin, in his Church Government,[2] argues this independency from the fact that an isolated church has this power, and the establishment of neighbor-churches cannot institute an entire and distinct and diverse sort of government over that original church. Hooker, in his Survey,[3] asserts that each particular church is complete and independent, for the exercise of all acts and dispensations belonging to a church, without reference to any other congregation. And Mitchell[4] says: "The independence of the churches is a necessary part of their self-government. Their powers become a nullity, if they resign themselves to a superior jurisdiction. Our Saviour himself gives the ultimate power to the church, Matt. xviii. 17, 18. He does not say, If the offending member neglect to hear the church, let it be carried up to some higher tribunal, but the case is to be terminated there." See ib. 68—70. — See CHURCHES *subject to no external jurisdiction.*

[1] In Han. i. 7. [2] Page 134. [3] Part i. 221. [4] Guide, 66, 67.

INDEPENDENCY *endangers monarchy.*—Prynne, a Presbyterian, in the fourth of his Twelve Considerable Questions, asks:[1] "Whether the grounds and reasons principally insisted on for an independent church government be not such as, if duly examined, will, by necessary, inevitable consequence, subvert, dissolve, or at least embroil or endanger, all national and provincial churches, councils, and synods, and all settled monarchical, aristocratical, or oligarchical government, in nations," &c.? Here, alone, Burton, his Congregationalist opponent, seems to be put to the worse in his argument. In his reply,[2] he only seems to confirm Prynne's awful objection, though he labors hard to overthrow it. The truth is, Prynne's argument is unanswerable. Lord Brooke, in his discourse on Episcopacy,[3] labors hard, and is evidently in great trouble, to prove that church liberty has not a tendency to introduce republican civil government. Even Hanbury[4] says: "It cannot be proved that Independency leads necessarily to republicanism." He, however, found himself hard pressed with the fact, that the existence of the Commonwealth was exactly coeval with the triumph of Independency in England. American Congregationalists will agree with him, that it "cannot be proved," because they perceive that it is self-evident. Robinson, in his Answer to Helwisse,[5] found himself pressed with the same argument; and Punchard remarks, that "it could not but be a difficult task to show that their church government was not popular." That Robinson, with his clear mind, was endeavoring to evade the argument against ecclesiastical democracy, and to make it equivalent to civil monarchy, may be clearly seen from the continuation of his reasoning.[6] Our forefathers were sincere, loyal monarchists, and brought in the ruling elders to make a mixed government. These, centaur-like, appear in their system neither one thing nor another, and went into disuse just as fast as republican principles advanced in the colonies. Rev. Jonathan Mahew[7] says of himself: "And having learnt from the Holy Scriptures, that wise, brave, and virtuous men were always friends to liberty; that God gave the Israelites a king in his anger, because they had not sense and virtue enough to like a free commonwealth." Eliot, speaking of the mission of Bradstreet and Norton to England in 1662, says:[8] "It was well known that they were actuated by republican sentiments, and were Puritans of a strict denomination, with no kind of reverence for bishops or *nobles*." Letchford, in his Plain Dealing,[9] compares Independency to democracy in civil government. He predicts that the "elective course will soon lead to disorder and ruin." He says that he and others do *know* (*! !*) that it is not fit nor *possible* (*! !*) to be continued *long in New England* (*! ! !*). John Milton[10] says: The kings of this world have ever instinctively hated the church of God. Is it because they fear liberty and equality, or because themselves belong to another kingdom? He says:[11] "King Charles set himself to the removal of those men whose doctrine and desire of church discipline he feared would be the undoing of his monarchy." Henry Jacob[12] shows that his opponents thought that popular church government led to making the civil government conform to it. — See Punchard's View, 240—243.

[1] Page 3. [2] In Han. ii. 411. [3] Ib. 125. [4] Ib. iii. 379. [5] In Punchard's Hist. 337, 340; and Works, iii. 134—138. [6] Ib. 347—349. [7] In Eliot, Biog. Dict. 321. [8] Ib. 82. [9] In Hist. Soc. Col. series iii. vol. iii. 127. [10] Eikonoklastes, 132. [11] Ib. 134. [12] In Han. i. 222.

Whoever wishes to learn what means were used to put down Independency in England should consult Hanbury, vol. ii. 218—220, and vol. iii. 101, and learn it from the pens of their opponents, particularly Baillie, who invoked a Scotch army, fifteen thousand strong, to give force to Presbyterian arguments in the Westminster Assembly. He complains that the "Independents there plead for toleration for others as well as themselves"!!

INDIFFERENTS *to be decided by the church, not by rulers.* — Lord Brooke shows,[1] that, if indifferent matters are to be decided by church rulers, they will soon decide all things indifferent to be absolutely necessary. It was thus that they decreed the absolute necessity of the habits, ceremonies, &c., and enforced conformity under the most severe penalties. Bradshaw says:[2] "Those who have power to join to the sacrament of baptism the sign of the cross, have authority also, no doubt, to join to the sacrament of the Supper, flesh, broth, butter, or cheese."

[1] In Han. ii. 120, 121. [2] Treatise on Divine Worship, 10.

INSTALLATION, *is it indispensable?* — Cotton Mather[1] says: "Ministers coming from England were usually re-ordained; but, some of them scrupling, the churches have elected them and embraced them, and so, solemnizing the transaction with fasting and prayer, have enjoyed them to all evangelical intents and purposes, without their being re-ordained at all.

[1] Magnalia, ii. 209.

INSTALLATION, *mode of.* — Cotton Mather[1] says, a minister removing from another church, "a day of prayer is kept, the choice renewed, and the charge accepted, in the presence of delegates from other churches; and no further imposition of hands is used in his instalment. He says[2] that "installations are conducted as ordinations, except the imposition of hands." Cambridge Platform[3] intimates that imposition of hands should be used in installation, since Paul twice received it from Ananias. — See Upham's Rat. Dis. 124; Punchard's View, 166. See IMPOSITION OF HANDS.

[1] Rat. Dis. 41, 42. [2] Ib. 169, 170. [3] Chap. ix. sect. 7.

INSTITUTIONS OF THE GOSPEL, *what.* — Owen, in his Catechism,[1] enumerates the principal of these to be — "calling, gathering, and settling churches, with their officers; prayer; singing psalms; preaching; sacraments; and discipline."

[1] In Works, xix. 502.

INTERMISSIONS, *Sabbath, how spent in New England.* — Cotton Mather[1] says: "The more faithful and watchful pastors have been put upon using their contrivances that their employments may be most serviceable to the interests of holiness. It has been proposed, that repetitions of, or conferences on, the word of Christ, may be some of their employments." Thus they were in advance of Raikes in devising virtual Sabbath-schools. — See SABBATH-SCHOOLS.

[1] Rat. Dis. 45.

JESUS CHRIST *is the only lawgiver to his church.* This is one of the first principles of Congregationalism. It is directly asserted by Henry Jacob, in his Divine Beginning of Christ's Visible Church.[1] John Davenport, in his Power of Congregational Churches,[2] says: "The absolute supremacy of power is in Christ. That which the Church hath is only delegated from Christ." — See LEGISLATION.

[1] In Han. i. 228. [2] Ib. ii. 64.

JURISDICTION *of churches in the people.* — John Wise, in his Quarrel of the Churches Espoused,[1] says: "Our New England government grants a juridical power to the fraternity, and makes them the proper judges in all ecclesiastical cases and administrations." The Answer of the Boston Synod of 1662 says:[2] "Every church . . . hath received from the Lord Jesus Christ full power and authority ecclesiastical, within itself, regularly to administer all the ordinances of Christ, and is not under any other ecclesiastical jurisdiction whatever." — See Churches *subject to no external jurisdiction;* Consociations; Councils; Independency *of churches;* Synods; Keys; Power, *church;* and the like topics.

[1] Page 108. [2] Pages 113, 114.

KEYS, *power of, what.* — Hooker says:[1] "By power of the keys we understand the power of ordination, excommunication, &c." He shows[2] that even Rutherford admitted that an isolated church had the power of excommunication in itself. John Cotton says:[3] "The keys of the kingdom are the ordinances which Christ hath instituted to be administered in his church."

[1] Survey, part i. 231. [2] Ib. 240. [3] Keys of Heaven, 20.

KEYS *granted only to embodied churches.* —Goodwin[1] says: "The *jus executionis*, Matt. xviii. 16, Christ doth not give it to the saints and officers simply, but as formed up into bodies. Matt. xvi. holdeth that they are to be saints making confession, as Peter did; but Matt. xviii. holdeth forth how that these saints be formed up into several bodies or churches, and so to execute this power." The whole of the fourth chapter of his second book is on this point. Davenport, in his Power of Congregational Churches,[2] shows that this doctrine follows from the fact that all they do as embodied churches proceeds from this power. Hooker[3] shows that "a church congregational is the first power of the keys." He says, however, that it was *the* question of that day, "whether all ecclesiastical power be impaled, impropriated, and rightly taken into the presbytery (i.e. the bench of elders in a church) alone; causing great thoughts concerning presbytery, how shall they retain their power? and the people, how shall they retain their rights?" (See ELDERS.) Owen, in his Nature of a Gospel Church, chap. iii.[4] says: "The keys were originally given to the whole church, in distinction from the officers of it." John Cotton[5] says: The power of the keys is a liberty purchased to the church by the blood of Christ, and should not be parted with at a less price.

[1] Ch. Gov. 55. [2] In Han. ii. 63, 64. [3] Pref. to Survey. [4] In Works, xx. 389. [5] Way of the Churches, 50.

KEYS, *power of, claimed for particular churches with elders.* — This was strenuously maintained by Goodwin.[1] The presence of elders with the church was held to be necessary, because the power to receive, excommunicate, &c., was supposed to be with them, while they might not do it without the "free consent of the brotherhood."[2] Cotton, in his Keys,[3] argues this same point, placing the key of power in the brethren, and [4] the key of authority in the elders. Thus, here, as everywhere else, we find a guarding against democracy, by placing the executive power wholly in the elders. So Cambridge Platform [5] places the power of office in the elders, and the power of privilege in the brotherhood (see chapters v. and x.); making the elders subject, however, to the power of the church "in case of mal-administration." Eaton and Taylor maintain [6] that the power of government is distinctly given to the church: "Tell it to the church." Also the power of excommunication was in the church, and not even in the apostle. So, too, argues Isaac Chauncy, in his Divine Institution of Congregational Churches.[7] He shows conclusively that the keys were given to the church through Peter, as it is usual to name one or more individuals in all charters. — See ELDERS, *is one or more necessary to church action?*

[1] Ch. Gov. 111—116. [2] See Bradshaw's Eng. Puritanism, in Neal, i. 249. [3] Pages 36—48. [4] Ib. 49—54. [5] Pages 28, 41. [6] Defence, 85, 95. [7] Pages 102—104.

KINGSHIP OF CHRIST *immediate.* — Goodwin[1] shows that this should be maintained, "not merely as our liberty, but as Christ's prerogative, which we, as his courtiers, are not to see encroached upon or diminished." Consequently, he holds that none have a right to direct us contrary to God's commands, nor have we a right to obey such wicked directions. — See JESUS CHRIST *is the only lawgiver to his church.*

[1] Ch. Gov. 258.

KNEELING, *why not practised at communion.*— Robinson, in his Answer to Hall,[1] asks: "Where learned you your devout kneeling to or before the bread, but from that error of transubstantiation?" Neal[2] represents the Puritans as excepting against the injunction of kneeling at the sacrament of the Lord's Supper, as not agreeable to the example of Christ, having no foundation in antiquity, and having been grossly abused to idolatry. He represents them[3] as declaring that it arose from the notion of the transubstantiation of the elements;—that the Papists admit they would be guilty of idolatry in kneeling before them, if they did not really believe them to be the real body and blood of Christ; and that it is a gross hypocrisy for us to pretend more holiness, reverence, and devotion in receiving the sacrament than the apostles, who received it from the immediate hand and person of Christ himself. Lord King, in his Inquiry,[4] shows from the fathers, that, in whatever other position it was received in the ancient churches, it could not have been kneeling. Cartwright, in his Answer to Whitgift,[5] shows that there is the same dangerous tendency to idolatry in kneeling at the sacrament as in receiving the wafer-cake.

Bradshaw, in his Treatise on Worship and Ceremonies,[6] advocates the same sentiments, showing that, if it is in reverence to God, it is will-worship, i.e. not required; and, if in reverence to the bread, it is idolatry. In the Dispute concerning Kneeling at the Sacraments, published in 1608, it is asserted,[7] that "kneeling in reverence to the bread and wine would have justified the angel and Peter in receiving homage out of reverence."

[1] In Punchard's Hist. 379; and Han. i. 194; and Works, iii. 411. [2] Neal's Puritans, i. 107. [3] Ib. 246, 247. [4] Part ii. 113. [5] Page 165. [6] Pages 90—105. [7] Page 162.

LAWS, *New England, concerning religion.*—Lambert, in his History of the Colony of New Haven, says[1] the Plantation Covenant was for more than a year their only civil and religious compact; in this they agreed "to be ordered by the rules which the Scriptures hold forth." Eliot, in his Ecclesiastical History of Massachusetts,[2] asserts, that, soon after 1651, it was ordered by General Court, that no minister should be called into office without the approbation and allowance of some of the magistrates, as well as some of the neighbor-churches. In a petition of the Church and Town of Woburn in 1553,[3] the petitioners complain of a late order of court, "that those who preach constantly be approbated, either by a council of neighbor-churches, or by *the county* court." (See further, under Approbation *to preach.*) In 1695 it was enacted, that, when a parish do not concur with a church in the choice of a pastor, the church may call a council; and, if they approve, he shall be the minister of the parish. This was argued in point in the Springfield case. (See Answer to Hampshire Narrative, 37.) In the Answer of the General Court to Dr. Child and others, in 1769,[4] they assert that, according to the fundamentals of Massachusetts, "all persons, orthodox in judgment and not scandalous in life, may gather into a church state. Zabdiel Adams, in his Answer to a Treatise on Church Government, admits that a parish may refuse the result of a council negativing their dismission of a minister; but, in that case, they must pay his salary according to contract. These are a few of the things that were of old in New England religious laws. — See Acts and Laws of his Majesty's Province in Massachusetts Bay, published in 1742, pages 14, 15, 17, 18, 27, 36, 41, 68, 70, 81, 94, 153, 154, 155, 156, 211, 213, 215, 216, 231, 264, 265, 266, 267, 324, 331, 332.

[1] Page 44. [2] In Mass. Hist. Soc. Col. series i. vol. x. 25. [3] Ib. series iii. vol. i. 35—42. [4] Hutchinson's Mass. Col. of Papers, 201.

Dr. Perry's forthcoming work will doubtless contain much valuable information concerning present New England ecclesiastical laws.

LEGISLATION *not the prerogative of churches.* Punchard, in his History,[1] shows that this was a fundamental doctrine of some of the purest early dissenting churches, — as the Paterines, who say, "a church has no power to frame any constitutions;" and the Albigenses and Waldenses, who declare "that Christ has given his church no authority to make laws for the government of his people." Neal,[2] in Reply to Hooker ("the judicious"), says: "As far as any church is governed by the laws and precepts of the New Testament, so far it is the church of Christ; but when it sets up its own by-laws as terms of commuion, or works the policy of the civil magistrate into its constitution, so far it is a creature of the state." Cotton says:[3] "All legislative power in the church is in Christ, and not from him derived to any other; James iv. 12; Isa. xxxiii. 22. He only can create and ordain a true constitution of a church estate." Samuel Mather says:[4] "I may not fear to assert that a great part of those disorders which have arisen in the Christian world have been by usurping legislative power over the churches." Owen, in his Original of Churches, chap. ii.[5] asserts that no legislative ecclesiastical power is left to men, and that assuming such power is dangerous. Watts, in his Foundation of a Christian Church,[6] maintains that churches may not appoint any new rules of admission. Welde, in his Answer to Rathband,[7] shows it to be a principle of the New England churches, "that the church has no power to make laws, but only to observe those laws which Christ has given and commanded." He, however, shows, against the cavils of his opponent, that they have a power to determine needful things for themselves, but not to legislate. Mitchell[8] says, some think that it is expedient to have written rules of discipline and practice; but care should be taken, in forming them, that they be not of a legislative character, but only declarative. Congregationalism as Contained in the Scriptures, &c.,[9] says: "This description of a church (in the Platform) excludes from it every thing of the nature of legislation." — See CREEDS.

[1] Pages 102, 109. [2] Puritans, i. 207. [3] Keys, 65. [4] Apology, 29. [5] Works, xx. 92. [6] Works, iii. 235. [7] In Han. ii. 321. [8] Guide, 139. [9] Page 6.

LETTER OF DISMISSION; *has every member, not under discipline, a right to one?* — See Affinity; Dismission.

The principles laid down in these articles indicate that he has a right to a dismission, if not *disciplinable,* but not to avoid merited discipline. Nor has he a right to any other recommendation than the church can conscientiously give him, based on all the facts in the case, whereupon the church applied to are to exercise their discretion as to receiving him. But, unless the church proceed immediately to discipline, he has a right to dismission without unnecessary delay.

LIBERTY *of conscience to be allowed.* — Thomas Goodwin[1] expatiates largely on this point, asserting "that saints, or persons professing Christ, though they differ, yet, being in Christ, they ought not to judge or despise, but forbear one another;" enforcing his arguments by the commands to bear the infirmities of the weak, love one another, &c. He takes an appeal from the law of persecution to the law of God, and sues out execution for the day of judgment. — See Conscience, Toleration, Fellowship, Creeds, Uniformity, Union.

[1] Ch. Gov. 399—408.

LICENSE *to preach.* — Formerly, individual pastors introduced whom they thought proper into their pulpits, and churches made long trial of the gifts and fitness of candidates for the pastoral office. In 1705, an unsuccessful effort was made to have none thus employed as candidates, who are not "recommended by a testimonial under the hands of some association."[1] Wise[2] strenuously maintains that this would be an infringement on the rights of the churches. Cotton Mather[3] regards the want of a formal licensing power as a defect, and quotes his Proposals, published twenty years before, but says: "They are not to this day (1726) fully executed." From the Records of Boston Association, it appears that the late Dr. Gray of Roxbury was the first approbated by that body, in 1792; and that it was matter of long deliberation whether they should proceed to give such approbation according to the vote of the Convention of 1790. March 15, 1804, that association appointed a committee "to prepare rules to be observed by association in future, with respect to the examination and *approbation* of candidates for the ministry." The subsequent reports of this committee, and the doings of the association thereon, reveal to the practised eye much of the workings of "the hand of Joab," on the question whether association should grant *license*, or merely *approbation*. It was decided that "the moderator shall put (to the association) this question,—Do you approbate?" and that the "credential" shall be of the following "tenor: . . . We approve as qualified for the work of the gospel-ministry . . . ; we accordingly recommend him to the acceptance and employment of the churches."

A highly esteemed correspondent, who has devoted much labor, and brought uncommon resources of learning, to the investigation of the usages of the churches, writes substantially thus: According to a fundamental principle of Congregationalism and long-established usage in New England, license to preach is the express or implied authority granted by a church to preach to them the gospel. They refused submission to or acknowledgment of any assumed authority as a pre-requisite to the office of preaching the gospel in any church. Yet they prudently availed themselves of such information from good and discerning men, and especially settled ministers, as might aid them in coming to a wise decision in licensing to preach to them on any occasion of need or convenience. Such letters of credit or *approbation*, coming at first from one or more ministers in their individual capacity, in process of time came from ministers convened in associations, whose approval was thus expressed, rather for convenience than from a designed assumption of power to themselves, or a denial of it to the churches. The import of such approbation was not understood, either by associations or churches, as conferring a power or a right to preach, or in any manner qualifying the individual whom they thus approved for the office of a public teacher. No association has formally claimed the right to license. None could vindicate such a claim by any authority. The term *license* now extensively current, as if signifying a grant by associational authority to preach, is unknown to the records of the older associations, except as a recent usurper, or, as in the Boston Association (the oldest in the country), under virtual condemnation. The Mendon Association, which has just completed its first century, is yet a stranger to giving license to preach, and scrupulously refrains from the use of language importing an authority which belongs exclusively to churches. Still more recently has sprung up the practice of licensing for a limited term; a practice for which there is no authority, unless the term license is used, as it is in some associations, to signify a mere recommendation, which the receiver is not allowed to use after the expiration of the limited time.— Mitchell[4] and the Congregational Manual[5] now claim licensing as the right of ministers in their associated capacity; but the practice is of recent origin.— See APPROBATION *to preach;* PREACH, *who may?* PROPHESYING.

[1] Wise's Quarrel of the Churches Espoused, 120. [2] Ib. 121—128. [3] Rat. Dis. 117, 121. [4] Guide, 232. [5] Page 29.

LIMITS *of churches.*— Goodwin[1] limits them to so many as can meet in one place, because "the same assembly is to meet for discipline that meets for worship; because of the time that is instituted for their worship, viz. the Lord's day, and because of the duties of the elders to preach and rule;" with several other considerations. This is the universal sentiment of Congregationalists.— See CHURCH, *may one have branches?* CHURCHES *distinct bodies.*

[1] Ch. Gov. 67.

LITURGY.— Cotton Mather[1] shows that "the New England churches have no liturgy composed for them, much less imposed upon them. . . . Our Saviour and his apostles never provided any prayer-book but the Bible for us. . . . The first planters hoped that the second coming of our Saviour will arrive before there will be received among them any *liber officialis* (book of authority) but the Sacred Scriptures." He shows that liturgies were invented when the bishops, assembled in councils, were many of them so illiterate that they must get another to subscribe their names for them.

[1] Rat. Dis. 46—52.

LORD'S PRAYER: *we are not tied to the form, but only to the spirit of it.*—Greenwood, in his Answer to Giffard,[1] says: "Christ did not say, Say these words by rote, but after this *manner* therefore pray ye." The adverb is one of similitude: Christ teaches to ask for the object of individual wants, as a child asks bread of a father. This was a matter of long dispute between the Nonconformists and the Episcopalians; the former maintaining that there was no necessity of having the words even of the Lord's Prayer imposed on men. Increase Mather, in his Order of the Churches of New England Justified,[2] shows that it is lawful, but not required, to use the words of the Lord's Prayer.

[1] In Han. i. 68, 69. [2] Pages 117—136.

LORD'S SUPPER, *a church ordinance.* — Goodwin[1] argues this point at length, endeavoring to prove it by necessary inference from other Congregational principles, and by the Holy Scriptures.

He maintained that it must be in a congregated church, and by a preaching elder (see further on *Must it be administered by an ordained minister?*); — that the recipient must be a member of some organized church; and that a number of congregated church members, not with a church, have no right to this ordinance.

[1] Ch. Gov. 350—356.

LORD'S SUPPER, *should it be administered to any who are not members of churches?* — The Answer of the New England Elders to the Nine Positions,[1] shows that the means of judging of piety are wanting, unless the communicants join themselves to some church. Goodwin[2] says: "One apostle and one other man could not receive the Lord's Supper together, because they could not make a church, 1 Cor. x. Allin and Shepard, in their Answer to Ball,[3] agree that there are privileges which belong to a believer as such, but not instituted privileges. These only are rightly to be obtained in the way of the institution. Dr. Watts, in his Terms of Communion, Quest. vi.,[4] maintains that those not members of churches ordinarily ought not to come to the communion, but that there are exceptions. A church may refuse to receive a troublesome Christian (?) to membership, and yet admit him to communion!! By further reference to the Answer of the New England Elders to the Nine Positions, as quoted in Hanbury,[5] we find them declaring; "Church communion we hold only with church members, admitting to the fellowship of the seals known and approved and orderly recommended members of any true church." This they maintain by seven considerations, among which is this: They that are incapable of the censures are incapable of the privileges. Those not in covenant are incapable of the censures, therefore of the seals as privileges.

[1] Page 70. [2] Ch. Gov. 233. [3] In Han. iii. 40. [4] Works, iii. 256. [5] Vol. ii. 27.

LORD'S SUPPER *not for the known wicked.*—Johnson, in his Treatise on the Reformed Churches,[1] quotes from Chrysostom: "No small punishment hangeth over you, if, knowing a man to be wicked, ye suffer him to be a partaker at this table: his blood shall be required at your hands." One of the Queries to the Church of Scotland[2] is this: "If he that eateth and drinketh unworthily, eateth and drinketh his own judgment; and all English souls are bound to eat and drink . . . at sixteen, who sees not . . . that the body of the people are compelled by law to eat and drink, at sixteen, their own judgment?" Cotton Mather[3] argues that they should not be admitted who do not give evidence of serious piety, upon which "all turns." Upon this point there was, however, much doubt and diversity in his day. They, however, agreed that the weakest Christian, if sincere, should not be discarded. The half-way covenant doctrine led consistently to the admission of the unregenerate to the communion.

[1] In Han. i. 316. [2] Ib. ii. 247. [3] Rat. Dis. 82—84.

LORD'S SUPPER *should not be privately administered.* — Sparke and Travers, in their conference with the Bishop of Winchester,[1] objected to private communion. Cotton Mather[2] says: "It being a main scope of the Lord's Supper to be a seal of that mystery, the communion of saints (?), the churches of New England judge it not so proper for one or two, by a bedside or the like, to celebrate this ordinance."

[1] Neal's Puritans, i. 167. [2] Rat. Dis. 102.

LORD'S SUPPER, *should it be administered by any but ordained ministers?* — The Savoy Confession[1] says: "No persons may administer the sacrament but such as are ordained thereto." And this is agreeable to present, and, so far as I can learn, past practice of Congregationalists. How much of the principle of apostolical succession and holy unction is countenanced by this practice, may be a question. Samuel Mather[2] quotes Fabritius, with apparent approbation: "If any man, even a laic, be appointed by the church to administer the sacrament, if he does it, he does nothing but his duty, and neither offends against the faith nor against good order." Andrew Fuller, in his Address to a Young Minister,[3] says: "Ordination seems originally intended for guarding against bad characters. I have therefore been much concerned to see the practice of administering the Lord's Supper obtain prior to it, which tends to set it aside, and will, I am persuaded, be the source of many mishaps in the churches." Yet on the same page, in his Reply to a Baptist Church in Edinburgh, he says: "I had long been of the opinion that there was no Scripture for confining the administration of the Lord's Supper to a minister. . . . I could wish that every church, when destitute of a pastor, would attend to the Lord's Supper among themselves." — See SEALS; MINISTERS, *may they administer seals, &c.?*

[1] In Neal's Puritans, ii. 179. [2] Apology, 61. [3] Works, ii. 662.

LORD'S SUPPER, *is baptism an indispensable pre-requisite to?* — Andrew Fuller, in his Letter to Ward,[1] argues the affirmative from Christ's requirement of baptism. Robert Hall, in his Terms of Communion, everywhere maintains the negative.

[1] Works, ii. 667, 668.

LORD'S SUPPER, *should the bread and wine in it be consecrated?* — Nathaniel Mather, in his Discussion on a Pastor's Officiating in Other Churches,[1] says: "No man should bless and separate the elements, so as to make them sacramental, without power from Christ, whose work alone it is, by his poor minister, to effect that special union, which there truly is in the sacrament, between the elements and Christ's body and blood." Upham[2] speaks of the consecration of the sacramental elements in prayer, and no wonder, in these days of consecration of burial-grounds, and dedication of meeting-houses; but the quotation from Nathaniel Mather above smells strangely of Rome for a Congregational writer of those times. This does not seem to have been a subject much discussed by the fathers; but their sentiments on parallel doctrines may be seen under the heads CEREMONIES, HABITS, IDOLATRY, KNEELING. One of the Genevan Disputants (Peter Carpenter, "a low countrieman") says[3] of the consecration of the emblems of the Lord's Supper: "They are to be condemned who attribute some holiness to the signs; and, as for those who worship them, these we utterly detest as open idolaters."

[1] Page 19. [2] Rat. Dis. 235. [3] Page 164.

LORD'S SUPPER, *how often should it be administered.* — Goodwin devotes the fifth chapter of his seventh book on Church Government to prove that it should be administered every Lord's day. His arguments are powerful and ingenious, if not conclusive. He demands a warrant[1] for singling out special days for this purpose of attending to a divine institution. Cotton Mather[2] says: "The time for celebrating this ordinance in New England is various, and the pastors reserve the liberty of altering the times as they judge fit, upon emergencies." Hopkins[3] says: It does not follow from Acts xx. 7, that the disciples always came together on the first day of the week to break bread. — See Upham's Rat. Dis. 236, 237.

[1] Page 342. [2] Rat. Dis. 95. [3] System, ii. 347.

LORD'S SUPPER, *we should not neglect, for wrong in others.* — This is so plain a principle of Scripture that it seems strange that it should ever have been lost sight of; yet multitudes seem to

20

feel that they are excused from obeying Christ when they are angry with their brethren. Cambridge Platform[1] shows that no member should punish himself on account of wrong in any of his brethren. If discipline is neglected, and the church cannot be reformed, they may use their liberty to withdraw and go to other churches, when they cannot remain without continuing in sin, according to chapter xiii. section 4. Mitchell[2] shows that such a forsaking the communion is a disciplinable offence. Cotton Mather[3] quotes Cambridge Association, who assert that it is schism and scandal to withdraw on account of wrong in others, and should be dealt with as unruly and walking disorderly. In Winthrop's Journal[4] is recorded an instance of the church in Watertown dealing with, and excluding a member for thus absenting himself, in 1632.— See Upham's Rat. Dis. 143, 144, 237, 238; also Isaac Chauncy's remarks under article SUSPENSION.

[1] Chap. xiv. sect. ix. [2] Guide, 112—115. [3] Magnalia, ii. 221. [4] Vol. i. 81.

LOT, *when we may lawfully decide by it.* — Foxcroft, in his Discourse preparatory to the choice of a minister,[1] recommends the lot where two or more candidates divide a people relative to the choice of a pastor, "that the Lord may show which he has chosen." Cotton, in his Letter to Leavitt,[2] says: "Carding and choosing valentines are an appeal to the lot, in which God is the Disposer." And to appeal to him and his immediate providence for the dispensing these *ludicra* seemeth to me a taking of his name in vain.

[1] Pages 24—47. [2] In Hist. Soc. Col. ser. ii. vol. x. 183.

MAGISTRATES, *may they make laws establishing religion?* — Burton, in his Answer to Prynne's Twelve New Interrogatories,[1] says: "Those patriarchs and princes of Israel, before the law and under the law, from Adam to Christ, never had this power or prerogative to make ecclesiastical laws or binding canons." He further presses the point,[2] that neither synods nor parliaments have this power. Magistrates are to punish for overt acts, not for opinions. Baillie, in his Dissuasive,[3] vehemently accuses the Independents of esteeming all matters of religion free and exempt from the magistrate's sword and power. Edwards, in his Gangrænæ,[4] represents the Independents of the army as unwilling that the Parliament should set up even Independent government: they held liberty of conscience; that in matters of religion no man should be bound, but every one left to follow his own conscience. Cambridge Platform[5] encroaches on this broad ground: though it maintains the general principle, yet it makes a fatal exception, by allowing magistrates to punish, where the matter is perfectly clear, for heresy and venting corrupt opinions that destroy the foundation. It does not here distinguish between disturbing the peace and venting what the judges say it is clear are pernicious opinions. Bastwick, in his Treatise on Church Government,[6] accuses the Independents of holding that the magistrate might not inflict corporal punishment for matters of religion. It seems that the loss of his own ears had not brought him to his senses. Possibly, as his own party came into power, he remembered the maxim, "An eye for an eye, and a tooth for a tooth;" adding, — and an ear for an ear. Philip Nye, in his lawfulness of the Oath of Supremacy,[7] says, "ALL MEN ARE BY NATURE EQUAL;" yet he argues the supremacy of the king and his government in ecclesiastical affairs. Upham, in his Century Sermon,[8] informs us that Hugh Peters reproved Sir Harry Vane for his conduct towards Mrs. Hutchinson and her company, and "plainly insinuated, that, if governors would concern themselves only with the things of Cæsar, the things of God would be more quiet and prosperous." — See Upham, Rat. Dis. 293. See PERSECUTION; TOLERATION.

[1] In Han. ii. 408. [2] Ib. 414, 415. [3] Ib. iii. 150. [4] Ib. 187. [5] Chap. xvii. [6] In Han. iii. 93. [7] Page 17. [8] Page 46.

MAGISTRATES *should punish rioters.* — This was, and is, the universal doctrine of Congregationalists. The Fifteen Propositions to Parliament for Gathering Independent Churches[1] has the following: "That such persons who shall disturb the people of God, . . . when they are congregated to worship him in his ordinances, may be punished according to their demerits."

[1] In Han. iii. 248.

MAGISTRATES, *should they have a voice, as such,*

in the doings of the churches?— Cambridge Platform,[1] after denying their power to restrain churches, maintains that their help and countenance, when it may be had, should not be slighted. As they were usually consulted about the formation of new churches, no wonder that they took it in dudgeon when a church was gathered without their consent, as the Massachusetts records abundantly evince. All this may, however, be accounted for by their loyal attachment to monarchical and magisterial government. No American advocates the affirmative of this question since the consummation of the Revolution.

[1] Page 61.

MAJORITIES *have a right to govern in the church.*— Isaac Chauncy[1] says: "Whatever passes in the church by a majority of the brethren is a church act." Letchford, in his Plain Dealing,[2] says: "In the Bay, the churches govern each by all the members unanimously, or else by the major part, wherein every one hath equal vote and superspection with their ministers." In Portsmouth, in the early part of the last century, the majority of the church removed to a new place of worship at the north part of the town, while the rest remained, and organized themselves into a distinct church. The majority retained the name of the First Church.[3] See UNANIMITY.

[1] Divine Inst. Cong. Churches, 105. [2] In Mass Hist. Soc. Col. series iii. vol. iii. Epist. to the Reader. [3] Eliot, Biog. Dict. 410, art. Rogers, Nathaniel.

MAJORITIES, *where they ought to forbear exercising their natural right.* — Watts, in his Foundation of a Christian Church,[1] shows that the greater number must always rule, but that they are, in certain cases, under moral obligation not to insist on their right; as, for instance, in receiving a new member to the church when a portion seem conscientiously dissatisfied. Hopkins[2] shows that majorities must govern, and minorities ought to rest satisfied, save in cases of conscience, where they should protest. See Upham's Ratio Disciplinæ, 145, note. It is understood to have been recently decided by a council, in a case in Salem, Mass., that a majority have no right to disband a church and divide the property. On the one hand, the sovereignty of the majority was pleaded; and, on the other, that the majority have no right to repudiate their own covenant engagements. — See CHURCH, *majority constitute;* UNANIMITY.

[1] Works, iii. 240. [2] System, ii. 350—352.

MARRIAGE *not the office-work of pastors.* — Robinson, in his Apology,[1] says: "We cannot assent to the received opinion, and practice answerable, in the reformed churches, by which the pastors thereof do celebrate marriage publicly and by virtue of their office." The pastor's office, he argues, is peculiar to the Christian religion, and ought not to be stretched to any thing else but what is peculiar to Christians; which marriage is not, being common to them and the Gentiles. In his Answer to Hall,[2] he objects that making it a part of a minister's work is making it a sacrament. Jacob's Church Confession, art. xxiii.,[3] says: "Concerning marriage and burying the dead, we believe that they are not actions of a church minister, because they are no actions spiritual, but civil. Neither are ministers called to any such business, nor is there so much as one example of it in the whole book of God, . . . without which warrant we believe it to be unlawful." And this, we find,[4] was the practice in New England in 1633, though they could not make a law to hinder ministers from marrying, because that would be against the common law of England. Letchford[5] says: "Marriage in New England is by magistrates, and not by ministers." So Punchard, in his View, 191. The Plymouth Colony laws[6] enacted in 1671, that none should be joined in marriage but by magistrates, or such persons as the court should appoint where no magistrate is near.

[1] In Punchard's Hist. 349, 350; and Works, iii. 45. [2] In Han. i. 196; and Works, iii. 412. [3] Ib. 300. [4] Winthrop's Journal, i. 323. [5] In Hist. Soc. Col. series iii. vol. iii. 94. [6] Page 272.

MARRIAGE, *may it be solemnized by ministers?* — Johnson, in his Christian Plea,[1] maintains that the requiring of it by ministers, with prescribed liturgies, tended to confirm the Papists in their error of its being a sacrament; yet he suggests whether it *may* not be solemnized by ministers as well as others, so as it be not imposed upon them, nor observed with superstition. Cotton Mather[2] asserts that in New England, in his day, it was usually solemnized by pastors, though formerly it was always done by magistrates. Massachusetts Province Laws[3] made provision for its solemnization by ministers as early as 1692.

[1] In Han. i. 319, 320. [2] Rat. Dis. 111, 112. [3] Page 19 (Ed. 1699), *et al.*

MARRIAGE, *may it be solemnized on the Lord's day?* — Cotton Mather[1] declares that "the churches of New England wholly decline them" on that day. He quotes Zepperus, Voetius, and an army of others, to show that it is wrong to do it on the Sabbath.

[1] Rat. Dis. 112, 113.

MEETING-HOUSE. — Cotton Mather[1] declares that this was the term usually employed by New England Christians to designate a place of worship, but that they did not admit the idea of a holiness in places. Isaac Chauncy[2] asserts that "there is no just ground from Scripture to apply such a trope (as church) to a house for a public assembly." It must, however, be admitted that this trope was in early use among the churches,[3] though I deem it an improper use and productive of evil, in conveying a false impression of holiness in places. — See CONSECRATIONS; DEDICATIONS.

[1] Rat. Dis. 5. [2] Divine Inst. Cong. Churches, 2. [3] See Lord King's Enquiry, part i. 4, 5.

MEMBERS, *church, should consist of experimental Christians.* — Robinson, in his Apology,[1] says that it behoveth every one to believe and "know (?) that he is a true Christian," before he can hope to please God in the performance of this or that particular Christian work. Burton, in his Protestation Protested,[2] says: "A particular church, rightly collected and constituted, consists of such as are living members of Christ the head." Hooker, in his Survey,[3] answers Rutherford, who plead that nothing more was necessary to admission, except that they profess before men the faith, desire the seals, and crave fellowship with the visible church, saying: "The apostle commanded to turn away from such as, having the form of godliness, deny the power thereof." The Rejoinder to Prynne's Reply[4] says: "The matter of a church should be saints. The apostle wrote to the churches as saints." Isaac Chauncy[5] says the elders ought to inquire of the candidates the reason of their hope, whether it be grounded on the fundamentals of Christian doctrine; and whether their conversation answer to their profession. Increase Mather, in his Vindication of the Order of the New England Churches,[6] says: "A church ought to consist of true believers." Pierce, in his Vindication of Dissenters,[7] says: "Wickliffe defined a church to consist only of persons predestinated." With the above principles agree Cotton's Plea for the New England Churches, in Hutchinson's History of Massachusetts, i. 370, 371; Increase Mather's Disquisition on Ecclesiastical Councils, preface, vi.; Propositions to Parliament, in Han. iii. 247; Congregational Union of England and Wales, Principles of Discipline, ib. 600; Richard Mather's Church Government and

Church Covenant, 9; Cotton's Way of the Churches, 57; Punchard's History, 47, 109; Cambridge Platform, chap. xii. sect. 2; and Owen's Nature of a Gospel Church, in Works, xx. 357; with *multis aliis.* — See Upham's Rat. Dis. 51—54, and Punchard's View, 38, 44. See next article; also HALF-WAY COVENANT.

[1] In Han. i. 384; and Works, iii. 65. [2] Ib. ii. 73. [3] Part i. 32. [4] Page 3. [5] Div. Inst. Cong. Churches, 106, 107. [6] Page 13. [7] Pages 4—6.

MEMBERS *satisfy the church at admission.* — Richard Mather[1] says: Paul was not received till the church was satisfied of his conversion. And,[2] The church have a right to choose both their officers and brethren. (True, if they proceed according to the rule, and receive or reject as Christ does. The churches are the earthly judges to admit or reject him.) He quotes[3] Zepperus, De Politia Ecclesia, and R. Parker, Politia Ecclesiæ, showing that the reformed churches received their baptized children only when they professed piety, and were propounded in the assembly. Cotton, in his Holiness of Church Members, says:[4] The church . . . cannot lawfully receive members, . . . but such as are, in a charitable discretion, esteemed saints by calling. In his Keys[5] he says the brethren of the church have power and liberty of propounding any just exception against any such as offer themselves to be admitted into their communion; and he quotes the case of Saul, and the proposition of Peter, concerning Cornelius: "Can any forbid water?" The

Saint's Apology[6] says: The matter of this is a company of saints of whom . . . the church that admits them ought to judge of every one of them, that Christ has begun a good work in them, and will finish it." The Low Country Exiles, in their Confession, art. xxiv., say:[7] "Christ hath given power to receive in or cut off any member to the whole body together, in any Christian congregation;" by which they mean covenant-church. Dr. Stiles, in his Convention Sermon,[8] says: "There was never an instance of admission to the churches without the votes of the brethren," because of the spirit of liberty in the churches. The authors of Gospel Order Revived say:[9] A church has no more right to debar those who refuse to relate their Christian experience, than to require oaths and subscriptions and conformity to a thousand more ceremonies. But this was never the generally received doctrine. From Upham's Life of Sir Henry Vane the Younger[10] we learn that Winthrop maintained "that the churches had power to receive or reject at discretion;" but Vane thought it was "only at the discretion of Christ." Cambridge Platform, chap. xii. sect. 22; Hooker's Survey, part i. 47, 54, 93; Owen's Original of Churches, in Works, xx. 185; and Watts's Foundation of a Christian Church, in Works, iii. 200, advocate the necessity of their satisfying the members of personal piety.

[1] Apology, 18. [2] Ib. 23. [3] Ib. 34, 35. [4] Page 24. [5] Page 38. [6] In Han. ii. 231. [7] Ib. i. 95. [8] Page 64. [9] Page 8. [10] In Sparks's Am. Biog. iv. 152, 153.

MEMBERS, *examination of, for admission.*— Welde, in his Answer to Rathband,[1] shows how these were conducted,— by the elders in private with the more bashful, and by a public relation with those that were able. And though some few be dissatisfied, they used to submit to the rest, and sit down satisfied, unless their reasons be such as may convince the church. (See MAJORITIES; MINORITIES.) Hooker in his Survey,[2] describes the method of applying to the elders, who propound them, if, on inquiry, they consider them fit. The church should then repair, and inquire of them, in separate companies, and see if they live in no known sin, and can give a reason of the hope that is in them. They may converse with the women privately, though women may speak publicly to give a reason of their hope, and confess their sins. Increase Mather, in his Vindication,[3] shows that they ought to be tried; but their examination should be so tender that the weakest Christian may be admitted. Eliot (in his Ecclesiastical History of New England, in Historical Society's Col lection, series i. vol. ix. 3), and Neal (History ot New England, i. 273—275), treat this subject es sentially in the same way.

[1] In Han. ii. 302. [2] Part iii. 4—6. [3] Page 17, 19.

MEMBERS, *church; mode of receiving.*— Cotton Mather[1] describes this to be "by vote of the church, and assenting to the covenant." Ames, in his Marrow of Sacred Divinity,[2] says: "None are rightly admitted to the church but by confession of faith and promise of obedience." Letchford, in his Plain Dealing,[3] shows the manner to have been much as at the present day, save that the men usually declare the mode of their conversion in public, and the women have the relations of their experience read, as taken by the elders at their examinations. He asserts[4] that the members were voted into the church at the time that they were admitted. Morton, in his New England Memorial,[5] says: "Some were admitted by expressing their consent to the written Confession of Faith and Covenant; others did answer questions about the principles of religion, that were publicly propounded to them; some did present their confession in writing, which was read for them; and some, that were able and willing, did make their confession in their own words and way." See Upham's Rat. Dis. 98. — See CONFESSIONS; COVENANT; CREEDS.

[1] Rat. Dis. 91. [2] Page 141. [3] In Hist. Soc. Col. series iii. vol. iii. 67, 68. [4] Ib. 71. [5] Page 146.

MEMBERS, *scandalous, not received by recommendation from other churches.* — Richard Mather[1] says those emigrants who are known to be godly are all admitted to some church on their own desire, unless they have given offence by their walk: in this case, they must give evidence of repentance. Hooker[2] shows, that, if two or three witnesses show a recommended member to be scandalous, he is to be rejected.

[1] Ch. Gov. and Ch. Cov. 8. [2] Survey, part i. 241.

MEMBERS, *removing; should they be examined, confess, and covenant anew?* — Richard Mather[1] affirms that they should; "for the former church may have erred in receiving them." Hooker[2] says they may be received without, if their praise is in all the churches; or the church may examine, and, if they are scandalous, should reject them. Winthrop[3] shows that Cotton was thus examined when he was received to the church in Boston. Mitchell[4] declares the right to examine, but says that it is not generally practised. Milton[5] says the covenant should be repeated, unless the church have ample testimonials from some other orthodox church. — See PROFESSION *of faith.*

[1] Ch. Gov. and Ch. Cov. 30. [2] Survey, part iii. 7. [3] Journal, i. 110. [4] Guide, 224, 225. [5] Chris. Doc. ii. 202, 203.

MEMBERS *remove with consent.*—Welde[1] shows Rathband that they should first consult the church with whom they are in covenant, but the church *never* holds one a member against his will. He shows that, in extraordinary cases, there should be a council; but the church cannot act against their own consciences, and say they are satisfied when they are not. Cambridge Platform[2] says: "They who are joined with consent may not depart without consent, unless forced thereto. If a member's departure be manifestly unsafe and sinful, the church may not consent thereto; for, in so doing, they should partake of his sin. If the case be doubtful, . . . it seemeth best to leave the matter to God, and not forcibly to detain him." Isaac Chauncy[3] says:

"A member may not depart to non-communion, or to the communion of another church, without the leave of the church of which he is a member. Such a deserter is a *felo de se*, and doth disfranchise and excommunicate himself." See Upham's Rat. Dis. 147; Punchard's View, 173. — See AFFINITY; DISMISSION; WITHDRAWING.

[1] In Han. ii. 324. [2] Chap. xiii. sect. 2, 3. [3] Divine Inst. Cong. Churches, 116, 117.

MEMBERS, *may they ever be received from other churches without dismission and recommendation?* — Increase Mather, in his Vindication,[1] shows that dismission and recommendation are scriptural and reasonable, and that "a church ought not to receive a member from another church, without endeavors of mutual satisfaction of the churches concerned." I. Chauncy[2] says: If, upon the use of all due means, the church will grant no dismission, the member refused may join another church as a non member. Cotton Mather, in his Ratio Disciplinæ,[3] lays down a rule for a case which he says "perhaps never happened," in which a church refuse to receive a member where a council advise to it, viz. that he be received to some other church in the neighborhood. Cleveland, in his Narrative of the Conduct of the Fourth Church in Ipswich,[4] quotes from Watts's Foundation of a Christian Church: "If particular persons cannot agree with the major part, they may withdraw, if the church refuse to dismiss them; for Christian churches must have all voluntary members, and are not to be turned into prisons."

Cleveland adds: "A member has a right to seek his edification where he can best obtain it." This is particularly allowable to members in corrupt churches. Cambridge Platform[5] points out the way for such to proceed, viz. by calling a council of neighbor-churches, and, with their advice, offering themselves to the fellowship of another church. Owen, in his Answer to Stillingfleet, sect. 3,[6] points out the proper course of such members as are in a church with defective rules, viz. to try peaceably to introduce a right state of things; consider whether they are required to do any thing unlawful; if so, and no forbearance is allowed, they must not condemn them (if they are Christians), but peaceably withdraw. This was the principle on which the true Congregationalists separated from the Episcopal church, because it required them to do what they deemed wrong. — See AFFINITY; DISMISSION; CEREMONIES; LITURGIES; HABITS; SEPARATION; SCHISM; NONCONFORMITY; WITHDRAWING; Mr. Davenport's case, in PASTOR *not lightly removed.*

[1] Pages 109—113. [2] Page 121. [3] Page 161. [3] Page 38. [5] Chap. xv. sect. 2. [6] In Works, xx. 321.

MEMBERS, *pious ones of heretical and scandalous churches to be received.* — Cambridge Platform[1] directs that such should be received to wonted communion; "for it is not equal that the innocent should suffer with the offensive;" — a principle which would, if applied, help out of difficulty those who scruple the regularity of a church to which some credible saints belong.

[1] Chap. xv. sect. 2.

MEMBERS *continue such of the former church, till received by the church to which they are recommended.* — Cotton Mather[1] shows this, and it is the universal principle acknowledged by Congregationalists.

[1]Rat. Dis. 140.

MEMBERS *removing should transfer their membership to the churches where they remove.* — This is another universally approved principle. Cotton Mather shows its propriety, and[1] says: If they do not ask it, the church sometimes sends it.

[1] Rat. Dis. 140, 141.

See further, for Members, under CHURCHES, *censures, &c. in the people; Members have equal rights.*

MINISTERS, *what.* — Thomas Goodwin[1] defines them "under-rowers to the church," a literal translation of 1 Cor. iv. 1; and "servants of Christ," Rom. xv. 16; "dispensers of the gospel," Gal. iii. 5, 11; Rom. xv. 16.

[1] Catechism, 10, 11.

MINISTERS, *are they successors of Jewish priests?* Punchard[1] shows from history, that the doctrine that they were their successors, as it prevailed in the second century, was one great means of corrupting the churches, giving rise to the different grades, bishops, priests, and deacons (soon it was found more analogous to have one high priest). He quotes Mosheim, showing that this doctrine soon led to other errors, among which was this,— an official elevation and sacredness in the clergy, which Christ never authorized. Owen, in his Duty of Pastor and People,[2] chapters iii., iv., shows that appropriating the title *priest* to ministers is of Roman origin.— See Neander's Planting and Training of the Church, 84; and his Church History, i. sect. 2, page 150.

[1] Hist. 22. [2] Works, xix. 24—35.

MINISTERS *not successors of the apostles by ordination.*— See BISHOPS; ORDINATION *by direct succession unnecessary.*

MINISTERS, *of equal rank.*— This doctrine was received by the Paulicians in the seventh century, though it had been abandoned. In 1572, Mr. Charke of Peter House, Cambridge, said that "there ought to be a parity among ministers," &c.; for which he was expelled the University. The same year, Mr. Field and Mr. Wilcox were shut up in Newgate for *petitioning* parliament on this subject. The cry was, that levelling the bishops would lead to levelling all the nobility in the land.[1] The first claim to an inequality (*jure divino*) in England was set up by Dr. Bancroft, at St. Paul's Cross, January 12, 1588, and at once aroused all the conforming Puritans in opposition. Sir Francis Knollys took the lead, and "wrote to the learned Dr. Reynolds of Oxford for his opinion." Dr. R. at once cited a host of English Episcopal authors, maintaining their equality save by the queen's mere civil appointment. Among these he quotes Bishop Jewell, who cited Jerome, Ambrose, and Austin to their equality. He (Dr. R.) also directly and indirectly quotes a score or more of eminent reformers and English prelates to the point of their equality by divine appointment; and says: "All who have labored in reforming the church for five hundred years (and this was nearly three hundred years ago) have taught, that all pastors, be they entitled bishops or priests, have equal authority and power by God's word."[2] Dr. Chauncy, in his Dudlean Lecture,[3] shows that the apostles instituted but one order of ministers; gave no instructions concerning the fitness for different orders of it, and no different rules for those who were to ordain ministers of different grades. No ministers are found in the apostles' times but of one order; and "bishop" and "presbyter" are used interchangeably in the Greek in Acts xx. 17 and 28. The Reviewer of Sparks's Letters in Answer to Wyatt's Sermon[4] says the arguments adduced for three orders would prove the existence of six or seven, as apostles, prophets, evangelists, elders, &c., &c. — See French Confession, and Confession of Low Country Exiles, in Hanbury, i. 92. See Bishops

[1] Neal's Puritans, i. 121, 122. [2] Ib. 186, 187. [3] Pages 13—25. [4] Page 9.

MINISTER, *calling; in what does it consist?* — Owen[1] says that it arises from Christ's institution of the office; from God's providential designation of the person; and from the church's call, election, or appointment; and their acceptation. Richard Mather[2] says the outward calling of a minister consists in election by the people; which he sustains by quotations from Mornay and from Chrysostom. Yet he says the calling of many ministers (Episcopal) in England may be excused because they were accepted by the people. In his Apology[3] he shows that ministers have power over the churches only by virtue of their choosing them to rule over them. (See ELDERS *rule as moderators.*) Jacob's Church, in their Confession (art. x.),[4] say: "We believe that the essence of a minister's call under the gospel is the congregation's (i.e. church's) consent." They assert,[5] in their Plea for Toleration, that ministers' calling is by the consent of the several congregations. Holding that a minister must be made by a bishop or another minister, is to hold "that a minister is before and greater than a church; a great and harmful error, and contrary to 1 Cor. iii. 21—23." Increase Mather, in his Vindication of the Order of the New England Churches,[6] enumerates among those things ("which to espouse is to give up the whole of Congregationalism"), "that a minister's call consists not in election, but in the imposition of hands." With this doctrine agree Increase Mather (Disquisition on Ecclesiastical Councils, preface), who quotes many authors to sustain it; and Trumbull (History of Connecticut, i. 296), where he declares that "such was the opinion of the principal divines who settled New England and Connecticut." Cambridge Platform declares explicitly[7] that it consists, not in his ordination, but the church's election and his acceptance. — See CALLING; ELDERS; IMPOSITION *of hands;* ORDINATION; PASTOR.

Works, xix. 70. [2] Ch. Gov. and Ch. Cov. 67. [3] Page 24. [4] In Han. i. 296. [5] Ib. 307, 308. [6] Page 8. [7] Chap. ix. sect. 2.

MINISTERS, *authority of, what.* — Goodwin[1] shows that they have the "*rule over*" the church in these three things: "To declare to them the mysteries of the kingdom of God; so that, whether they exhort, teach, or admonish, they do it with authority; to call the church assemblies together, and to dismiss them, and *moderate* matters in the assembly;" and "they are the mouth and hands of the church, by which they execute the power of the censures." This is the doctrine which has been hitherto maintained by Congregationalists; yet they have a remedy in the case of mal-administration of ministers, — all power coming back into their own hands at their own election. Ainsworth, in his reply to Clyfton,[2] says: "To give votes in deciding of controversies, and judging of sinners, is not a part of government, but of power and right that saints out of office have." Watts, in his Foundation of a Christian Church,[3] says the rule of ministers is to lead in worship, not to impose odd inventions. Paul had no dominion over men's faith. The judge has no power to make law: he explains, and the jury decide. Ministers have no power to command any thing but what is found in the Bible. — See ELDERS *rule as moderators;* GOVERNMENT, *church, in the people;* POWER, *church, installed in the ministry or the brethren?*

[1] Catechism, 12. [2] In Han. i. 249. [3] Works, iii. 218, 219, 226.

MINISTERS, *people may do their work for them if they neglect it.* — John Robinson, in his Justification of Separation, says:[1] "Yea, even where officers are, if they fail in their duties, the people may enterprise matters needful, however you make the minister the *primum movens*, and would tie all to his fingers." Jacob's Church,[2] in their Confession (art. xiv.), say: "Officers have nothing more than what the congregation doth commit unto them, and which they may, when need requireth, take from them, yea, to their utter deposing and also rejection out of the church, if such necessity be." Welde, in his Reply to Rathband,[3] however, maintains that they must first depose him before they can take his office-work from him; "but in no case, while he abides in office, to resume their power, and enter upon his work." — See ELDERS, *is one or more necessary to church acts?* OFFICERS *abdicate when they refuse to do the duties pertaining to their office;* JURISDICTION; GOVERNMENT, *civil;* RESISTANCE.

[1] In Han. i. 212; and Works, ii. 148. [2] Ib. 297. [3] Ib. ii. 317.

MINISTERS *should submit to the censure of the church.* — Goodwin[1] shows this from the example of Peter. — See PASTOR, *is he censurable by his church?* ELDERS, *is one or more necessary to church action?*

[1] Catechism, 11.

MINISTER, *how dismissed from his pastoral charge.* — Punchard, in his View,[1] gives the details of a proper procedure, save that he makes it regular for a people who want to dismiss their pastor to send a delegation to suggest the expediency of his asking a dismission; thus putting a false coloring on the whole matter, representing that the first movement originates with him rather than with them. See Upham's Rat. Dis. 124—133; and Bacon's Church Manual, 139, 140. — See next article.

[1] Pages 175--177.

MINISTERS, *how deposed.* — The Answer of the New England Elders[1] asserts that the church, in the name of Christ, gave their minister power to be what he is; and they may on as good grounds depose him from it, as they called him to it. Robinson, in his Reply to Barnard,[2] says: "If the ministers will deal corruptly, . . . the brethren are to censure, depose, reject, and avoid them." In the Appendix to Mr. Perkins,[3] he says: "If an officer be found unfaithful, he is by the church to be warned to take heed to his ministry, . . . which if he neglect to do, by the same power (the church's) which set him up, he is to be put down and deposed." Wise[4] quotes Cyprian: "When bishops prove wicked or heretical, the churches have power to degrade and depose them, and to choose others in their room." Cambridge Platform[5] says: "In case an elder offend incorrigibly, . . . as the church had power to call him to his office, so they have power, according to order (the council of other churches, where it may be had, directing thereto), to remove him from his office." Hooker[6] shows, that, in case the officer is heretical and obstinately wicked, the church have power to reject him, and make him no officer; for a church is before its officers. He shows[7] that they who have power to "depose" their officers have the power of judgment over them. Hutchinson, in his History of Massachusetts,[8] lays it down as the received opinion of the fathers of New England, that it is in the power of churches to call their officers, and remove them from office, — the advice of neighbor-churches, where it may conveniently be done, being first had. Samuel Mather devotes the fourth chapter of his Apology to prove this right in the churches. He quotes from Clement, Origen, and Cyprian, to the point; and maintains the right from the power of self-preservation and the principles of the Platform. The Massachusetts Convention of 1773, in their Observations on the Plan of Church Government,[9] assert that the churches have power to depose, but are morally culpable if they do it without or contrary to a council.* The power resides in *them only*, and not in any synod or ecclesiastical council. In exercising it without counsel, they act contrary to order. Baynes, in his Diocesan's Trial,[10] says: "If their own churches have no power over them, it will be hard to show wherein others have such

* This was about the time of the controversy concerning veto-power; and, if we cannot see how they are "morally culpable" for using their rightful power, we may reflect that "that which is crooked cannot be made straight."

power and jurisdiction over persons who belong not to their own churches." — See Bacon's Church Manual, 140, 141.

[1] Page 77. [2] In Punchard's Hist. 330; and Works, ii. 174. [3] Ib. 353; and Works, iii. 431. [4] Vindication, 13, 14. [5] Chap. x. sect. 6. [6] Survey, part i. 93. [7] Page 196. [8] Vol. i. 381. [9] Pages 6, 7. [10] Page 88.

MINISTERS, *their character not indelible.* — This was the doctrine of the Brownists.[1] The early Congregationalists also held the same. The New England Elders[2] say: "We have no such indelible character imprinted on a minister, that he must needs be so for ever, because he once was so. His ministry ceasing, the minister ceaseth also." Allin and Shepard, in their Defence of the Nine Positions,[3] inquire, "What authority has he to minister to any church, if they will not hear him?" A dismissed minister, they maintain, is no longer an officer in any church of God; and the reason is, a minister's office in the church is no indelible character. Cambridge Platform[4] says: "He that is clearly loosed from his office-relation to that church whereof he was a minister, cannot be looked at as an officer, nor perform any act of office in any other church, unless he be again called to office." Cotton Mather[5] quotes John Owen: "We have no concernment in the figment of an indelible character, . . . yet we do not leave the minister when we go from home." He distinguished between an officer of a church, and one providentially called to preach the word. John Robinson, in the Appendix to Mr. Perkins,[6] says: Those that are out of office, we are told, are to feed the flock in the exercise of prophecy, which, it is said, is proved by examples in the Jewish church, Luke ii. 42, 46, 47; iv. 16, 18; Acts viii. 4; xi. 19—21; xiii. 14—16; xviii. 24—26; and by the command of Christ and his apostles, Luke ix. 1; x. 1; Rom. xii. 9; 1 Peter iv. 10, 11; 1 Cor. xiv. 1, &c.—See next article; also PREACH, *who may?* PROPHESYING; OFFICERS, *their office, qualifications, and jurisdiction.*

[1] Neal, i. 150. [2] Ans. 77. [3] In Han. iii. 42. [4] Chap. ix. sect. 7. [5] Magnalia, ii. 205. [6] In Punchard's Hist. 253; and Works, iii. 432, 433.

MINISTERS, *may they administer seals where they are not pastors?*—The early Congregationalists generally maintained the negative. The New England Elders[1] declare that a minister may not perform a ministerial act in any other church. Goodwin devoted the seventh chapter of his seventh book to show that they could not lawfully be administered anywhere but in a particular church, by their own ministers, and that they might not have them administered to different branches successively. Paget (a Puritan Conformist) inquires:[2] "If members may lawfully receive the Lord's Supper in another church, . . . why may not pastors administer it also in another, when need so requireth?" Ainsworth replies:[3] "A Christian joineth himself to a flock where the pastor feedeth them," when he comes among them. Show you a like warrant for elderships to do the work in other elderships and churches. Hooker, in his Survey, says[4] a pastor only of one flock can do no pastoral acts (referring to seals, &c.) in another: "Those whom a pastor cannot judge over, over them he can exercise no pastoral act." Nathaniel Mather published a Disquisition on purpose to prove the negative of this question. In his Epistle to the Reader, he says a minister is to feed *the* flock over which the Holy Ghost has made him *overseer;* otherwise we shall justify the conduct of those who call lay brethren to administer it. "If he does it as pastor, then he does it as pastor of his own church, and then one church may make a pastor for another." He maintains[5] that a pastor may not administer seals to another church, though the church asks it and he consents. This principle, he claims, leads churches to furnish themselves with pastors, which if they are too poor to do, their sister-churches should give them pecuniary help, not officers. He claims the majority of Congregationalists with him. His illustrious relatives, it seems, espoused the other side of the question. The same is true of the modern Congregationalists generally. They hold that administering the seals is not an act of ministerial power; having gone over to the democratic doctrine so dreaded by the fathers. Cotton Mather says[6] the Platform denies not the power of a minister to administer communion in another church besides his own. Mr. Phillips of Watertown did administer it to Mr. Wilson's of Boston when he was gone to England. Ancestus thus requested Polycarpus to administer it. Cambridge Association[7] early decided that they might so administer it, by the request of the church. In his Ratio Disciplinæ,[8] he says of this question: "It has been very publicly and practically answered that they may." He claims Dr. Goodwin, Dr. Owen, and the first fathers of New England, as with him. The opinion of Samuel Mather may be clearly inferred from his principle, that a church may lawfully appoint a lay brother to administer them. It is on this principle alone, the consent of the church, that dismissed ministers and evangelists now administer seals. We may see, then, that the administration of the Lord's Supper by ecclesiastical and voluntary assemblies is out of order. It should be wholly under the direction of the church where they assemble. Increase Mather maintains this side of the question in his Vindication,[9] argues that they may administer on invitation, and quotes Cambridge Platform, chap. xv. sect. 4; Norton's Answer to Appolinius; Shepard and Allin's Answer to Ball; Richard Mather, Cotton, and Goodwin. Cotton,[10] however, did not baptize his child at sea, because he believed that a minister could not lawfully administer seals out of his own congregation; and also that they should be administered in an organized church. See Upham's Rat. Dis. 217, 236. — See LORD'S SUPPER, *may it be administered by any but ordained ministers?* OFFICERS; SEALS; PLATFORM, *Cambridge.*

[1] Ans. 78. [2] In Han. i. 331, 332. [3] Ib. 344, 345. [4] Part ii. 61, 63. [5] Pages 50, 70, 75. [6] Magnalia, ii. 204. [7] Ib. 205. [8] Pages 134—136. [9] Pages 112—117. [10] Winthrop's Journal, i. 110.

MINISTERS *should give themselves wholly to their work.* — Thomas Goodwin shows at length[1] that God thought fit to make it the sole business of men, enabled with the greatest gifts that were ever poured out upon men, to attend and look to the bringing up of his children, and to give themselves continually to the word and prayer. Every private member is to advance his brother; but it is the minister's work to do it. So Bradshaw, in his English Puritanism.[2] Hooker, in his Survey,[3] shows that he must take up no employment but what fits him for his main work, and not entangle himself, Acts vi. 2—4. Cotton Mather,[4] in his Sermon to a Part of the Persons engaged in a Just War against the Northern and Eastern Savages, apologizes for his lack of preparation, and says: "Nothing is more fulsome and nauseous than for a preacher to value himself on such a crime as his not spending much time in study." — See next two articles.

[1] Ch. Gov. 265—272. [2] In Neal, i. 249. [3] Part ii. 27. [4] Epistle Dedicatory.

MINISTERS *should not be magistrates.* — Hooker, in his Survey,[1] says: "The minister should give the whole man to the work; hence it is unlawful for him to be a magistrate, for he has not the ability to discharge the duties of both offices." Jacob's Church Confession (art. xxiv.)[2] says: "We believe that joining of pastoral ministry and magistracy together in one person is simply unlawful, and contrary to the text of the New Testament." To the same effect they profess in art. xxvii. Lord Brooke, in his Discourse on Episcopacy[3] comes out largely on the evils of this practice, in the case of the lords bishops of England. Bradshaw, in his English Puritanism,[4] says: "No pastor ought to exercise or accept of any civil jurisdiction, . . . but ought to be wholly employed in spiritual offices and duties." Cartwright, in his Reply to Whitgift,[5] says that a minister may not have a civil office. He may not so much as be diverted to bury his father, nor rule to divide an inheritance. So, too, argue the overseers, &c. of the English Church at Amsterdam.[6] Increase Nowel resigned his ruling eldership in Charlestown, because it was decided that it was inconsistent with his holding the magistracy.[7]

[1] Part ii. 26. [2] In Han. i. 301, 302. [3] Ib. 118, 119. [4] In Neal's Puritans, i. 249. [5] Page 206. [6] Apology, 37—61. [7] Eliot, Biog. Dict. 343.

MINISTERS, *maintenance of.* — Goodwin devotes the fourth chapter of his seventh book on Church Government to this subject. He defends their right to it on the principles of common justice; pleads that it should be ample because of the necessary expenses; because it is the labor of the mind, which spends the best spirits, and preys upon the vitals; their education is long and expensive; and it brings the greatest of all blessings. He shows that it should be a fixed stipend, mutually agreed upon, and that the people have no right to dictate alone what to give (yet he argues for raising it by voluntary contribution); and he shows abundantly, that it is not a matter of courtesy, but a minister's right. The Confession of Jacob's Church, art. xxvi.,[1] maintains that voluntary tithing is not unlawful, but that it is better that it should be by voluntary contribution, by every one as God has prospered him. Rathband[2] asserted, that, in New England, ministers were in the habit of requiring a stipulated salary, else they would not preach. Welde denies the charge, and says our ministers' maintenance must be honorable; not as alms and coveting, but as debt and duty. But for settled and stinted maintenance there is nothing done that way, except from year to year. The Massachusetts colony laws in 1651 enacted that every inhabitant shall contribute to all charges in church and commonwealth, and provides that they may be compelled thereto by assessment and distress, and strengthened the same in 1654 and 1660. The Massachusetts Province laws in 1692, and the Plymouth Colony laws in 1657, provide for the support of ministers by law. Hooker, in his Survey,[3] after asserting that he must give himself wholly to his work, adds: "They should provide for him and his family, not as a matter of liberty or courtesy, but of justice. He asserts[4] that it cannot be raised out of a contribution to it and the poor; because one is a matter of mercy, the other of justice. If a member fail to support, it is a breach of a known rule of duty. The church determine how it is to be raised, and the deacons see to the execution of it. Isaac Chauncy, in his Divine Institution of Congregational Churches,[5] shows that Christ sent not his ministers without scrip, as common beggars, but there was moral justice that they should be remembered by the people. The Apology of the Overseers, &c. of the English Church at Amsterdam[6] argues, that they should be maintained by voluntary contributions. Eaton and Taylor[7] argue that such a contribution should be taken every Lord's day. Increase Mather, in his treatise concerning the Maintenance due to those who Preach the Gospel, comes to these conclusions: An honorable maintenance is due them; the reformed churches have many of them been faulty in this matter; there is something due to God out of every man's estate, and the tenth of his income is the least that may be supposed; tithes are not, by the divine law, due to ministers of the gospel, but the surplus should be applied to other benevolent objects. Mitchell, in his Guide, 178—210; Upham, Rat. Dis. 109; and Punchard, View, 188—190, treat of this subject in its modern bearings and usages.

[1] In Han. i. 301. [2] Ib. ii. 333. [3] Part ii. 27. [4] Ib. 30, 31. [5] Page 138. [6] Pages 37—61. [7] Defence, 60.

MINISTERS, *refusing to support, disciplinable.* — Mitchell[1] shows this on the ground that it is *covetousness, injustice, and disobedience to Christ*, and betrays such indifference to the gospel as is not far from *denying the faith.* — See preceding article.

[1] Guide, 100.

MINISTERS *set apart to the work, and to preach to those without.* — Goodwin[1] shows this, though they have no power to judge those that are without.

The Brownists held a minister's whole duty to be to take care of the church.

[1] Ch. Gov. 310—313.

For the whole subject of ministers, see also ELDER, ELECTION, INSTALLATION, OFFICER, ORDINATION, PASTOR, PREACH, TEACHER.

MINISTRY, *a learned and able, to be provided for.* — This was one of the first cares of the New England Planters. Accordingly, four hundred pounds were voted by the General Court in 1630 to begin the enterprise of establishing Harvard College. This, considering the deep poverty of these Puritans, must have cost a great sacrifice. But, as Cotton Mather says, "Without such provision for a sufficient ministry, the churches of New England must have been less than a business of one age." Our fathers came here for Christ and the church, and owe their prosperity under God to sowing bountifully to enable their ministers to be workmen that need not to be ashamed.— See this matter wisely stated in Mather's Magnalia, ii. 67.

MINORITIES, *their rights.* — Trumbull[1] informs us that the General Court of Connecticut called a Council at Hartford in 1657; but the minority would not accept the result, because the council was forced upon them by legislative authority. Watts, in his Foundation of a Christian Church,[2] shows that the majority are to choose the minister, and a minority should sit down satisfied unless it be against their consciences; in which case they should withdraw. — See MAJORITIES.

[1] Hist. Conn. i. 315. [2] Works, iii. 216.

MISSIONARY WORK. — In Mourt's Relation[1] is this reflection, "Seeing we daily pray for the conversion of the heathen, we must consider whether there be not some ordinary means and course for us to take to convert them; or whether prayer for them be only referred to God's extraordinary work from heaven." He presses this consideration, as a reason for removing to New England. Dr. Ware, in his History of the Old North and New Brick Churches, Boston, asserts[2] that one of them in 1726 contributed £60 for the propagation of the gospel. Robinson and Owen, and their coadjutors, just as distinctly recognize the obligation of aggressive missionary movements as do Worcester and Evarts, and the Missionary Boards of the present day.

[1] In Hist. Soc. Col. series ii. vol. ix. 67. [2] Page 50.

NEGATIVE VOTE. — See CHURCHES *begun without officers;* PASTOR, *has he a negative vote?*

NEW ENGLAND, *tribute to first settlers of.* — The authors of the Apologetical Narrative in the Westminster Assembly, speaking of their own helps to understand the true system of church government, say:[1] "Last of all, we have had the example of the ways and practices (and those improved to a better edition and greater refinement by all the forementioned helps) of those multitudes of godly men of our own nation, to the number almost of another nation; and among them some as *holy* and *judicious* as this kingdom hath had, whose sincerity in this way hath been testified by the greatest undertaking, but that of our father Abraham out of his own country, and his seed after him; a transplanting themselves many thousand miles into the wilderness, merely to worship God with more purity;" — no mean praise to come from the greatest lights of the seventeenth century.

[1] In Han. ii. 223.

NON-COMMUNION, *grounds for.* — Goodwin shows[1] that this should be only for such sins as render the individuals of the church rejected, worthy of excommunication.

[1] Ch. Gov. 238.

NONCONFORMISTS, *Independents among them were for universal toleration.* — Neal[1] shows that this was their wish in 1662, after the Restoration; while the Presbyterians objected to including the Papists, and thereby defeated the whole object. — See TOLERATION.

[1] Puritans, ii. 247.

NONCONFORMITY, *reasons for.* — A good account of these is given in Neal's History of the Puritans, vol. i. chap. 4. He gives[1] an abstract of them, handed in by the ministers who first refused subscription, entitled, Reasons grounded upon the

Scriptures, whereby we are Persuaded not to Admit the Outward Apparel and Ministering Garments of the Pope's Church; as, 1. "Our Saviour says: Take heed that ye contemn not one of these little ones." They show that conforming here may lead these to idolatry, and thus wound their weak consciences. 2. "We may not do any thing that is repugnant to Christian liberty, nor maintain an opinion of holiness where none is, nor consent to idolatry, nor deny the truth." They show many other evil things which they should do by conforming to the habits. 3. They vindicate their course by the testimony of the fathers. The Letter of some Aged Non-conforming Ministers touching the Reasons of their Practice,[2] gives, in substance, the following: They do not like the Prayer-book; Christ gave no authority to impose such a book on us; much of it is taken from the Mass-book; it is faulty in form; requires things not true nor good, as holy days, baptismal regeneration, the funeral service, sending all the baptized to heaven, &c.; it decrees human traditions, the cross in baptism, kneeling at the sacrament, &c. In short, they adduce almost all the arguments of dissenters in a condensed form. — See HABITS, CEREMONIES.

[1] Ib. 99. [2] Pages 7—23.

NONCONFORMITY, *obstacles to.* — Prince[1] informs us that not more than one in forty of the Catholics refused to conform in Elizabeth's reign, so that the Puritans had to contend not only against the ceremonies, but also against disguised

Papists. The preface to the History of Nonconformity (attributed to Neal), after stating other persecutions of non-conforming ministers, says: "Are they willing to lay down and live peaceably among their neighbors? They shall not so much as have liberty to do that within five miles of any corporation, unless they will *swear never to endeavor* any alteration in church government." — See PERSECUTION; TOLERATION.

[1] Chronology, 228.

OATH, *mode of taking*. — Increase Mather, in his Discourse on Common Prayer, Worship, and Kissing the Book in Swearing,[1] maintains that it is unscriptural to kiss the book, the Scripture form being with uplifted hand; that it is symbolizing with Popish idolatries. The Papists say: So help me God and these holy evangelists. Pareus says: It is Popish superstition in swearing to touch the Gospels with the finger. Burroughs, Voetius, and Thomas Goodwin are cited, condemning the practice as idolatrous. Rev. S. Willard, on the Ceremony of Laying the Hand on the Bible in Swearing, says:[2] "Whatever is sworn by is not a medium, but an object, of worship." It is in the oath of supremacy "an invocation to God, and swearing by the contents of the book."[3] In ib., Epistle to the Reader by M. I. (probably Increase Mather), Goodwin, Nye, and Burroughs are quoted as opposed to this rite. Kissing in a religious way is a gesture of adoration.

[1] Pages 39—43. [2] Page 5. [3] Ib. 6.

For the general subject of Oaths, see Savoy Confession, art. xxiii. It may be found in Upham's Rat. Dis. 271, and also bound with the Cambridge Platform, edition of 1808; the Confession being published in 1812, also in various other works.

OFFENCES. — Hooker[1] says that private ones should be covered as far as possible, and healed. — See DISCIPLINE.

[1] Survey, part iii. 34.

OFFERINGS. — See GIFTS; COLLECTIONS.

OFFICE *does not reside in electors.* — Owen, in his Nature of a Gospel Church, chap. iv.[1] shows that election only gives the power of office as Christ directs, but does not transmit power from the electors to the elected.

[1] In Works, xx. 424.

OFFICER, *may a church call one of another church occasionally to preside over them?* — Goodwin[1] seems tacitly to admit that they may, though he shows that it is by virtue of the special call of the church, and not of his office in the other church. — See MINISTERS, *may they administer seals, &c.?*

[1] Ch. Gov. 232.

OFFICERS, *church; what they are.* — Burton, in his Rejoinder to Prynne's Full Reply,[1] makes them to be pastors, teachers, ruling elders, and deacons. So, too, the Leyden Church,[2] Lord Brooke,[3] the Independents in the Westminster Assembly,[4] the Proposers to Parliament for gathering Independent Churches,[5] the principal divines among the first settlers of New England.[6] Widows were added to these by Thomas Goodwin,[7] and afterward by other Congregational writers. (See these several officers under their own appropriate heads.) The Congregational Union of England and Wales [8] believe that they are only bishops and deacons, and with this agree the present general belief and practice. President Stiles [9] says: "Several churches, in compliance with the sentiments of their pastors, had ruling and teaching elders at first; yet they at length disused the ruling elder; and the teaching elder, as distinct from pastor, is now dropped." Dr. Dwight [10] says: "Whatever church officers the Scriptures have established, as standing officers, are appointed by God himself: . . . all others are of human institution."

1 Page 4. 2 In Punchard's Hist. 362. 3 Discourse on Episcopacy, in Han. ii. 127. 4 Ib. 224. 5 Ib. iii. 248. 6 Trumbull's Hist. Conn. i. 295. 7 Catechism, 28. 8 In Han. iii. 600. 9 Conv. Serm. 64. 10 Works, Serm. cl.

OFFICERS, *church; their office and qualifications.* Nathaniel Mather, in his Disquisition,[1] says, to be an officer in a church is to be Christ's substitute. It is not an indelible office-power, imparted to a man, go where he will; but is a spiritual relation, to which the institution of Christ gives being; and does not extend to those over which the Holy Ghost has not made him overseer. He shows [2] that churches may be without officers, but officers cannot be without churches. The Vindication of the Preacher Sent[3] maintains that some gifted unordained men are gospel preachers; and that officers sustain not a relation as officers to the universal church. The New England elders, in their Answer to the Nine Positions,[4] say: "The office is founded in the relation between the church and the officer; wherefore take away the relation, and the office ceaseth." Bradshaw, in his English Puritanism,[5] asserts "that ecclesiastical officers or ministers in one church ought not to bear any ecclesiastical office in another." The True Description of the Visible Church, published in 1589,[6] says a pastor should be "apt to teach," and watchful over the flock; a doctor apt to teach, to edify; the elders should have wisdom, judgment, and should be able to prevent and redress evil. Lord Brooke, in his Discourse on Episcopacy,[7] asserts that it is not in the power of officers to decide cases when the church is together. Why tell it to the church, if the officers are to decide? "All officers vail bonnet when the party giving power is present." Goodwin[8] maintains that he carries with him the power of order, as of a minister to preach (i.e. by authority), but not a power of jurisdiction, which ceases when and where his official relation to a particular church ceases. Cambridge Platform[9] says: "Church officers are officers to one church even that particular church over which the Holy Ghost has made them overseers." A council at Concord, in 1637,[10] decided that ministers, come from England, were no ministers till they were called to another church, though they were ministers before they were solemnly ordained. See Suppressed Directory of the Early Nonconformists, in Neal, ii. 440; also Goodwin, Church Government, book vi. 282—290. — See MINISTERS, *is their character indelible? may they administer seals, &c.?* OFFICERS *limited to those qualified.*

[1] Pages 3, 4. [2] Page 7. [3] In Han. i. 357. [4] Ib. ii. 29. [5] Neal's Puritans, i. 248. [6] In Han. i. 30. [7] Ib. ii. 128. [8] Ch. Gov. 230. [9] Chap. ix. sect. 6. [10] Winthrop, i. 217.

OFFICERS *not the church.* — Goodwin[1] says: "They are never called the church in the New Testament. The officers are said to be set in the church, but they are not called the church." He quotes[2] from Parker's Ecclesiastical Polity, "It may be denied that the name *church* is ever in the Scriptures restrained only to the priests;" and he shows from Clemens Romanus, that he wrote to the church, and not to the elders as such. The whole of chap. vii. book ii. argues that the elders are not the church.

[1] Ch. Gov. 66. [2] Ib. 74.

OFFICERS, *church, chosen by the people.* — This is everywhere maintained as fundamental to Congregationalism. Mosheim[1] affirms unhesitatingly, "that the people were undoubtedly the first in authority . . . it was therefore the assembly of the people that chose their own rulers and teachers." The Desires of the Independents[2] has this, "that godly, able ministers, *chosen by the people*, exercise their ministry." Bartlett's Model[3] has a "brief view for choosing officers by the whole church." The sixth of the Propositions to Parliament[4] is, "that every congregation . . . have full and free power to choose their own officers." Cotton's Keys, 37; Cambridge Platform, chap. viii. sect. 5, 6; Wise's Vindication, 50, 51; Samuel Mather's Apology, 35—50; and Davenport's Apologetical Reply, 37, all maintain and defend the same doctrine. Owen, in his Nature of a Gospel Church, chap. iv.[5] shows that the apostles are recorded in Acts xiv. 23 to have ordained elders in every city *by the lifting up of the hands, or election of the brethren,* translated as it is by force of law, to answer a special purpose. He[6] answers specious objections to the choosing of them by the people (as that they are incapable), showing that they are not precluded from taking advice, but they must choose for themselves. Dr. Bentley, in his Description of Salem,[7] shows that Mr. Nicholet was called to Salem by a vote taken in the congregation, and not in the church. "Governor Leverett and others declared their disapprobation, as contrary to the law of the jurisdiction and the usages of the church." Letchford, in his Plain Dealing,[8] asserts that "the churches elect their own officers." Lord Brooke, in his Discourse on Episcopacy,[9] says by God's rule the officers' election is to be by the people. See Upham's Rat. Dis. 102—104; Punchard's View, 57, 123, 134; and especially Coleman's Primitive Church, chap. iv. — See Pastors, *power to elect, in the church.*

[1] In Han. i. 9. [2] In ib. iii. 44. [3] Ib. 246. [4] Ib. 247. [5] Works, xx. 415. [6] Ib. 422. [7] In Hist. Soc. Col. series i. vol. vi. 263. [8] Ib. series iii. vol. iii. 64. [9] In Han. ii. 126.

OFFICERS, *church, chosen for life.* — The sixth of the Propositions for Reforming the English Churches includes this:[1] "Let them ordain officers for life, and not for one year only." Their rotation was one of the objections of the exiles to the Dutch churches. — See ELDERS, *is their office perpetual?*

[1] In Han. ii. 578.

OFFICERS *limited to those qualified.*— Cambridge Platform[1] says they should be first tried and proved, in respect to those gifts and virtues which the Scripture requireth in men that are to be elected to such places; specifying their qualifications, and naming the Scripture proofs. Owen, in his Nature of a Gospel Church,[2] says it is not in the power of the church to communicate office-power to one who has not the required qualifications. After repeating substantially the above,[3] he maintains that it is duty to withdraw from churches that have deficient pastors, and join to others. — See OFFICERS, *their office and qualifications.*

[1] Chap. viii. sect. 3, 4. [2] Works, xx. 432. [3] Ib. 455.

OFFICERS, *all elected ones are truly officers.* — Hooker[1] shows this point, and adds: "The Scribes and Pharisees sit in Moses' chair. They must therefore be heard, though unworthy." He evidently means only that they should be heard while continued in office, and we continue with the church, which is an important but often neglected truth.

[1] Survey, part ii. 45.

OFFICERS, *God's gift, and not to be multiplied.*—Goodwin[1] shows this most conclusively, making it appear that to appoint officers in the kingdom of heaven, which Christ has not appointed, is to usurp his authority. He tells us, in his word, what officers he has set in the churches, and requires (1 Tim. vi. 14) that his commandment be kept unrebukable till the appearing of the Lord Jesus Christ. Cambridge Platform says:[2] "The instituting of all these officers in the church is the work of God himself; . . . and therefore such officers as he hath not appointed are altogether unlawful to be placed in the church, or to be retained therein." Hooker[3] shows that there should be no more officers than are appointed by Christ. "These are from heaven."—See Church, *officers of;* Committees, *church;* Standing Committees.

[1] Ch. Gov. 267—269. [2] Chap. vii. sect. 6. [3] Survey, part ii. 4.

OFFICERS *necessary because of God's appointment.*— Goodwin[1] shows this in a masterly argument, setting at nought the wisdom of those who would have no pastors; officers which God has set in the churches.

[1] Ch. Gov. 264—269.

OFFICERS, *may they be deposed for sins not deserving of excommunication?*— Goodwin[1] discusses this point at length, and concludes in the negative: showing that the Scriptures require them to be treated "with peculiar tenderness," whereas the present practice is to treat them with "peculiar severity."

[1] Ch. Gov. book vii. chap. 10.

OFFICERS, *servants of the church.* — Goodwin[1] says: "It is necessary that there should be many officers in every church, to whom the exercise of church power be especially committed, though the power itself be wholly in the church itself, whose servants and helpers they are, 1 Cor. i. 24, and not lords over them." — See ELDERS, *servants of the church.*

[1] Ch. Gov. 267.

OFFICERS *abdicate when they refuse to do the duties of their office.* — Wise[1] maintains the application of this as a general rule to those pastors who refuse to call the church together. Goodwin,[2] speaking of the delinquency of officers, says: "Then doth their power return again to the church, from whence they first received it." — See MINISTERS, *people may do their work for them, &c.;* GOVERNMENT, *civil, &c.;* particularly quotations from Bridge and Chief Justice Holt, in ib.

[1] Quarrel of the Churches Espoused, 91. [2] Catechism, 23.

ORDINANCES, *perpetuity of, in the churches.* — Goodwin devotes the fifth chapter of his first book to demonstrating this doctrine; proving it from the existence of the ancient churches and from the declarations of the Scriptures. Bridge, in the preface to his Vindication of Ordinances, argues the sanctity of the Lord's day from the fact that religion flourishes most when it is most observed. He shows[1] that ordinarily men are converted under the public ministry. The alleged fact, that persons have greater enjoyment in private devotions than in public ordinances, is no more an argument against ordinances than it is against taking their daily food, because they may enjoy their private devotions more than their ordinary meals.

[1] Page 14.

ORDINATION, *what.* — Isaac Chauncy, in his Divine Institution of Congregational Churches,[1] says: Ordination, in the Old or New Testament, applied to men, signifies the installing in the office to which they are called. In the places where our translators thus use the word, there is not the least mention of the imposition of hands, though the word rendered *ordaining* signifies the uplifting of the hands, by way of suffrage, in the election of officers. Increase Mather, in his Sermon at the Ordination of Mr. Appleton,[2] says: "Mutual election is that which doth essentiate the relation of a pastor to this or that particular church." Hall, in his Puritans and their Principles,[3] argues that to "ordain elders means simply to establish them," and has reference to no external ceremony. He demonstrates, by several references to Greek authors, that the word rendered *ordained* in Acts xiv.

23 refers to the election of the people by the lifting up of hands. Declaration of Discipline (probably Udal's), published in 1574, says in the table: "Ordination is a solemn investing or installing into office." The point is discussed in ib. page 66. Cambridge Platform says:[4] "This ordination we account as NOTHING ELSE but the solemn putting a man into his place and office in the church, to which he had a right before by election." The Congregational Manual says:[5] "Ordination is a public consecration of a man to the work of the ministry, an admission of him to the order of elders or bishops, and a solemn putting of him into his place and office as pastor of the church, like the installing of a magistrate." Dr. Watts, in his Foundation of a Christian Church,[6] shows that there is no instance of ordination recorded in Scripture, save for extraordinary officers, and intimates that it is doubtful how many of these practices should now be retained. Hooker, in the preface to his Survey, says: "Ordination is the installing of an officer into office, to which he was previously called." — See IMPOSITION OF HANDS; ORDINATION, *is any besides election indispensable? by presbytery.*

[1] Page 68. [2] In his Practical Truths, 122. [3] Page 305, 306, 321. [4] Chap. ix. sect. 2. [5] Page 29. [6] Works, iii. 206.

ORDINATION *must be to a particular church by election.* — This was maintained by Axton in the court of Archbishop Parker.[1] In the debates in the Westminster Assembly[2] is the question, whether certain ministers in London may not be appointed to ordain others *jure fraternitatis.* The Independents dissented, unless the ordination was attended by the previous election of some church. It is asserted [3] that there was a debate in the same assembly, "whether ordination might precede election to a particular cure or charge." Goodwin, Nye, Bridge, and the rest of the Independents, "replied to the arguments from the ordination of Timothy, Titus, and Apollos," that these were extraordinary officers; and it appeared absurd to ordain an officer without a province to exercise his office in. The grand difficulty lay here, that ordination without election to a particular charge seemed to imply a conveyance of office-power, which, in their opinion, was attended with the difficulties of a lineal succession. The same doctrine is advanced in the Nonconformists' Directory in the days of Queen Elizabeth.[4] Hooker, in the preface to his Survey, says: "There ought to be no ordination of a pastor at large, i.e. such as should make him a pastor without a people." He [5] quotes several authors to show that the pastoral office is constituted by election. He also shows that in the beginning the people chose their officers, and then presented them to the apostles for ordination. The Declaration of Discipline asserts [6] that "ancient synods made a decree, that no man should be ordained an elder without a title, that is, a church." The Congregational Manual proposes [7] to adhere to these ancient usages, except in the case of missionaries and professors in colleges and theological seminaries. Clemens Romanus [8] says: The apostles ordained officers "with the good liking and consent of the church." The Savoy Confession, on the Institution of Churches, art. xv.,[7] says: "Ordination alone, without election, or a precedent consent of the church, . . . doth not constitute any person an officer, or consummate office-power unto him." Isaac Chauncy, in his Divine Institution of Congregational Churches,[10] says: Christ never constituted such a ministry, but what were set in a particular church by election. The apostles were set first in the church at Jerusalem. If there be a catholic visible church, there should be a catholic visible pastor. Increase Mather, in his Vindication,[11] shows at length that pastors may not be ordained except to particular churches. The contrary was an innovation of the bishops. Many ancient councils objected against it, and deemed it null and void. Such an officer is a sinecure, and his particular church cannot depose him from his office. Rev. Stephen Badger was ordained a missionary at Boston, with special reference to the Indians at Natick;[12] but he was called and ordained the pastor of a church gathered there.[13] Dr. Coleman was thus ordained in London for Brattle-street Church, Boston, in 1699; but this excited opposition, and led one to call the church a "Presbyterian brat."[14] — See Upham's Rat. Dis. 13. — See EVANGELISTS.

[1] In Neal's Puritans, I. 113. [2] Ib. 494. [3] Ib. ii. 8. [4] Ib. Appendix, 440, 441. [5] Part ii. 40, 41. [6] Page 39. [7] Page 29. [7] Epistle to the Corinthians, 23. [9] In Han. iii. 547. [10] Pages

18, 19. [11] Pages 100—107. [12] Title to Dr. Appleton's Ordination Serm. of id. [13] Do. to Dr. Sewall's Charge, and Mr. Abbott's Right Hand to do. [14] Eliot, Biog. Dict. 125.

ORDINATION *of missionaries.* — See EVANGELISTS ; also the next preceding arricle ; also Upham's Rat. Dis. 86—94.

The following has been kindly furnished by Rev. Dr. Anderson, Sec. A. B. C. F. M., for the stereotype edition of this work : —

"The *present* usage in ordaining missionaries is not described with entire accuracy by Prof. Upham in his Ratio Disciplinæ. At first, and for some time, the Prudential Committee were accustomed to call the ordaining council. But, for many years past, the whole matter of ordination has been left with the candidate to arrange with the church to which he belongs, or with some other church to which he sustains a providential relation. The letters-missive are issued in the name of the church, inviting sister-churches to come, with their pastors, and ordain the candidate, if they think proper, as a missionary to the heathen. Where circumstances have been peculiar, the candidate has himself sometimes communicated his wishes, by letter, to certain pastors and churches, and asked them to assemble and ordain him, in case they saw no objection. I am speaking of such as are ordained Congregationally. The ordination of Presbyterian missionaries is of course by their Presbyteries." *

* The communication from which the above was taken was expected in season for a correction of the article EVANGELISTS *not to be ordained for the conversion of infidels.* It seems that this

ORDINATION *by direct succession unnecessary.*— Owen, in his Nature of Schism,[1] inquires why in doctrine we should succeed the persecuted woman, while in office we must succeed the persecuting beast. In his Review of the same,[2] he maintains that there should be a succession through the elders of the same church, where there are any, but not back through Rome. Hopkins[3] argues for direct succession, and maintains, very inconclusively, that every minister may consider himself in direct succession, in the absence of evidence to the contrary. See ORDINATION *by ministers; by the people.*

[1] In Han. iii. 441. [2] Ib. 450. [3] System, ii. 233—240.

article left the impression on the mind of Dr. A. that the authorities quoted would not allow missionaries the right of administering seals, gathering churches, &c., till they were actually constituted pastors of mission-churches. Now, Dr. Owen, in the immediate context to the quotation cited, expressly recognizes their right to this, founded on Acts xiii. and other passages. The simple question at issue is whether they should receive such ordination as to constitute them a distinct class of church officers? They surely should possess all the authority which Barnabas had after he and Paul were separated to the work, unless the laying on of hands had connection with the imparting of miraculous gifts, (see IMPOSITION OF HANDS, *is it necessary?*) and all which Luke had after that he was chosen (χειροτονηθεὶς, 2 Cor. viii. 19) or ordained *of the churches* to travel with Paul and Timothy. This seems to be very nearly imitated in our present missionary ordinations, according to the above article. The object of the author is simply to elicit inquiry as to the idea of office-power conferred on evangelists by ordination. The Congregational Dictionary is designed to be *reformatory* and *progressive* in its influence, recognizing the Holy Scriptures as the only standard of authority. It is not apprehended that this tends to any *revolutionary* movements, our churches being already based on the Rock of Ages, according to the divine word.

ORDINATION *conveys no spiritual power.* — Dr. Price[1] says of the Independents in the Westminster Assembly: "They were distinguished from the Presbyterians by . . . and denying the communication of spiritual power in ordination." Hooker[2] maintains that Timothy received not office-power, but spiritual gifts, by the laying on of Paul's and the presbytery's hands. He is exhorted to stir up, not his office-power, but the gift that was in him. Imposition of hands did not add to his office, but only confirmed it. — See IMPOSITION OF HANDS.

[1] In Neal's Puritans, i. 462, note. [2] Survey, part ii. 55—59.

ORDINATION, *is a council necessary to?* — R. Mather[1] says: "It is the practice, in ordaining and deposing ministers, to call in the aid of other churches; but it is not lawful nor convenient to call in such assistance (viz. by way of authority or power of the ministers of other churches)." Cotton[2] says, the Presbytery of that church, if they have one, if not two or three others of the gravest of the brethren, being deputed by the body, ordain him, with imposition of hands. He says:[3] "Ordination is a work of church power. . . . The power of the keys is a liberty *purchased to the church by the blood of Christ," and should not be parted with at a less price.* The views of the fathers undoubtedly were, that a council was very desirable for advice, and safety from impostors, but that the power of ordination was in the church. — See ORDINATION *by the people.*

[1] Ch. Gov. and Ch. Cov. 41. [2] Way, 41. [3] Ib. 50.

ORDINATION, *none besides election indispensable.* Archbishop Cranmer took this ground in an early period of the English Reformation. He says:[1] "He that is appointed a bishop or a priest needeth no consecration by the Scriptures; for election or appointing thereto is sufficient." Cambridge Platform[2] says: "The essence and substance of the outward call of an ordinary officer doth not consist in his ordination, but in his voluntary and free election by the church, and his accepting of that relation. . . . Ordination doth not constitute an officer, nor give him the essentials of his office. The apostles were elders without imposition of hands by men. Paul and Barnabas were officers before that imposition of hands." Owen, in his Nature of a Gospel Church, chap. iv.,[3] shows that the elders were ordained by the choosing of them by the people, by the lifting up of their hands, according to the Greek of Acts xiv. 23. He maintains, however,[4] that they should be solemnly set apart; and says that the light of nature proclaims this, as it does the coronation of kings, which gives them not their title, but proclaims it. At an ordaining council at Concord in 1637, it was decided, that, upon election, ministers were such before they were ordained.[5] Isaac Chauncy, however, held to the necessity of ordination. He says:[6] "The consummation of a call is made by the free acceptance of the person called; but this doth not constitute a person in the ministerial office, any more than a private contract doth constitute man and wife." Increase Mather, in his Sermon at the Ordination of Mr. Appleton,[7] and Mr. Pemberton, in his Discourse at the Ordination of Mr. Sewall,[8] hold the same doctrine. See Samuel Mather's Apology, chap. ii.; Upham's Rat. Dis. 111; Robinson's Works, iii. 39. — See CALLING; TRANSLATION.

[1] In Punchard's Hist. 200. [2] Chap. ix. sect. 2. [3] Works, xx. 415. [4] Ib. 424. [5] Winthrop, i. 217. [6] Divine Inst. Cong. Churches, 65. [7] In his Practical Truths, 124. [8] Page 3.

ORDINATION *by ministers.* — Robinson, in his Justification,[1] says: "We acknowledge, that, in the right and orderly state of things, no ministers are to be ordained but by ministers. . . . If ordination had been so prime a work, Paul would have tarried himself in Crete to have ordained elders there, and sent Titus, an inferior officer, about the inferior work of preaching." To this agrees Congregational practice everywhere. Ministers seem the proper persons for such public performances; but when this practice is perverted to mean that the officiating ministers give the church a minister or withhold him at pleasure, are more than counsellors, and control more than their own acts, then it is time for the churches to stand fast in their liberty; as they did in various instances in the early settlement of Massachusetts and Connecticut. (See two preceding and two succeeding articles.) Dr. Stiles[2] says: "It was a mistaken notion of our fathers, that the power of ordination was in the church by the elders;" (might not the church then be overruled in their choice?) "also that, where there are no elders, it might be performed by delegated brethren." He traces all through the bishops, and thus argues a lineal succession *via* Rome. Though the bishops did not intend to impart to presbyters the power of ordaining, yet they did (by unintentional contagion, I suppose!) give them full presbyterial powers. "Dead flies!" Rev. Joseph Webb, in his Letter to Cotton Mather,[3] expresses great fears of the evils growing out of the lay-ordinations. But, in the Letter of the Boston Ministers on the Duty of the Distressed Churches, they scout these fears, saying:[4] "They will have none owned for ministers of Christ but such as Antichrist has ordained for him, such as the paw of the beast hath been laid upon, that they pretend succession from." Barrowe, in his Discovery of a False Church,[5] shows that to make ordination pertain to ministers only, is a "trick to stop" a real election by the people, and make it really depend upon the classis, while the people have their eyes blinded in the matter.

[1] In Han. i. 215; and Punchard's Hist. 333; and Works, ii. 430, 437. [2] Election Serm. 59—64. [3] In Hist. Soc. Col. series ii. vol. ii. 132, 133. [4] Ib. 134. [5] In Han. i. 47.

ORDINATION *by presbytery.* — Goodwin says:[1] "The Scriptures in plain terms attribute the act of ordination to a presbytery, i.e. a company of elders united in that relation" (referring to the elders of one particular church). His definition, however, virtually begs the question. The chapter on discipline in the Savoy Confession says:[2] "The way of ordaining officers is, . . . after their election by the suffrage of the church, to set them apart with fasting and prayer and imposition of hands of the eldership of the church; though, if there be no imposition of hands, they are nevertheless rightly constituted ministers of Christ." Barrowe, in his Refutation of Giffard,[3] says: "It is to be performed by the eldership of the church, if there be one in it; if not, by the help of the elders of some other faithful congregation." Richard Mather, in his Reply to Rathband,[4] says: "We willingly do grant, that, where elders are not wanting, imposition of hands is to be performed by the elders." So say the Independents in the Westminister Assembly.[5] "There is a sufficient presbytery (for ordination) in every congregation." Cambridge Platform says:[6] "In such churches where there are elders, imposition of hands in ordination is to be performed by those elders." It was thus that Mr. Cotton was installed in Boston.[7] Isaac Chauncy[8] argues, that, as "the elders of one church cannot perform an authoritative act in another church," therefore, if ordination is to be by elders at all, it should be by elders of the same church. Increase Mather[9] maintains that it is one of the fundamentals of Congregationalism, that ordination of pastors must be by the approbation of neighbor-churches or elders. He states[10] that it was an old doctrine in New England, that a church which has no elders should desire neighbor-churches to assist in ordination. He supposes lay-ordination not decent, though valid, because no imposition of hands is necessary, but only election. Mr. Pemberton, in his Discourse at the Ordination of Mr. Sewall, maintains[11] that the power of ordination is in the presbytery. — See IMPOSITION OF HANDS; INSTALLATION.

[1] Ch. Gov. 54. [2] In Neal's Puritans, ii. 179. [3] In Han. i. 57. [4] Ib. ii. 186. [5] Ib. 511. [6] Chap. ix. sect. 3. [7] Hubbard's Hist. of Mass. 188. [8] Divine Inst. of Cong. Churches, 69. [9] Vindic. of N. Eng. Churches, 8. [10] Ib. 100. [11] Page 11.

ORDINATION *by the people.* — Barrowe, in his Answer to Giffard,[1] says: "If the apostacy be so general that there are not anywhere to be found any true elders, yet then hath the church . . . power to ordain their ministers by the most fit members and means they have." The Confession of the Low Country Exiles, art. xxiii.,[2] says: "Every Christian congregation hath power and commandment to elect and ordain their own ministry." Ainsworth, in his Reply to Johnson,[3] says: "That ministers of one particular church should ordain elders for another church is more unorderly than when every church ordaineth them itself." Davenport, in his Power of Congregational Churches,[4] says: "Their ordination of officers, by deputing some out of their own body thereunto . . . in a want of officers, is an act of this power of the keys residing in them." Richard Mather and W. Tompson, Answer to Herle,[5] say: "Where elders cannot conveniently be borrowed from any other church, imposition of hands may lawfully be performed by some principal men of the congregation, though they be not elders by office." So also Mather's Reply to Rutherford,[6] Propositions attributed to John Cotton,[7] and the

Petition of the Independents in the Westminster Assembly.[8] In the grand debate in the Westminster Assembly,[9] "the Independents maintained the right of every congregation to ordain its own officers;" and when it was voted "that no single congregation, that can conveniently associate, assume to itself the sole right of ordination," Thomas Goodwin, P. Nye, J. Burroughs, S. Simpson, W. Bridge, W. Greenhill, and W. Carter entered their dissent. Cambridge Platform[10] maintains the same doctrine. Hooker[11] says: "It is most comely that those of the same congregation should exercise it" (ordination), but they may invite others. He[12] reiterates the same sentiment, and shows that if a classis is composed of those sent by churches, then congregations first provided ministers, for they did not first receive them from classes; and, if presbyters first made a bishop, they were before him, and did not receive their office from him. Hutchinson, in his History of Massachusetts,[13] says: "The church in Charlestown chose Mr. Wilson for their teacher, and ordained him;" and[14] "Mr. Higginson was ordained by two deacons and a private brother in Salem," though it appears that they had sent for a delegation from Plymouth, who were detained. Mr. Hooke was ordained at Taunton by a schoolmaster and one of the other brethren.[15] There was such an ordination, in 1642, in Woburn. A number of ministers were present; but "the people were tenacious of their right to ordain, supposing that yielding it might lead to dependency, and so to presbytery."[16] Another, Israel Chauncy's, took place in Stratford, where, Eliot says,[17] "by forgetfulness (I rather think in contempt of habits and ceremonies) the elder imposed his hand with a leather mitten upon it." Cotton Mather, in his Magnalia,[18] represents ordination by "lay-brethren, orderly chosen by the church thereunto," as having, in his time, gone into disuse. Samuel Mather, in his Apology,[19] shows that the Bohemian Churches commenced on this (lay-ordination) principle; and[20] he shows that "even a famous bishop of Salisbury" held it in his Exposition of the Thirty-nine Articles. He argues the point at length and very conclusively;[21] and indeed in the whole of his second chapter. Watts, in his Foundation of a Christian Church,[22] shows that popular ordination is valid, and sometimes necessary, but not often expedient. Davenport, in his Power of Congregational Churches,[23] says: The churches have power to ordain their own officers by some deputed out of their own number, in case of the want of officers. Isaac Chauncy[24] answers the question: "Who shall ordain when there are no elders?" saying: "Who should do it but the church that called him?" The power is in the church, if necessary, to lay on hands by some brother delegated and appointed thereto; for foreign ministers cannot do an authoritative act in that church. He argues[25] that the church is superior to all the ministers thereof; hence that the church may ordain them: and that[26] a person should be ordained by the church that calls him, being no more than the public solemn recognition of their call and his acceptance. It ought to be performed decently and to the honor of God, with solemn prayer; delegates from other churches being present as witnesses. Increase Mather, in his Vindication of the New England Churches,[27] quotes from Owen: "Where elders cannot be had, ordination may be performed by those not elders." Lambert, in his History of New Haven Colony,[28] says, Mr. Prudden, of Milford, records his own ordination by three brethren, "designed by ye church for that work, ye 18 of April, 1640." Bentley, in his Description of Salem,[29] shows that the church there, in the beginning, determined that the authority of ordination should not rest in the ministry, but depend entirely on the free election of the church. They were careful to record that they acknowledged no jurisdiction in the church of Plymouth, when they invited them to Mr. Higginson's ordination. Eliot, in his Ecclesiastical History of Massachusetts,[30] says that in 1642 Mr. Carter was ordained in Woburn by the church, who would not call the elders of other churches to do it, *lest it should lead to presbytery and dependence of churches.* Dr. Eckley, in his Dudlean Lecture,[31] says: "We differ from our episcopal brethren as respects the right of any particular church to elect and consecrate its own officers, no less than to perform the other acts of jurisdiction, without the aid of presbyters, bishops, or pastors of other churches; and to the special propriety of these measures, whenever, through any extraordinary occurrences, the assistance of such ministers cannot be obtained. . . . Not only the independence, but the very existence, of a Christian society would be lost, in the event of its denial." Hunter, in his Life of Oliver Heywood,[32] asserts that it is a fundamental principle of Congregationalism, that it was not the intention of the founders of Christianity that all who take upon them the Christian name should form one vast society; but that every organized society, with pastor and deacon, was a true Christian church, which may call a pastor, and invest him with office, without ordination by bishop or any body of presbyters; though ministers might witness the act, and make (invoke) a divine blessing upon it. He asserts [33] that Goodwin, Bridge, Nye, Simpson, and Burroughs were nearly of this opinion. Letchford, in his Plain Dealing,[34] says: "They appoint some of themselves to impose hands on their officers." And [35] "Mr. Hooke was ordained in Taunton by a schoolmaster," and Mr. Hooke joined in ordaining Mr. Streate. He says [36] that the elders in Boston replied to his question, saying: "If the people have power to choose their own officers, they have power to ordain them." Upham, in his Dedication Sermon,[37] says: "The Salem church themselves laid hands on their ruling elder; he on the teacher, and both in the same form on their pastor." In the Appendix to the same,[38] he reiterates Eliot's above-quoted assertion relative to the power of ordination residing in the people, and asserts [39] that when John Higginson was ordained, in 1660, "Major Hawthorne and the deacons imposed hands upon him, in the presence of the neighboring churches and elders." The same is repeated in his Second Century Sermon, page 39, and Eliot's Biographical Dictionary 255. Dr. Emmons[40] says: "People have a right to choose their own officers, and then install them into office. . . . The right is primarily and solely in the church; and when ministers ordain, it is because they are invited and appointed by the church to do it." So, too, Ainsworth, in his Answer to Clyfton;[41] and Lord Brooke, in his Discourse on Episcopacy.[42] — See Bacon's Ch. Manual, 138, 139. — See Imposition of Hands, *by whom;* Councils, *can they ordain and depose?*

[1] In Han. i. 58. [2] Ib. 94. [3] Ib. 252. [4] Ib. ii. 64. [5] Ib. 175. [6] Ib. 188. [7] Ib. 578. [8] Ib. iii. 44. [9] In Neal's Puritans, ii. 8. [10] Chap. ix. sect. 5. [11] Survey, part ii. 59. [12] Ib. 78. [13] Vol. i. 370. [14] Page 374. [15] Ib. [16] Hubbard, 408. [17] Eliot, Biog. Dict. 101. [18] Vol. ii. 209. [19] Page 58. [20] Ib. 60. [21] Pages 56—60. [22] Wks. iii. 210. [23] Page 104. [24] Div. Inst. Cong. Chs. 70. [25] Ib. 72. [26] Ib. 78—83. [27] Page 96. [28] Page 101. [29] In Hist. Soc. Col. series i. vol. vi. 242. [30] In ib. series i. vol. ix. 39. [31] Pages 15, 16. [32] Page 58. [33] Ib. 39. [34] In Hist. Soc. Col. series iii. vol. iii. 64. [35] Ib. 96. [36] Ib. 108. [37] Page 22. [38] Page 52. [39] Ib. 55. [40] Vol. v. 448—450. [41] In Han. i. 252. [42] Ib. ii. 126.

ORDINATION, *mode of.* — Cotton Mather[1] describes it as differing in his day from the present usual mode, in that the letter missive often designated persons to perform the several parts, except the right hand of fellowship. Usually the person ordained preached; sometimes another. The vote of the church and the acceptance of the call were repeated at the ordination. (This was practised since the remembrance of the compiler.) Hands were also imposed during the giving of the charge, and a prayer succeeded it. Isaac Chauncy, in his Divine Institution of Congregational Churches, shows[2] that a ruling elder or delegated brother (of the church) repeats the questions as to the call and acceptance; the brethren voting by the lifting up of the hand, the pastor elect assenting. Eliot, in his Ecclesiastical History of Massachusetts,[3] shows that at first there was no sermon at ordination, though afterwards the minister ordained usually preached. (He attributes the change to John Cotton.) Mr. John Higginson preached his own ordination sermon in 1660; Thomas Prince, in 1718; (five years before, Mr. Pemberton discoursed at the ordination of Mr. Sewall, his colleague;)[4] Mr. Maccarty at Worcester, in 1747. Mr. Rogers of Ipswich[5] preached at his own ordination as early as 1638. For modern mode, see Upham's Rat. Dis. 117; Punchard's View, 164. — See CHURCH, *mode of constituting.*

[1] Rat. Dis. 22—42. [2] Page 82. [3] In Hist. Soc. Col. series i. vol. ix. 13. [4] The printed discourse itself. [5] Eliot, Biog. Dict 408.

ORDINATION, *method of keeping a day of.* — Cotton[1] shows that it was kept with preaching, prayer, humiliation, and fasting, "till near the close of the day," when the ordination-services were performed. The Description of the Visible Church,[2] and Mather's Rat. Dis.[3] maintain that "it should be kept as a sacred fast unto the Lord."

[1] Way, 40. [2] In Punchard's Hist. 366. [3] Page 24.

ORDINATION, *mode of objecting to.* — A council at Springfield,[1] about 1736, decided that they expected the dissatisfied should not only present objections but proofs, and that there should not be a public hearing of the matter, unless some appeared as accusers.

[1] Ans. to Hampshire Narr. 59, 64—67.

ORDINATION, *should it be repeated?* — Isaac Chauncy says[1] that the contrary "conceit . . . is a Popish error; for churches are no more prisons to ministers than to people, . . . and one church's ordination of a man cannot make him pastor of another."

[1] Divine Inst. Cong. Churches, 83.

PARISH, *not a Christian church.* — Euring, in his Answer to Drake's Ten Counter Demands,[1] shows this conclusively: "Your parish assemblies do not gladly receive the apostles' doctrine." — See Upham's Rat. Dis. 38, 317—323.

[1] In Han. i. 362, 363.

PASTOR, *his official duties.* — The True Description of the Visible Church[1] describes them somewhat figuratively. I epitomize thus, — To feed the sheep; guide and keep them; draw them to him; look into their souls; discern their diseases; cure them by appropriate medicine; give warning, that they may orderly proceed to excommunication; watch over and defend the flock. Cambridge Platform[2] distinguishes his office from that of teacher, in that it is the pastor's special work to attend to exhortation, and that of the teacher to doctrine;

and either of them to administer seals, and preach the gospel. Goodwin refines at large on the distinction.[3] Jacob's Church Confession[4] maintains that he should be trusted to rule in all ordinary affairs of the church; "yet so that, in matters of weight, the whole congregation (i.e. church) do understand thereof, before any thing be finished, and also that the congregation do not manifestly dissent therefrom. Owen, in his Eshcol, or Rules of Walking in Fellowship, rule vii.[5] maintains, from Acts xiv. 27, their right to call the church together. In his Nature of a Gospel Church, chap. v.[6] he makes his duties to be, to preach the word, pray for the flock, administer seals, and[7] visit the sick. He argues[8] that it is not the *pastor's* duty to go up and down preaching for the conversion of strangers, though he occasionally should. Hooker, in his Survey,[9] makes it his duty to work on the will and affections, to win and woo the soul, to lay open the loathsome nature of sin, and quicken the renewed soul to every holy work. Davenport, in his Apologetical Reply,[10] argues that pastors govern by feeding the church of God, not by having the church depend on their authority. He quotes Ames on 1 Pet. v. 3 to sustain him. From the votes of the church and doings of a council in Dorchester,[11] it appears that in 1774 the church negatived the motion of the pastor for a church meeting, at a given time; that the pastor refused to attend another church meeting, because it was not of his appointment; that the church refused to proceed to business at another time, when called to by the pastor;

that he attempted to dissolve a church meeting by his own power, and that he frequently refused to attend church meetings which he declined to appoint. The council did not sustain the pastor.

[1] In Punchard's Hist. 368. [2] Page 30. [3] Ch. Gov. book vi. chap. viii. [4] Art. xiv. in Han. i. 298. [5] Works, xix. 77. [6] Ib. xx. 433. [7] Ib. 450. [8] Ib. 445. [9] Part ii. 19, 20. [10] Page 298. [11] Pages 5—8.

PASTOR, *has he a negative vote in the church?*— Increase Mather, in his Disquisition on Ecclesiastical Councils,[1] incidentally intimates that the Platform gives him this power. Eliot, in his Ecclesiastical History of Massachusetts,[2] says: "After the Platform, some ministers claimed more than it gave them, and some claimed a power to negative the proceedings of the church." Zabdiel Adams, in his Answer to a Treatise on Church Government,[3] says: "The keys are so lodged with elders and brethren as never to be used but by mutual consent." He maintains,[4] that, since ruling elders have ceased, the whole power of the bench of elders rests with the pastor. Eliot[5] asserts that in these matters he took a position which could not be maintained by the Platform, nor any just sentiments of religious freedom. See also Allen's Biographical Dictionary, art. Adams, Zabdiel. The History of Sterling[6] shows, that Mr. Mellen held, that, if there were some to rule, there were others to obey; and applied it to the negative vote, causing much trouble and his own dismission. President Stiles, who was extensively acquainted with the churches,[7] says: I know of no more than one church, where the pastor has a negative vote. Some pastors have claimed it over Congregational churches; but, except being moderator, the pastor has but the authority of a private brother, according to the true principles of Congregationalism. He says:[8] "The churches would not bear a negative of the eldership." Dr. Emmons[9] says, if the pastor might negative all the doings and votes of the church, they would have no power at all. He is a mere moderator, and, with respect to voting, stands on the same ground with a private brother. See Upham's Rat. Dis. 83—85, 107.—See CHURCHES *begun without officers, &c.*; MEMBERS *have equal rights*; MAJORITIES.

[1] Page 14. [2] In Hist. Soc. Col. [3] Page 83. [4] Ib. 76—80. [5] Biog. Dict. 17, 18. [6] In Wor. Mag. ii. [7] Conv. Serm. 68. [8] Ib. 64. [9] Vol. v. 451, 452.

PASTOR, *power to elect him is in the church.*—Cotton[1] says, that, though his office is from Christ, the power to elect is in the church. But he asserts,[2] that they do it with the approbation of other churches, because in the multitude of counsellors there is safety. He quotes[3] Cyprian, lib. i. epist. 41: "*People* have the power of choosing worthy bishops, and of rejecting the unworthy." Clemens Romanus[4] says the apostles appointed officers "with the good liking and consent of the church." Robinson, in his Answer to Helwisse,[5] says: "For the choice of officers, we do take for our direction the practice of the apostles and apostolical churches, grounded on perpetual equity, that men should choose them under Christ, unto whose faithfulness, under the same Christ, they are to commit their souls." This doctrine is maintained in the Apology of the Overseers, &c. of the English Church at Amsterdam. Foxcroft, in his Sermon Preparatory to the Choice of a Minister,[6] asserts that "none but members have a just right to vote in ecclesiastical affairs. . . . A good deal of prudence is necessary to consult the congregation, while the right of the church to election is asserted and exercised." Dr. Ware, in his History of the Old North and New Brick Churches,[7] asserts that Cotton Mather's church, in 1697, sent a letter of admonition to the church in Charlestown, for betraying the liberties of the churches, by putting into the hands of the whole inhabitants the choice of a minister.— See ELDERS *chosen by the people;* OFFICERS *chosen by the people.*

[1] Way, 43. [2] Ib. 45. [3] Ib. 64. [4] Epistle to the Corinthians, 23. [5] In Punchard's Hist. 338; and Works, iii. 135. [6] Pages 17, 20. [7] Page 18.

PASTOR, *mode of election of.* — Cotton Mather[1] shows the mode of proceeding in his time, much as at the present day, first by the church, and then by the parish concurring, as described by Mitchell in his Guide, 175, 176. Barrowe, in his Refutation of Giffard,[2] asserts that every member should have the privilege of assent or dissent, showing his reasons. — See Punchard's View, 114.

[1] Rat. Dis. 14—22. [2] In Han. i. 57.

PASTOR, *how dismissed.* — See MINISTER, *how dismissed;* also Punchard's View, 175. Some special cases might be cited, as those of Bolton and Stirling; but it would seem much more necessary to inform people generally how to *keep*, than how to *dismiss*, a pastor.

PASTOR *should not be lightly removed.* — Cambridge Association[1] intimated that God frowns on rash removals of ministers. They, however, admit that they may be removed, "when benefit from their ministry is to be despaired of; . . . in case it be necessary for the common good; . . . in case they want sustenance, . . . or have chronical diseases which may not be removed." Owen, in his Nature of a Gospel Church, chap. v.,[2] says the ancient church made great provisions against it. He thinks, however, that there may be occasions for their removal, with the consent of all concerned. A pastor cannot voluntarily lay down his office for mere age or weakness, because he is not required to do more than he can; nor for weariness and despondency. But it is lawful on an incurable decay of mental abilities, incurable divisions in a church, neglect of support, or when the church will not do important duties. He may then retire to private life, or take office in another church. Cotton Mather, in his Ratio Disciplinæ,[3] shows that the translation of a pastor was then accomplished with the greatest difficulty. He should have it in his heart to live and die with his people. When there was but one pastor, and he ever so great, and his people ever so small, nobody scarce durst whisper about his removal. The people were jealous of such efforts, as though ROBBERS OF CHURCHES were assaulting them. But in some cases a council have recommended a removal, notwithstanding the people's dissent. Eliot, in his Ecclesiastical History of Massachusetts,[4] says that the magistrates and ministers aided in the removal of Mr. Norton to Boston, thinking that it would be an advantage to have him here. Wisner, in his History of the Old South Church, informs us[5] that the church in New Haven would not dismiss Mr. Davenport; but, as he would not be persuaded, they would not further oppose him. And[6] they "ceased, saying, The will of the Lord be done." They left him and the church in Boston to make what use of it (their inaction) they could, without giving him a letter, though they dismissed his wife and son and son's wife. Dr. Ware informs us, in his History of the Old North and New Brick Churches,[7] that the New Brick Church grew out of a controversy about calling a minister already settled (Rev. Peter Thacher of Weymouth). The ministers of Boston opposed, and requested not to be invited on the ordaining council. The Boston ministers, in connection with their answer to a question, say[8] that they look on such removals as directly tending to unsettle and disquiet churches. See Upham's Rat. Dis. 161—164.

[1] In Magnal. ii. 215. [2] Works, xx. 458, 459. [3] Pages 167—170. [4] In Hist. Soc. Col. series i. vol. ix. 30. [5] Page 7. [6] Ib. 75. [7] Pages 25, 26. [8] Objections to the Rev. Peter Thacher's Ordination, 22.

PASTOR, *is he censurable by his church?* — Richard Mather, in his Church Government and Church Covenant,[1] argues that every pastor is censurable by his own church. Robinson, in his Answer to Bernard,[2] says: "If elders . . . may displace a pastor by their authority, they may also set him up by their authority." The Low Country Exiles, in their Confession, art. xxiii.[3] maintain the same doctrine, and add: "Yea, if the case so require, to cut them off by excommunication." Ainsworth, in his Answer to Clyfton,[4] argues that his people (who put him in) may put him out of the pastoral office; "and why may they not put him quite out of the fold of Christ, that is, excommunicate him?" Jacob's Church Confession, article xiv.[5] says: "They have nothing more than what the church doth commit unto them, and which they may not, when need requireth, take away from them, yea, to their utter deposing and rejection out of the church itself, if such necessity be." Davenport, in his power of Congregational Churches,[6] says: "Nor doth it make the people rulers of their rulers, . . . that the church hath power over them, in case of delinquency; for excommunication is not an act of the highest rule, but of the highest judgment. . . . If the ministers become delinquents, then, as members, they are under the whole." Wise, in his Quarrel of the Churches Espoused,[7] comments pointedly on the first "Proposals" to take Congregational ministers from the watch and discipline of their churches, and commit them to associations. Hooker, in his Survey,[8] says, every brother, and therefore Archippus the elder, if he be a brother, is liable to church censure. Samuel Mather, in his Apology,[9] quotes Zanchy: "No one is exempted from this discipline, whether he be an elder or pastor or magistrate, unless he would be exempted from the number of the brethren, and therefore of the sons of God." Goodwin, in his Catechism,[10] says: "If Peter himself offend, and Peter will not hear thee, tell the church of Peter: Christ alone and his church is king and judge in such a case." Isaac Chauncy, in his Divine Institution of Congregational Churches;[11] Eaton and Taylor, in their Defence;[12] and Baynes, in his Diocesan's Trial,[13] argue in the same strain. Mitchell, in his Guide,[14] supposes that the doctrine of Saybrook Platform, which gives discipline to associations in such cases, is the general usage. If so, it must be by recent innovation. Cambridge Platform, after showing how he may be deposed by his church,[15] adds: "And being now but a member, . . . the church, that had power to receive him into their fellowship, hath also the same power to cast him out that they have concerning any other member." It is obvious that a minister ought still to be amenable somewhere, and not to cease to be a member of Christ's church. See Upham's Rat. Dis. 170, 176; Punchard's View, 182, 270.— See next article; see also CHURCHES, *proceedings when pastors offend;* MINISTERS, *how deposed.*

[1] Page 48. [2] In Punchard's Hist. 331, 332; and Works, ii 239. [3] In Han. i. 94. [4] Ib. 251. [5] Ib. 297. [6] Ib. ii. 65. [7] Pages 118—120. [8] Part iii. 3. [9] Page 98. [10] Page 23. [11] Page 104. [12] Page 58. [13] Page 88. [14] Pages 232—235. [15] Chap. x. sect. 6.

PASTOR, *is he a member of his church?* — Welde, in his Answer to Rathband,[1] says it is our universal and constant course not to organize a church till they have one amongst themselves fit for a minister, whom, with all speed, they call into office. Cotton Mather, in his Ratio Disciplinæ,[2] speaking of election and ordination, says: "There is a seasonable care taken, that, if the candidate were a member of some other church, he have his dismission (his relation declared to be transferred); that, as near as may be, according to the primitive direction, they may choose from among themselves." Cotton, in his Way,[3] says, destitute churches look out from among themselves such as are qualified to be officers. Isaac Chauncy, in his Divine Institution of Congregational Churches,[4] says the person called ought to be a member; for to constitute a non-member in office is contrary to the rules of any corporate society. So[5] "none can be an officer of a corporation, but he that is incorporate first as a member." Dr. Dwight[6] maintains that *a pastor should not be a member of his church.* Mitchell, in his Guide,[7] has a chapter on the membership of ministers, and complains severely of Upham for asserting that they are members and censurable by the brethren, denying that such is general usage, unless in Upham's own locality. He thinks him to have been influenced by consulting old writers. His well-informed readers may think so too, especially by Trumbull's Connecticut, which shows that the Saybrook plan was not claimed in the beginning, even by its friends, to be pure Congregationalism. See

Upham's Rat. Dis. 127—130; Punchard's View, 270—272. — See last preceding article, particularly quotation from Cambridge Platform; also CONSOCIATIONS.

[1] In Han. ii. 329. [2] Page 22. [3] Page 39. [4] Page 65. [5] Ib. 104. [6] Works, Serm. clvii. [7] Pages 237—242.

PASTOR, *colleague.* — Mr. Foxcroft settled as colleague with Mr. Wadsworth in 1717,[1] and Dr. Chauncy was ordained colleague with Mr. Foxcroft in 1727.[2] Mr. Foxcroft, the senior pastor, was then but thirty years of age. Previous to about this time, the distinction had usually been that of Pastor and Teacher.

[1] Mr. Foxcroft's Sermon at his own Ordination. [2] Sermon of ib. preparatory to the Choice of a Minister.

PEACE. — This has always been considered by Congregationalists as very desirable, so far as it may consist with truth; but the doctrine of the league with iniquity seems to be a modern whim. Burroughs, in his Irenicum,[1] says: "Let us all be for peace, *yet so not to be befooled into bondage by the name of peace.* Now God hath by his mighty arm helped us, let us not be put off with a bubble, and made to believe that it is the pearl. We know with whom we have to deal." This was written at the time that Cromwell's army began to make their power dreaded by the Presbyterial domination, to whom the Independents had been recently petitioning in vain for a mere toleration.—See RESISTANCE.

[1] In Han. iii. 125.

PERFECTION *in churches impracticable.*— Robinson, in his Apology,[1] says: "Foolish were we, if we knew not these things; impudent, if we denied them to be true; and unequal, if we acknowledged not . . . that many . . . blemishes . . . will creep into churches in our days." Even so rigid a Separatist as Canne says, in his Reply to Dayrel:[2] "Whereas Mr. Barrowe, Ainsworth, and others do show from the Scriptures what a true church is, whereof gathered, how every member should walk, and how abuses are to be reformed, &c.; he either, through ignorance or malice, or both, still inferreth from their writings, that they held perfection of churches; that there can be no hypocrite or reprobate in the church; things groundlessly collected by him." And even Roger Williams, in his Hireling Ministry None of Christ's,[3] says: "God hath covered the failings, and accepted his own grace, in such men as Calvin, Luther, &c., as he did the polygamy and sin of the patriarchs of Israel."

[1] In Han. i. 386; and Works, iii. 72. [2] Ib. 521. [3] Page 10.

PERSECUTION, *what amount of, justifies dispersion?* — Goodwin, in his Church Government,[1] maintains that the spoiling of goods is not a sufficient justification. The church should bear it joyfully, remain and testify; but, when it comes to the endangering of life, then they may disperse. God will have mercy, and not sacrifice. Simpson, before the House of Commons,[2] maintained that persecution must never hinder confession, though it may profession of some things which are good.

We must own God, even though the point be at the breast, and the dagger at the heart; but we need not attend all positive ordinances at such perils.— See FLIGHT.

[1] Page 262. [2] Han. ii. 212.

PERSECUTION *for Congregationalism.*— Many of our intelligent people seem little aware of the amount of persecution which our fathers endured for their faith. Let such learn from Neal's History of the Puritans, the deprivations, imprisonment, exile, and various sufferings of the thousands of such men for their nonconformity; and, in Punchard's History of Congregationalism, chap. xiv., of the martyrdom of Barrowe, Greenwood, and Penry, for the same cause. Then there was the slow martyrdom of the multitudes of men, women, and children, who perished for it in the English prisons, in Elizabeth's, the James's, and the Charles's reigns, throwing into the shade all the sufferings by the fires of Smithfield, in that of the bloody Mary. These are the best antidote against longings for the fleshpots of Egyptio-English prelacy in Congregationalists. Even in New England, Rev. J. Moody was imprisoned by Gov. Cranfield, of New Hampshire, in 1684, because he administered the communion not according to the way of the Church of England. He then forbade his preaching, which was the occasion of his coming to Boston.[1] Neal, in his History of New England,[2] says that, in 1573, ministers were examined, "whether the Book of Common Prayer were good and godly, every tittle of it grounded on the Holy Scriptures? and whether the thirty-nine articles were agreeable to the word of God or not? Whether we must of necessity follow the primitive church in such things as are used and established or not? and whether all ministers should be equal? and for not giving satisfactory answers, many were cast into prison." — See SEPARATION; AUTHORITY, *human.*

[1] Eliot, Biog. Dict. 327. [2] Vol. i. 55.

PLATFORM, *Cambridge; its import.* — Hon. S. Haven[1] says: "When the Platform was framed, the community consisted partly of those who held the power of the church to be in church officers, and partly of those who held it to be in the brethren." President Stiles[2] says, three or four of the ministers who formed the platform were Presbyterian, i.e. for giving church presbyters all power; several for giving a negative vote to the elders; and the rest agreed with the almost universal sense of the brotherhood in the *pure and unmixed idea of a Congregational church,* viz. all disciplinary power vested in the fraternity. And[3] he asserts that the authors of the Platform agreed on a different course of procedure in the churches holding different principles. He says[4]: "Though the compilers of the Cambridge Platform hoped to have introduced a triumvirate presbytery in each congregation, . . . yet the authority of such presbytery was confined to such churches as received it." It was received with a multitude of interspersions, securing the independency and uncontrollable power of churches, and was adopted at last by a compromise. Neal, in his History of New England,[5] says: "All did not agree to the Platform, but all acquiesced in it." One thing concerning which they differed was the power of ministers to administer seals where they were not pastors.

[1] Proceedings of the First Church and Parish of Dedham, 62. [2] Conv. Serm. 57, 58. [3] Ib. 66. [4] Ib. [5] Vol. i. 273—275.

PLATFORM, *Saybrook, import of.* — Dr. Stiles asserts,[1] that the first principles laid down in the Saybrook Platform, and some of the evident interlining, often clash with each other, — the first giving uncontrolled power to the churches; and the other, controlling power to consociations; and that it is to be supposed that the churches adopted it in a sense subordinate to the first principle.

[1] Ib. 73, 74.

PLATFORMS, *of what authority?* — Welde, in his Answer to Rathband,[1] says: "We hold it not unlawful to have a platform; . . . yet we see no ground to impose such a platform on churches, but leave them their liberty therein." (See CREEDS.) Rathband wonders "how the New England churches fell into so exact a discipline without a platform!" Welde informs him, that it was "because they had their discipline from the Scriptures," the best and the most consistent directory in the world. Hubbard[2] treats of the opposition of some to the first synod, for forming Cambridge Platform, as the ground of "fear that it was intended to have ecclesiastical laws to bind the churches," and of Mr.

Norton's success in overcoming the opposition, by laying down the authority of a synod as "consultative, declarative, and decisive, not coercive." Mitchell[3] says of our platforms and confessions: "They were never set up as standards . . . they are lights, which all are free to use or not as they please." Samuel Mather, alone of all the old Congregational authors to my knowledge, maintains[4] that the Platform is "a holy pact or covenant," renewed and transmitted by the successive councils, synods, and right hands of fellowship, performed by virtue of it; as though these things could not be done, according to the Scriptures, agreeably to the Platform, without receiving the whole Platform as a code of ecclesiastical laws. His reasoning is the more remarkable, considering his rigid Congregationalism and lucid demonstrations of many principles totally subversive of this. His great-grandfather, who drafted the Cambridge Platform, held sentiments exactly the reverse of these. (See article CREEDS; first item.) Samuel Mather, however, in a note, p. 136, of his Apology, shows that our fathers did not bind themselves to perpetual conformity to the Platform, nor any human systems and forms. The Synod of 1679 approved of Cambridge Platform "*for the substance of it*," which, Cotton Mather[5] shows, means that they did not adopt the whole of it. He notes several particulars of their dissent, as a pastor's administering seals in another church, and the office of ruling elders. Dr. Stiles[6] says: "Our platforms were received by the body of the churches, only as plans of union and mutual fellowship." Mr. Norris, of Salem, persevered in a platform of his own church;[7] and Brattle-street Church was constituted on another platform.[8] In his Ecclesiastical History of Massachusetts,[9] Eliot informs us, that "the deputies of several congregations would not yield such a power to the civil magistrates, as they assumed by calling a synod: . . . they were jealous that such a power might be erected to impose a uniformity of practice." Cotton and his church for a time opposed, and the matter was compromised by its being "in the form of a motion, and not of command." Minot, in his History of Massachusetts,[10] says: Their platform united their churches to a certain degree, yet "exempted them from any jurisdiction by way of authoritative censure, or any church power extrinsic to their own."—See Upham's Rat. Dis. 36. For an exhibition of the play upon the ambiguity of Saybrook Platform by the same parties in and out of power, see Bacon's Hist. Discourses, page 270, and elsewhere.

[1] In Han. ii. 296. [2] Hist. Mass. 534—536. [3] Guide, 56. [4] Apology, 136—139. [5] Mag. ii. 204. [6] Conv. Serm. 49. [7] Eliot, Biog. Dict. 336. [8] Ib. 84, 269. [9] In Hist. Soc. Col. series ii. vol. i. 195. [10] Vol. i. 30.

POOR *of the church should be cared for.*—Ainsworth, in his Answer to Paget,[1] maintains this to be a duty, even to selling of goods and parting them as every man hath need. K. Chidley, in her Justification of the Independent Churches of Christ, tells T. Edwards[2] that the separatist English churches "maintain all their own poor," besides being taxed for the support of others. The question is an open one in our day, and under our circumstances.

[1] In Han. i. 283. [2] Ib. ii. 112.

POWER, *a church may give that which they do not possess.*— Hooker[1] shows that "those who have no office-power *formaliter* may give such power by voluntary subjection. . . . The power which a pastor hath is by election, and extends no farther than to his own people." Goodwin[2] shows that office-power is founded on mutual relation. This principle, carried out, will show how civil governments may have powers which individual electors have not.

[1] Survey, part ii. 72, 73. [2] Ch. Gov. 68.

POWER, *apostolical, did not descend to successors.* — Owen asserts and abundantly proves this, in the preface to his Nature of a Gospel Church.[1]

[1] Works, xx. 342.

POWER, *church, installed in ministry or brethren?* Ainsworth, in the preface of his Reply to Johnson,[1] says: "Two things have been heretofore controverted between Mr. Johnson and myself; one concerning the power of the Christian church, which he would have installed in the ministry thereof." Cambridge Platform[2] says the power of office is in the eldership, and the power of privilege in the brethren: "The latter is in the brethren formally, immediately from Christ; the former is not in them formally, but may be said to be in them, in that they design the persons to office." (See PLATFORM, *Cambridge;* ELDERS *rule as moderators;* PASTORS, *people may do their work, &c.;* OFFICERS *abdicate when, &c.*) Wise,[3] in his Vindication, shows that the people under the gospel are the first subject of church power, their government being a democracy. Even in electing an extraordinary officer, the apostles themselves referred the choice to the brethren. The process of discipline, from first to last, is by the brethren. Where there is any thing amiss, the fraternity is reprehended; and, where there is any thing worthy of credit, they are commended in the Scriptures. In his Quarrel of the Churches Espoused,[4] speaking of the Proposals (the germ of consociationism), he says "they give power to association to have the first cognizance of church cases: our government says, No, it belongs to particular churches." And[5] he quotes the passage above cited from the Platform, also chap. x. sect. 6, of the deposing of elders. By this means, he cuts up root and branch the Proposals, showing that they have the face of mere Presbyterianism, but contain the heart and core of Prelacy, if not of Papacy. Davenport, in his Apologetical Reply,[6] quotes from Parker: "The power ecclesiastical resides in the church." Robinson, in his Reply to Bernard,[7] says of ecclesiastical power: "We put it in the body of the congregation; . . . the multitude called the church." Elders he acknowledges as ordinary governors, only we may not acknowledge them as lords over God's heritage. Hooker[8] shows that "a church is before its officers; . . . else, as often as the officers die, the church dies." Mather, in his Answer to Rutherford, asks[9] if a church that has neighbors may not take upon itself entireness of jurisdiction, as well as one that has none; it being granted that a church isolated has supreme power in itself. President Stiles[10] asserts that there never was an instance of admission to a church (in Connecticut), without the votes of the brethren, because of the spirit of liberty in the churches. See Punchard's View, 56.—See MINISTERS, *how deposed.*

[1] In Han. i. 320. [2] Page 28. [3] Pages 44, 51, 56. [4] Page 104. [5] Ib. 118, 119. [6] Page 240. [7] In Punchard's Hist. 327; and Works, ii. 7. [8] Surv. part i. 93. [9] In Han. ii. 182. [10] Conv. Serm. 66.

POWER *of churches cannot be given away, nor taken from them.*—Samuel Mather, in his Apology,[1] says: "All jurisdiction ... should be confined to particular churches, in whose hands our Saviour hath left it. Nor may any particular churches ... deprive themselves of this power; for, in so doing, they would deprive themselves of a great trust. For, unless they have and keep this jurisdiction within themselves, they cannot faithfully discharge various other duties which are required of them by Jesus Christ, their lawgiver." Speaking in opposition to juridical power in councils, he says:[2] "The powers and privileges of particular churches are sacred things, by no means to be slighted and undervalued, nor to be left to the mercy of any classes, councils, synods, or general meetings." Owen, in his nature of a Gospel Church, chap. v.,[3] shows that church power is of such a nature that no essential part of it can ever be delegated. Hooker, in his Survey,[4] says: "It is not lawful for churches to give away their power, nor for others to take it from them." The principle on which all these assertions are based is, that the exercise of this power is the duty of the members themselves, and so cannot be devolved on others. — See Punchard's View, 108, 123, 142.

[1] Page 20. [2] Page 128. [3] Works, xx. 440. [4] Part i. 250.

PRACTICE *of the apostles the rule of church government.* — Goodwin argues this,[1] from the commission of Christ, "teaching them to observe all things whatsoever I have commanded you," with the title, preface, and matter of the Book of the Acts. The practices recorded in the Acts are evidently noted as hints and examples. These same practices were introduced into other churches: Paul mentions the offices of deacons and elders, as the command of Christ, in 1 Tim. iii. The apostles refer churches to their example. And, again, our Saviour, his apostles, and all the expounders of the moral law, thus argue from examples.

[1] Ch. Gov. 22—26.

PRAYER *prescribed unlawful.* — The supplication to King James I.[1] argues largely, and in some points conclusively, against the lawfulness of such prayers, especially in the Liturgy of the English Church, which "perverts the right use of Scripture." Robinson, in his Apology,[2] shows that the apostles did not use any set forms of prayer, and that the Lord's Prayer is not a model of any set form of words, but of the spirit of a prayer. (See LORD'S PRAYER.) Lord Say, in his Speech in Parliament,[3] says: "This is that which I am not satisfied in, that a certain number of men should usurp to themselves to form certain prayers and forms for divine service, and, . . . under the name of the church, enjoin them upon all persons, upon all occasions to be used, and none other." Cotton, in his Reply to Ball,[4] argues that a read prayer is no more his prayer than a read sermon is his preaching. He also says,[5] "A set form of prayer, prescribed to me for my prayer, maketh it to me a will-worship." Increase Mather, in his Lawfulness of Common Prayer Worship, &c. maintains[6] that its origin is popish and heathenish;[7] that it violates the word of God, by omitting some words, and putting others in their stead; and[8] that it advances the Apocrypha before the Holy Scriptures.

[1] In Han. i. 115, 116. [2] Ib. 375, 376; and Works, iii. 21—26. [3] Ib. ii. 134. [4] Ib. 158. [5] Ib. 162. [6] Page 2. [7] Page 13. [8] Page 14.

PRAYER *prescribed, may it be lawfully joined in?* — Lord Say, in his Speech in Parliament,[1] maintains that it may be with those who do not hold it indispensable. So hold all Congregationalists, in distinction from rigid Separatists. The Common Prayer Unmasked maintains the negative, from the name, matter, and original of it; the ridiculous manner of using it, and the evil effects of it.

[1] In Han. ii. 134, 135.

PRAYER *prescribed unprofitable.* — Jacob's Church, in their Confession, art. xxi.,[1] say: "Every form of prayer prescribed by men is not absolutely nor simply a sin; yet . . . it is not so profitable, but rather hurtful, in many cases of it, as making holy zeal and other gifts of the Spirit in many to languish." The Apologetical Narrative says:[2] "We practise, without condemning others, what all sides do allow, public prayers by ministers out of their own gifts." Cotton Mather[3] shows that "Christ never provided a prayer-book, but a Bible, for his people."

[1] In Han. i. 299. [2] Ib. ii. 225. [3] Rat. Dis. 48—51.

PREACH, *who may?* — Lord King, in his Inquiry,[1] shows that, in the ancient churches, laymen preached by leave of the bishops; and he quotes a letter from Alexander, bishop of Jerusalem, and Theoclestus of Cæsarea to Demetrius of Alexandria, defending this practice in the case of Origen, who, at the desire of the bishops, preached and expounded the Scriptures, though (in his language) not yet in holy orders. Hooker's Survey[2] asserts that a man may preach as a gifted Christian without pastoral power. Dr. Stephen Moore, preacher to parliament,[3] and the Savoy Confession,[4] maintain the same doctrine. Eaton and Taylor, in their Defence,[5] say: "Gifted men, not ministers, may preach." Acts xi. 19; viii. 14. The Army Scruples[6] assert that all men may read the Scriptures, and apply the sense for edifying. They that were scattered abroad, and went everywhere preaching the word, were not all ministers. The apostles "never forbade any to preach, but her that preached by the spirit of the devil;" and rejoiced when Christ was preached, even of envy. There is no difference between exhorting and preaching. If two persons may exhort each other, then a greater number may do so. The petitioners of the church and town of Woburn to the General Court[7] deny that it always requires a council to determine whether a man may preach. In 1630, there was no minister in the First Church in Boston; and Governor Winthrop, Mr. Dudley, and Mr. Nowel, the ruling elder, carried on the religious service.[8] John Milton, in his Treatise on Christian Doctrine,[9] says "the apostolical institution did not ordain that a particular individual, and he a stipendiary, should have the sole right of speaking from a higher place, but that each believer in turn be authorized to speak." He adds:[10] "Women are, however, enjoined to keep silence in the churches." The Apology of the English Church at Amsterdam[11] says: "Discreet, faithful, and able men, (though) not yet in the ministry, may preach the gospel and the whole truth of God." A sermon was preached in Plymouth, Mass., and printed in England, 1622, and reprinted in Boston, 1724, and Plymouth, 1785, by Robert Cushman, who was no minister.[12] — See APPROBATION *to preach;* LICENSE; PROPHESYING.

[1] Part ii. 14, 15. [2] Part iv. 33. [3] In Han. iii. 96. [4] Ib. 546. [5] Page 118. [6] Pages 3—13. [7] Hist. Soc. Col. series iii. vol. i. 40. [8] Eliot, Biog. Dict. 176. [9] Vol. ii. 203. [10] Ib. 204. [11] Page 37. [12] Eliot, Biog. Dict. 143.

PREACHING, *God's means of salvation.* — Goodwin has devoted the first chapter of his seventh book on Church Government, to show that preaching, in distinction from mere reading the word, is God's instituted appointment for the salvation of the hearers; arguing it from various Scriptures.

PREACHING, *is it lawful to hear, from Christian errorists?* — Robinson's Posthumous Treatise [1] was written on purpose to establish the affirmative of this question. It should be noted that this was the dividing point between the Congregationalists and the rigid Separatists. Roger Williams first broke with the churches in the Bay, because they would not acknowledge their sin in having heard the Episcopal ministers in England.

[1] In Han. i. 447—461; and Works, iii. 353—378.

PRELACY *does not prevent schism.* — John Milton [1] shows that it was not set up for this end, and accomplishes quite the contrary of preventing it.

[1] Treatise against Prelacy, in Works, i. 100.

PRESBYTERY, *what.* — In the Nonconformists' Directory [1] it is said: "There ought to be, in every particular church, a presbytery, which is a consistory, and, as it were, a senate of elders." The Independents in the Westminster Assembly [2] declare that the word occurs but three times in the New Testament, without any distinction of greater or less, as consistory, classis, synod, &c.; and the Scriptures hold out no such distinction of presbytery.

(See Elders, *ruling*.) The word *elder* means simply an old man. Dr. Stiles[3] says: "However fond they (our fathers) were of the power of presbyteries in the church, they were very opposite to the powers of classes, councils, and synods out of the church." Their idea (i.e. that of those who held to the rule of presbytery) was that of government by the bench of ruling elders in the church, and had no resemblance but in name to the rule of presbyteries, by way of appeal from church-sessions.

[1] In Neal's Puritans, ii. 440. [2] In Han. ii. 491, 492. [3] Conv. Serm. 60.

PRESBYTERY, *use of.* — Davenport, in his Apologetical Reply,[1] says: "The church commits those things to the presbytery which it cannot commodiously do by itself." Wise, in his Vindication, everywhere contends that it is necessary to the liberty of the brethren; not having yet discovered that his own favorite principle of pure church democracy would do away the whole need of presbytery, in the sense in which it was held by the advocates of a mixed church government.

[1] Page 241.

PRESBYTERY, *supposed power of.* — Cotton, in his Constitution of a Church,[1] defines it to be "to call the church together, and deliver the counsel of God to them with authority; to prepare matters for the church's hearing, and to propound and order them in the assembly; to administer ordination and the censures; and to dismiss the assembly with a blessing in the name of the Lord." Cambridge Platform[2] ascribes to it the same power, together with that of being moderators, and also examining candidates for admission and for office. — See ELDERS.

[1] In Han. ii. 156. [2] Page 40.

PRESBYTERY, *church has power over.* — Richard Mather maintains[1] that there is a presbytery in every church by its elders, but that the church has the ultimate and controlling power over them. Cambridge Platform[2] gives great power to elders; but, giving the church power to censure and depose one, it subjects them, necessarily, to an appeal to the whole body; they only ruling for the sake of order, and not as lords.

[1] Ch. Gov. and Ch. Cov. 49. [2] Chap. x. sec. 6—11.

PRIESTS, *ministers are not.* — See MINISTERS, *not successors of Jewish priests.*

PRINCIPLES *of Congregationalism.* — See CONGREGATIONALISM, *epitome of principles of.*

PRIVATE JUDGMENT, *right of.* — Neal[1] makes this one of the leading points of difference between the Puritans and Conformists, at the time of the separation, viz. "the natural right of every man to judge for himself, and make profession of that religion he apprehends most agreeable to truth, so far as it does not affect the peace and safety of the government they live under." This ground has always been defended by Congregationalists, and assailed by their opponents. — See Hanbury, i. 41, 53, 124, 171; ii. 47.

[1] Hist. Puritans, i. 108.

PROFESSION *of faith.* — Cambridge Platform[1] asserts that this should be made by members on their admission, and that nothing hinders that it should be made on their being received from other churches. — See CONFESSION OF FAITH; CREEDS; MEMBERS, *removing*.

[1] Chap. xii. sect. 5, 6.

PROPHESYING, *ordinary, i. e. expounding the word.* — In 1618 John Robinson published his "Plea for Prophesying, or Speaking after Sermon, in Reply to Mr. John Yates his Monopoly."[1] Punchard adds: "This practice was continued many years by the Leyden and Plymouth Church, and probably laid the foundation for the religious conference-meetings now so common among Congregationalists." In the Appendix to Mr. Perkins,[2] he says, such as are out of office are to feed the flock in the exercise of prophesying, which is proved — By examples in the Jewish church, Luke ii. 42, 46, 47; iv. 16, 18. Acts viii. 4; xi. 19—21; xiii. 14—16; xviii. 24—26. By the commands of Christ and his apostles, Luke ix. 1; x. 1. Rom. xii. 9. 1 Pet. iv. 10, 11. 1 Cor. xiv. 1. By prohibiting women, not extraordinarily inspired, to teach in the church; herein liberty being given to men their husbands, and others. By the excellent enas which by these means are obtained. Ainsworth, in his Communion of Saints,[3] says: "All men have not only the liberty, but are also to desire, that they may prophesy, i.e. speak to the church to edification, which is to be coveted rather than other spiritual gifts." Robinson advocates the same in his Answer to Helwisse.[4] Jacob's Church Confession, art. xviii.,[5] says: "We believe that the sober, discreet, orderly, and well-governed exercise of expounding and applying the Holy Scriptures in the congregation, by the apostle called *prophesying*, and allowed by him to every other understanding member of the church but women, is lawful now, convenient, profitable, yea, sometimes very necessary also in divers respects." Johnson, in his Christian Plea,[6] shows, touching the divers use of men's gifts, that they may be used either in office or out of office, Rom. xii. 6—8. Hanbury has[7] a long list of controversial works on this point. Goodwin shows[8] that by ordinary prophesying is meant "speaking out of the word to men's instruction. In 1 Cor. xiv. 1—3, prophesying is taken in opposition to gifts extraordinary, and is put for the ordinary expounding of the Scriptures; the word *prophesy* being not taken always to foretell, but also to declare, as Exod. vii. 1." Owen, in his Duty of Pastors and People, chap. vii.[9] shows that private Christians have a right to make known whatever is revealed to them out of God's word, and, if called in Providence, to preach the gospel. Cotton Mather[10] shows that in his time meetings for this purpose were kept up at private houses, after the manner of conference-meetings at the present day. Winthrop[11] cites prominent instances of the performance of this duty in the New England churches. So Letchford, in his Plain Dealing;[12] and Upham, in the Appendix to his Dedication Sermon.[13] Gov. Bradford's Letter[14] quotes Robinson's Apology, page 45: "First, in all churches . . . let the order of prophesying be observed, according to Paul's institution. Unto this are to be received, . . . yea, even of the multitude, who are willing to confer their gift, received of God, to the common utility of the church." Pierce, in his Vindication of Dissenters,[15] says Archbishop Grindal wrote the queen a letter in defence of prophesyings, for which he was confined to his house, and sequestered six months. Cotton Mather asserts[16] that the custom of asking questions after sermon, which had become the occasion of many contentions, underwent the condemnation of the Synod of 1637. — See PREACH, *who may?*

[1] In Han. i. 354—358; and Works, iii. 287; and Punchard's Hist. 343. [2] Punchard's Hist. 353; and Works, iii. 432, 433. [3] In Han. i. 281. [4] Ib. 261; and Works, iii. 134. [5] Ib. 298. [6] Ib. 317. [7] Ib. 356, note. [8] Ch. Gov. 279. [9] Works, xix. 43—47. [10] Rat. Dis. 192. [11] Vol. i. 91, 92, 130. [12] In Hist. Soc. Col. series iii. vol. iii. 75. [13] Page 52. [14] In Young's Pilgrims, 422. [15] Page 95. [16] Magnalia, ii. 446.

PROPHESYING *regulated by teaching officers.* — Robinson, in his Answer to Helwisse,[1] says: "The officers, after their ordinary teaching, exhort to the use and exercise of the like liberty (moving and propounding questions, and exhorting the people), and so, as there is occasion, open and explain things obscure and doubtful, reprove things unsound and impertinent, and so order, moderate, and determine the whole exercise. In this, I suppose, it appears unto all men that the officers govern." After what is quoted from the Appendix to Mr. Perkins in the last article, he adds: "This exercise is to be performed after the public ministry by the teachers, and under their direction and moderation, whose duty is, if any thing be obscure, to open it; if doubtful, to clear it; if unsound, to refute it; if imperfect, to supply what is wanting, as they are able." In his Apology,[2] he shows that they who speak should do it to edification, and first be allowed by the judgments of ministers and others. Cotton, in his Constitution of a Church,[3] says, after prophesying by the ministers, "if the time permit, the elders may call on any other of the brethren to speak a word of exhortation to the people." Welde, in his Answer to Rathband,[4] argues that it is not preaching with authority, and must not be practised by those not invited by the elders. So Goodwin and Nye, in their preface to Cotton's Keys.[5] Hubbard says[6] inaccurately, as we see above from Cotton's own hand, that prophesying was never practised in any of the churches except Plymouth; Cotton being jealous of it. Mitchell, in his Guide,[7] seems to feel great horror about lay-preaching, yet confesses it difficult to find where the "forbidden joint" lies; but, on the whole, concludes that it consists in an ordinary layman or a theological student taking a text, and making a formal discourse.

But he does not inform us whether the sin consists in the text or the formal method, or the theologico-chemical compound. Laymen, he admits, may pray, exhort, read, and comment on the Bible, warn the impenitent, reprove sin, and address a promiscuous assembly; but they must not preach. — See APPROBATION; LICENSE; PREACH, *who may?*

[1] In Punchard's Hist. 338; Han. i. 261; and Works, iii. 135. [2] In Han. i. 382; and Works, iii. 55. [3] In Han. ii. 156. [4] Ib. 316, 334. [5] Page 9. [6] Hist. Mass. 65. [7] Pages 273—277.

PULPIT *controlled by the minister.* — Mitchell, in his Guide,[1] reasons well on the right of a pastor, while he continues such, to the control of the pulpit untrammelled by the people.

[1] Pages 158, 159.

RECOMMENDATION, *need of.* — Cambridge Platform[1] states, that members unknown, and removing for a time, need letters of recommendation; and those permanently removing should have letters of dismission. Cotton Mather asserts[2] that pastors usually gave letters of recommendation to persons travelling, but admitted to occasional communion any who had any living testimony of their having been communicants in any of the reformed churches. See DISMISSION; MEMBERS.

[1] Chap. xiii. sect. 8, 9; and chap. xv. sect. 2. [2] Rat. Dis. 136, 137.

REPENTANCE *of offenders, how manifested.* — The True Description of the Visible Church[1] says the repentance of the party must be proportionate to the offence, namely, if the offence be public, public; if private, private; humbled, submissive, sorrowful, unfeigned. Cotton Mather[2] affirms that it is sometimes sufficient to confess before the church. Dr. Hopkins[3] maintains that it must always be public; because the offender, by his transgression, put out his light before the world. — See EXCOMMUNICATION, *public.*

[1] In Punchard's Hist. 371, 372. [2] Rat. Dis. 144. [3] Syst. ii. 360.

REPENTANCE, *churches judges of its genuineness.* — Goodwin[1] shows that this is indispensable to avoid gross imposition of offenders.

[1] Ch. Gov. 200.

REPENTANCE, *if manifested, may a church still exclude a flagrant offender?* — Owen, in his Nature of a Gospel Church, chap. x.[1] answers this question in the negative, unless they may reject whom Christ receives. The end of discipline is already attained.

[1] Works, xx. 560.

RESISTANCE *to oppression lawful.* — This was the doctrine of the separation, and of all the Independents; else Congregational churches had never outlived the storm of persecution. Bridge, in his Truth of the Times Vindicated (Answer to Fearne),[1] shows the correctness of this doctrine in the pending struggle with Charles I. He shows that the first source of civil power under God is in the whole people; that God appointed government, and left the children of men free to set up any way and form of government, still making the people the first receptacle of civil power; that people oppressed have other "remedy than crying and tears" (denied by his opponent), though "war is the worst of evils, and not to be undertaken but to prevent *gravissimum malum.* We say, if the prince do not perform his trust, the people may look to their own safety." Secretary Cooke alludes, on the scaffold, to his Monarchy No Creature of God,[2] and says the monarchists will be ashamed to oppose it. He assumes that monarchical government is no creature of God, and that the execution of the late king was one of the fattest sacrifices Queen Justice ever had. In Mr. Mayhew's Sermon to the West Church, Boston, on Lord's day after, Jan. 30, 1750,[3] he confutes the doctrine of passive submission to all who would bear rule. He shows that the duty of subjection to the higher powers is founded solely on their being the ministers of God for good to the people; and that, when governments fail to do this, it is duty to resist. Pierce, in his Vindication of Dissenters,[4] affirms that it is a doctrine of the church of England, that the magistrate is not upon any account whatever to be resisted. Dr. Ames, in his Cases of Conscience, says:[5] "War in the Scriptures is reckoned among the heaviest of God's judgments," but "is not always unlawful; . . . if so, . . . it had never been allowed of God in the Old Testament. . . . John Baptist exhorted soldiers not to cast away their arms, but to use them rightly." Bridge, in his Sermon to the Volunteers of Norwich and Great Yarmouth, says,[6] if parliament may send one sergeant-at-arms for one transgressor, they may send a thousand for a thousand such. Burroughs, in his Sermon to Parliament,[7] says: "When men in authority command any thing of their own wills, which is no law, it is not authority which doth command it. In this case, there is no resisting authority at all." Taylor, in his Vindication of Dissenters,[8] says: "We would not swallow their doctrine of passive obedience and non-resistance, as they stated it, in all cases whatsoever. . . . Why did not the bishops plead for it, when the Prince of Orange was coming over? We should not then have had the name of a Protestant Church, nor the shadow of an English parliament. If I can honestly help it, I will never, never be a slave to Kirk or Keysar." Withers, in his History of Resistance in the Church of England, shows that they have always held such resistance lawful. And he asserts[9] that the late Lord Chief Justice Holt, at the abdication of James II., maintained that "he that hath a trust, acting contrary, is a disclaimer of the trust." He maintains[10] that *exousia* means lawful power, to resist which is a damnable sin. "'Tis sin to resist the mayor in the lawful execution of his office; but, should he fall to cutting throats and firing houses, . . . he may be resisted." Paul's doctrine of non-resistance to the powers that be is limited, like Christ's, to resist not evil. Bradbury, in his Sermon entitled the Ass and the Serpent (from Gen. xlix. 15, 18), says:[11] "The foundation of all passive obedience is laid in stupidity." And[12] "God may deliver us up to the will of evil men; but to say that he would have us deliver ourselves up is to blaspheme his empire." He represents Issachar as stupidly crouching under burdens, when he had power to resist them. He shows[13] what they got who threw themselves into the hands of the tyrant Sennacherib, and says:[14] "There is nothing, in any one doctrine of Christianity, that will tie up the hands of an injured people. He that hath tasted that the Lord is gracious must have pity to the desolations of mankind: he cannot endure to see that nature marred by a tyrant that hath been honored by a Saviour. . . . As the kingdom of Christ extends itself, it will proclaim liberty to the captives." In the preface to his Lawfulness of Resisting Tyrants, he says: "If a prince break the fundamental laws that secure the rights and liberties of his people, 'tis just for them to take their remedy." He adds,[15] the people have a right in themselves to dethrone a tyrant. And[16] "David could say, 'there is no wrong in mine hand' while there was a sword in it." [17] They that out of weakness were made strong put to flight the armies of the aliens. "They bathe their sword in heaven, and it takes a celestial edge." In his Non-resistance Without Priestcraft,[18] he says the Scriptures state the case in this view: If God hath given us no capacity of resisting a tyrant, we must submit to it. If he hath, it is throwing away his favor not to use it. There is nothing ties the hands of an injured people but necessity. No law of God ever did make them slaves. Davenport, in his Royal Edict for Military Exercises, says:[19] "Without arms, and the exercise of them, the Commonwealth cannot be safe from dangers without. Neither God's power, nor his purpose, nor his promise, secures any man in the neglect of means. He did not feed with manna in Canaan." Mr. Emerson in his election sermon, entitled Piety and Arms, says:[20] "War between states is justified for the same reasons" as self-defence between individuals. Mr. Fish, in his Art of War Useful and Necessary, says[21] the art of war is lawful when it serves the defence of human rights, and not when it serves the purposes of sordid ambition. He proves from several considerations the absolute necessity for a Christian people to learn the art of war, even from the command, Thou shalt not kill. If we do not use means to preserve life, we are accessory to its destruction. The art is none the less useful because abused. Corbet, in his Principles and Practices of Several Nonconformists,[22] says: "When men's commands counteract the commands of God, it is God and not man that must have the pre-eminence in our obedience." Cotton Mather, in his Sermon to an Artillery Company,[23] says: "God is the God of armies, but is never called the God of thieves or the God of murderers." In his Discourse to Part of the Soldiers engaged in the Just War against the Northern and Eastern Indians, he says: "Gentlemen, it is the war of the Lord you are engaged in." R. Williams, in his Bloody Tenet,[24] says: "It is necessary with civil and earthly weapons to defend the innocent and rescue the oppressed." Samuel Adams exclaimed, on the 19th of April, 1775: "This is a glorious day for America."[25] Mr. Davenport preached about the time of the arrival of the pursuers of the regicide judges, from Isa. xvi. 3, 4. "Bewray not him that wandereth; let mine outcasts dwell with thee," &c.[26] Hugh Peters led a brigade into Ireland, and came off victorious.[27] Dr. Emmons[28] says: How many have believed in passive obedience and non-resistance because it was practised (?) under the law! Robert Hall, in his Village Preaching,[29] shows that there will be resistance to penal laws when they do not harmonize with public sentiment, nor approve themselves to conscience. — See GOVERNMENT, *civil.*

[1] In Han. ii. 190—197. [2] Ib. iii. 564. [3] In Appendix to Neal's Puritans, ii. 527—540. [4] Page 304. [5] Page 184. [6] Page 18. [7] Page 32. [8] Pref. i.—xii. [9] Page 19. [10] Ib. 23. [11] Page 3. [12] Ib. 8. [13] Ib. 12, 13. [14] Ib. 20. [15] Page 2. [16] Pages 9, 11. [17] Page 22. [18] Page 4. [19] Page 8. [20] Page 14. [21] Page 6. [22] Page 9. [23] Page 18. [24] Page. 34. [25] Eliot's Biog. Dict. 10. [26] Ib. 150, *et al.* [27] Ib. 374. [28] Vol. v. 439. [29] Works, ii. 191—199.

RESTORATION *of penitent offenders.* — Lord King,[1] after detailing the horrors of an ancient excommunication, shows how the penitents were restored, after a most abject humiliation, in amazing contrast with our Saviour's direction, And if he repent, forgive him; and Paul's, Ye ought to forgive him, lest such an one be swallowed up with much sorrow.

[1] Enquiry, part i. 125.

REVEREND. — Owen, in his Nature of Schism,[1]

speaks disparagingly of the title, saying that he had valued it little, since he considered that saying of Luther: *Nunquam periclitatur religio nisi inter Reverendissimos.* — See D.D.

[1] In Han. iii. 472.

SABBATH *a proper time for church discipline.* — Ainsworth, in his Reply to Johnson,[1] says: "The church judgments are the Lord's works, not ours; therefore fittest to be done on the Lord's day. . . . All churches baptize on the Sabbath, and excommunicate on the Sabbath: why should not the case be heard, as well as judgment executed, on that day?

[1] In Han. i. 251.

SABBATH-SCHOOLS. — The Rev. T. Robbins, D.D., in his Address at Williams College, p. 40, says that the earliest, of which he has seen an authentic account, was at Plymouth in 1669. — See INTERMISSIONS, *Sabbath.*

SAINT, *title of, avoided.* — Hutchinson, in his History of Massachusetts,[1] says the New England settlers never used the appellation of *saint*, to avoid approbation of the Pope and his power of canonization.

[1] Vol. i. 378.

SAVOY CONFESSION. — Mitchell[1] says of the Westminster and Savoy Confessions: "They never had the authority of standards with us, as some have supposed. . . . They were consented to for substance of doctrine by the New England churches. . . . They were never, to my knowledge, set up as standards, and made of the like authority with us, as confessions are with other communions. . . . They have the authority of *truth* with us, so far as they may agree with the Bible. . . . They have no other authority than this. The same may be said of our *Platforms:* they are lights which all are free to use or not as they please." — See AUTHORITY, *human, discarded;* PLATFORMS, *of what authority;* SCRIPTURES *a sufficient guide to order.*

[1] Guide, 55, 56.

SCHISM, *what.* — Owen, in his True Nature of Schism,[1] says that, "in its ecclesiastical sense, it denotes difference of mind and judgment, with troubles ensuing thereon, amongst men met in some one assembly, about compassing a common end or design." The arbitrary definitions of men, with their superstructures and inferences, we are not concerned in. He shows[2] that the definition of the word is *rending.* We hear nothing of schism in Scripture, save in the case of the church in Corinth. It refers to causeless disputes among brethren, and not to refusing subjection to bishops, councils, classes, &c. There is no mention of any withdrawing from the church, but not forbearing and forgiving one another. Withdrawing is not schism; nor is refusing to hold communion, nor even departure from a church, provided it be done without a variance, judging and condemning others. He shows that the Independents are willing to walk with the church of England in all things where their light will afford mutual peace. In his Review of the Nature of Schism,[3] he says it is impossible that a man can be a schismatic but by virtue of his being a member. And,[4] "Schism consists in division in a church, and not in separation from it;" and this is what the apostle dehorts from in the Epistle to the Corinthians, the only place where schism is mentioned in the Bible. Davenport, in his Apologetical Reply,[5] argues that schism sometimes means unjust secession from a church, 1 John ii. 19 (?), and sometimes contention in a church, 1 Cor. xi. 18. He shows[6] that secession is sometimes occasioned by injurious dealing of others. Hall's Puritans and their Principles[7] shows that it is not schism to break away from churches, but to make divisions in them. Taylor, in his Vindication of Dissenters,[8] shows that it is the church of England which causes schism, by cutting off all who affirm that there is any thing wrong in the Common Prayer or the Thirty-nine Articles. The preface of Defence of Mr. Henry's Enquiry into the Nature of Schism says that it consists, not in separation from communion, but in violation of love and charity. Rev. C. Turner, in his Anniversary Plymouth Sermon,[9] says: "If the church of England was schismatical in leaving Rome, we could heartily wish they had carried their schism to a greater length." In the Troubles in Frankfort,[10] Calvin's definition of schism was asserted to be a cutting off from the body of the church. Mr. Whittingham answered, "that he would prove that definition to be false, . . . and none of Calvin's; for if every cutting off from the body should be schism, then you and all who have once sworn to the Pope, and now have refused him, are schismatics."

[1] In Han. iii. 439. [2] In Works, xix. 122—127, and 222, 225. [3] In Han. iii. 444. [4] Ib. 454, 455. [5] Page 26. [6] Ib. 27. [7] Page 279. [8] Page 118. [9] Page 20. [10] Page 57.

SCRIPTURES *a sufficient guide to order.* — Punchard[1] says this principle was early lost sight of, and has never been fully regained. He asserts, however,[2] that, between the ninth and the thirteenth centuries, there were various bodies of dissenters who maintained that the Scriptures are an infallible and sufficient guide to the church of Christ; and that he has given his church no authority to make laws for the government of his people, but only to execute such as he has given in his word. He shows the difference between the Court Reformers and the Puritans to be substantially this: The one held the absolute right of the prince to determine rules and ceremonies; the other, that nothing should be required which was not deducible from the Scriptures, and no church officers be allowed which are not recognized in the New Testament. Goodwin[3] shows that there is much in the New Testament purposely written for the government of the churches, and the Scriptures are perfect in whatever they undertake to do, while they afford us direct rules on the subject. Cartwright, in his Controversy with Archbishop Whitgift,[4] maintained, in opposition to Whitgift, that the Scriptures are not only a standard of doctrine, but of government. The same doctrine is distinctly stated in the Nonconformists' Directory;[5] in Jacob's Church Confession, art. ii.;[6] Johnson's Treatise on the Reformed Churches;[7] and the Apologetical Narrative of the Independents in the Westminster Assembly.[8] Burton, in his Answer to Prynne's Twelve Considerable Questions,[9] says: "The Scriptures hold forth to us but only one form of church government and discipline, which ought not to be altered according to the diversity of human laws, as you affirm." So, too, Burrough's Irenicum;[10] Bartlett's Model.[11] The Congregational Union of England and Wales say, in their Principles of Church Order:[12] "The New Testament contains, either in form of express statute, or in the example and practice of the apostolic churches, all the principles of order and discipline requisite to constituting and governing Christian societies." Cambridge Platform [13] says: "The parts of church government are all of them exactly described in the word of God, . . . so that it is not left in the power of men, officers, churches, or any state in the world, to add, diminish, or alter any thing, in the least measure, therein." Hooker, in his Survey,[14] holds nearly the same language, and adds: It is not in the power of man to appoint an officer or an ordinance in his church. So Samuel Mather, in his Apology.[15] Hall, in his Puritans and their Principles,[16] quotes from the present good Bishop of Connecticut, commiserating those "who have the Bible alone for their standard of faith;" but a reviewer insists that it may yet be as well to hold on to the Bible till the good bishop provides us with something really better. Ames, in his Marrow of Sacred Divinity,[17] says: "Ministers ought not to do any thing in the church which they have not prescribed to them in the Scriptures." See the Third Petition of the Exiles and others to King James, on his Answer to the First Petition, in Han. i. 113; Mauduit's Case of Dissenting ministers, quoted under art. CREEDS; Dr. Kippis's, also ib.; Punchard's View, 30.— See GOVERNMENT, *church;* CHURCHES, *instituted bodies;* LEGISLATION.

[1] Hist. 39. [2] Ib. 109, 234, 235. [3] Ch. Gov. 13, 14, 16, 27. [4] In Neal's Puritans, i. 123. [5] Ib. ii. 440. [6] In Han. i. 294. [7] Ib. 315. [8] Ib. ii. 224. [9] Ib. 388. [10] Ib. iii. 115. [11] Ib. 242. [12] Ib. 599. [13] Chap. i. sect. 3. [14] Part i. 5, 6. [15] Pages 2, 3. [16] Page 59. [17] Page 155.

SEALS, *what.* — Congregationalists agree that the seals of the covenant are only Baptism and the Lord's Supper.

SEALS, *may a church authorize others than teaching elders to administer?* — This has ever been a disputed point. The Savoy Confession, chapter on Institution of Churches, art. xvi., says:[1] "But where there are no teaching officers, none may administer the seals, nor may the church authorize any to do so." With this agrees Hooker.[2] Watts, in his Foundation of a Christian Church,[3] says: "The church may appoint private members to administer seals rather than to neglect them. So taught Samuel Mather. — See BAPTISM, *who may administer it?* LORD'S SUPPER, *may any but ordained ministers administer?* MINISTERS, *may they administer seals where they are not pastors?*

[1] In Han. iii. 547. [2] Survey, part iii. 9. [3] Works, iii. 222.

SEALS, *all members have a right to.* — Hooker[1] shows that even the members of the church of Sardis had this outward right.

[1] Survey, part iii. 10, 11.

SEPARATION, *what.* — The Answer of the Independents in the Grand Committee of the Westminster Assembly[1] says: "If the purest churches in the world should impose, as a condition of receiving the Lord's Supper, any one thing which tender consciences cannot join in; if they remove from these churches, and have liberty from a state to gather other churches, this is no separation." John Howe[2] archly compares the ideas of some on this subject to the case of "a humorsome company, who should distinguish themselves by wearing a blue or yellow girdle, and call themselves mankind." So he thinks of those who style themselves "*The church,*" and the rest "Separatists."

[1] In Han. iii. 49. [2] Letter concerning Stillingfleet's Sermon, Works, 179.

SEPARATION *may not be schism.* — Barrowe and Greenwood, in their Answer to Giffard,[1] retort, that what would affix the blot of schism on them for separating from the church of England, would affix the same on the church of England for separating from the church of Rome. Johnson uses the same argument in his Treatise of Some Things which concern the Reformed Churches.[2] The Saints' Apology[3] says: "Luther made a separation from the external communion of all the churches in the world; . . . yet none but Papists, or such as long for a captain to lead them back again into Egypt, will accuse him of having made a schism; . . . for he separated, not from believers, but from unbelievers." Burton tells Prynne,[4] that John the Baptist (?), and even Christ himself, gathered churches out of the Jewish church. Owen, in his Nature of Schism,[5] says: "When a man's leaving the ordinary communion of any particular church for his own edification to join with another . . . is proved to be schism, I shall acknowledge it." Neal, in his History of the Puritans,[6] says: "There may be separation from a true church without schism, and schism within a church without separation." Cambridge Platform[7] quotes Dr. Ames's judgment, and says: "In this case, for aught we know, it passeth without exception. . . . If any, wronged with unjust vexation, or providing for his own edification, or in testimony against sin, depart from a church where some evils are tolerated, and join himself to another more pure, yet, without condemning of the church he leaveth, he is not therefore to be held as a schismatic, or as guilty of any other sin." — See AFFINITY; MEMBERS; SCHISM.

[1] In Han. i. 53. [2] Ib. 312. [3] Ib. ii. 232, 233. [4] Ib. 398. [5] Ib. iii. 444. [6] 1 Preface, xi. [7] Preface, xi.

SEPARATION, *reasons of.* — The Low Country Exiles[1] make the following objections to the church of England: "The whole land being received into the church; retaining the Popish clergy and prelacy, and the rest of the rabble, which they received from the Romish apostacy, about forty Popish offices being, at this day, in the church of England, not appointed by Christ in his Testament; the inferior clergy being unlearned, and cannot preach at all, and live in servitude of the bishops; the administration which is imposed on all; . . . they have gathered their service-book *verbatim* out of the mass-book." Robinson, in his Answer to Hall,[2] shows that the church are required to be separate from the world, and the English church have not made such a separation: "We have chosen, by the grace of God, rather to separate ourselves to the Lord *from it,* than *with it* from him." He enumerates[3] the Romish practices in the English church, and[4] says: "Where truth is a gainer, God, who is truth, cannot be a loser." So he quails not before the assertion of his opponent, that "whoremongers and murderers shall abide an easier answer than separation."[5] In his Apology[6] he represents the hierarchal government as overtopping by head and shoulders the Pope, the head only being cut off, upon whose shoulders some would place the civil magistrate; and that the field was, under the most severe penalties, purposely sown with tares.

[1] In Han. i. 93. [2] Ib. 187, 188; and Works, iii. 406. [3] In Han. i. 191—199; and Works, iii. 409—418. [4] In Han. i. 202; and Works, iii. 419. [5] Asserted in Han. i. 186; and Works, iii. 404. [6] In Han. i. 385.

SEPARATION, *cause of, in persecution to enforce conformity.* — The seeming little importance of the ceremonies has often induced the plea, that the Separatists ought to have conformed, and saved themselves from so much trouble, and the church of England from division. This they would have gladly done, had their consciences allowed, and had they not been required to swear belief in what they firmly disbelieved. Hooper objected to being made a bishop in the usual habiliments, because the common people would worship the garments, as they had been taught to do by the Papal priesthood. For this he was sent a prisoner to the Fleet.[1] The persecutions of Elizabeth threw those of Mary into the shade. They commenced with enforcing the acts of the queen's supremacy, of uniformity in common prayer, and the establishment of the Court of High Commission.[2] Then[3] we may see the successive steps of her demands, part of which were, the sacrament to be received kneeling; unleavened bread alone allowed; the wearing of copes, surplices, and square caps, by the ministers, which were all considered by the reformers as tending to idolatry, because the people had been required to adore them, and the posture of kneeling at the sacrament had been enforced as an act of adoration to the "breaden God." Elizabeth declared that she cared not for their consciences; but outward conformity she would have, or she would "hew them into shape." Passing over the many thrilling scenes that intervened, there passed, in 1592–3, the act which required every person above the age of sixteen to go frequently to the Episcopal Church, or abjure the realm; and if he returned, to suffer death without benefit of clergy. At this time, the prisons were full of persons confined and dying there for nonconformity. But, on the passing of this act, the doors were thrown open, and those who had chosen rather to die in prison than do violence to their consciences were permitted to go into banishment. Here was the origin of the Low Country Exiles, many of whom eventually became the planters of America, — an origin which promised something, and under God has accomplished wonders.[4] In 1604 the royal proclamation of King James I. declared all to be excommunicated, *ipso facto*, who should affirm that the Book of Common Prayer contained any thing repugnant to the Scriptures; that any part of the thirty-nine articles were superstitious or erroneous, or such as he might not "with a good conscience subscribe unto," with divers other points, equally and vitally important, and closing with, "or shall affirm that there are, within this realm, other meetings . . . of the king's born subjects than such as are established by law, that may rightly challenge to themselves the name of true and lawful churches."[5] In such circumstances, what could conscientious dissenters do? Ministers were required to swear to the royal supremacy over all matters civil and ecclesiastical; and there was no other alternative for them than perjury on the one hand, and separation, with imprisonment, exile, or death, on the other. It was under these circumstances that the Robinson Church went to Holland, amid every legal and illegal persecution, even parents and young children being separated by an armed band; and thus, through much tribulation, entered the kingdom of heaven.[6] Neal, in his Puritans,[7] informs us, that, in the early part of Elizabeth's reign, the rubric which declared that, in kneeling, no adoration was intended to any corporal presence of Christ in the bread, was expunged. Mr. Choules tells us, on the authority of Dr. Price,[8] that it was easy to tell the number of martyrs that Popery led to the stake, but no other than the Omniscient Being is competent to reveal the secrets of Whitgift's dark and loathsome prison-house; and the martyrdom of these prisoners was not one jot less wicked or cruel than that which Gardiner and Bonner practised. See a description of some of their sufferings in ib. 235—243. — See KNEELING; HABITS; CEREMONIES; PERSECUTIONS *for Congregationalism.*

Punchard's Hist. 207; and Neal's Puritans, i. 52—58. [2] Punchard's Hist. 228. [3] Ib. 229—243. [4] Ib. 293—295. [5] Ib. 310—312. [6] Ib. 314—322. [7] Vol. i. 76. [8] Note to ib. 236.

SEPARATION, *when required; how long to be forborne.* — Welde, in his Reply to Rathband,[1] quotes the Answer to the Thirty-two Questions: "When a man must himself conform to corruptions, then his standing is unlawful." Ainsworth, in his Communion of Saints,[2] says: "The saints should bear one another's infirmities and diversity of judgment, especially for the present, till the truth can be tried out either among themselves, or by the help of other churches, which was the practice in the apostles' days." Jacob's Church Confession, art. xv.,[3] says: "We believe, concerning mixtures of the open profane with some manifest godly Christians in a visible church, that what soul soever, in such a state, desireth to be in safety, ought, with all diligence, to leave that spiritual society." Owen, in his Nature of a Gospel Church, chap. i.,[4] argues that we should withdraw from a church where there is that which endangers the edification or salvation of the soul. Punchard, in his History,[5] shows from Robinson's Researches, that Tertullian and Privatus separated from the churches with which they were once connected, on account of the innovations in them. Watts, in his Foundation of a Christian Church,[6] shows the right to separate from even true churches. He says: "The churches must not be turned into prisons." Cambridge Platform[7] makes the just occasions for removal from churches to be, — if a man cannot remain without sin; personal or general persecution; or want of subsistence. Robert Hall, in his Terms of Communion,[8] says if communion with a Christian society cannot be had without compliance with rights and usages which we deem idolatrous and superstitious, or without a surrender of that liberty in which we are commanded to stand fast, we must, as we value our allegiance, forego, however reluctantly, the advantages of such a union. Lobb, in his True Dissenter,[9] says: "Those that are persuaded of the sinfulness of the terms ought not to communicate with the imposing church." — See next article.

[1] In Han. ii. 326, 327. [2] Ib. i. 284. [3] Ib. 298. [4] Works, xx. 366. [5] Page 48. [6] Works, iii. 227. [7] Chap. xiii. sect. 4. [8] Works, i. 290. [9] Page 130.

SEPARATION, *when condemned.* — The Saints' Apology[1] condemns all separation from the invisible church, "which cannot be done but by denying the faith," but commends separating from corruptions. Cambridge Platform[2] says: "To separate out of contempt of holy fellowship, for covetousness, or want of love, . . . or what . . . should be tolerated, . . . is unlawful and sinful." Burton, in his Rejoinder to Prynne's Reply,[3] says: "We separate from none we know to be true churches. If they would give us leave, in their communion, to protest against those corruptions which we think defile them, we should not scruple." Hall, in his Puritans and their Principles,[4] shows that Robinson was against separating from any churches of Christ, only from the national constitution and government of the English church. Robinson also maintained this in his Answer to Helwisse.[5] Robert Hall, in his Terms of Communion,[6] says: Divisions among Christians, especially when it proceeds to a breach of Christian union, is so fraught with scandal, and is so utterly repugnant to the genius of the gospel, that the whole Christian world have agreed in regarding it as an evil, on no occasion to be incurred but for the avoidance of a greater, — the violation of conscience.

Whenever by receiving we must sanction what the word of God condemns, we must come out. This justifies the separation from Rome, and from the church of England. The Low Country Exiles, in their Letter to Junius,[7] say: "We are persuaded that separation should not be made from any church, either rashly or at all, so long as we may remain with sound faith and consciences." In the Answer of the New England Elders to the Nine Positions,[8] it is said of those "who withdraw themselves from an able and faithful ministry as no ministry of Christ, and from godly congregations as no churches of Christ, because of some corruptions, from which, through want of light, not love of truth, they are not thoroughly cleansed, — *against such we have ever witnessed.*"

[1] In Han. ii. 232. [2] Chap. xiii. sect. 5. [3] Page 47. [4] Page 221. [5] In Punchard's Hist. 335; and Works, iii. 105. [6] Works, i. 334. [7] In Han. i. 139. [8] Ib. ii. 26.

SEPARATION *not made by Congregationalists.* Congregationalism, as Contained in the Scriptures and Explained by the Platform,[1] shows that "the churches of New England did not separate from the church of England, but were driven out by persecution." Owen, in his Nature of Schism,[2] says: "Unless a unity can be fixed, our departure cannot be proved." He maintained that he did not belong to the Bishop of Oxford, because he had never consented to, and so he did not separate from him; that if the bishop had a flock there, which he would attend, he should be glad of his neighborhood. He denies the charge[3] that he "unministers their ministers, and unchurches their churches," but does not thence justify and own their way, wherein they differ from the Congregational ministers of England. He disclaims the advocacy of any Independentism thus unchurching any true churches, while he advocates the peaceable proceeding of any people of God to join in the ordinances of Jesus Christ, reforming abuses, &c. Prince, in his Chronology,[4] quotes from Baillie, showing that Robinson was at first a separatist, but was brought to greater moderation by Dr. Ames and Mr. Parker, and became a principal overthrower of the Brownists and the author of Independency. (See BROWNISTS; INDEPENDENTS.) The Brownists in Leyden would hardly hold communion with Robinson; but Robinson held occasional communion with the Reformed churches.[5] Elder Brewster required no declaration of separation from the church of England.[6] Young in his Chronicles of the Pilgrims,[7] says: "Robinson was always against separation from any of the churches of Christ." Gov. Bradford, in his Answer to Lyford's Charge, denied that they were Brownists, or, like those sectarians, renounced the church of England.[8] Joshua Scottow, in his Narrative of the Planting and Training of the Massachusetts Colony, says:[9] They did not close with the hierarchy, . . . and were not with the rigid separation. See quotation from Neal's History of New England, in article CONGREGATIONALISM, *what.*

[1] Page 8. [2] In Han. iii. 442, 443. [3] Ib. 464. [4] Page 87. [5] Ib. 87. [6] Ib. 89. [7] Page 388. [8] Eliot Biog. Dict. 81. [9] Page 19.

SEPARATISTS. — It will be perceived by perusing a few of the preceding and the next succeeding articles, that this word was used in different senses, and is a somewhat comparative term. The Episcopalians usually called all the dissenters Separatists; whereas our fathers usually applied the term to those who denounced the English Episcopal congregations as no churches, and refused all spiritual communion with them. Francis Johnson, one of the most rigid Separatists, published, in 1608, Certain Reasons and Arguments, "proving that it is not lawful to hear or have any spiritual communion with the present ministry of the church of England."[1] The Letter accompanying the Answer to the Nine Positions shows that the New England churches were not rigid Separatists. They separated not from the churches of England as such, but from the corruptions which they conceived to be left in these churches; yet they left the few rigid ones among them "to the liberty of their own judgments without molestation."

[1] Han. i. 167. In a note may be seen how he was opposed by William Bradshaw.

SEPARATISTS, *semi.* — This was the title which our Congregational fathers at length received, when the distinction between them and the Brownists came to be better understood. H. Jacob, in his Plainer Opening of a Divine Beginning, &c.,[1] says; "I acknowledge that in England are true visible churches, . . . such as I refuse not to communicate with." Robinson, in his Treatise on Communion,[2] maintains that we must separate from the wrong things connected with the hierarchy, but not from the private communion with Christians in the church of England; and,[3] as Hanbury asserts, "goes on to show that the Lord's people may not communicate with them, in regard to government ecclesiastical, and the ministry thence derived." He asserts substantially the same things in his Posthumous Treatise,[4] showing that he cannot, however, communicate with their church order and ordinances, without being condemned of his own heart. — See SEPARATION; CATHOLICISM; COMMUNION.

[1] In Han. i. 230. [2] Ib. 259; and Works, iii. 105. [3] Ib. 264. [4] Ib. 451, 458; and Works, iii. 353—378.

SERMONS, *length of; studied; written.* — Cotton Mather[1] shows that the primitive preachers usually confined themselves to about an hour. He, moreover, says: "If they hear preachers boasting that they have been in their studies but a few hours, on a Saturday or so, they reckon that such persons rather glory in their shame. Sudden sermons they may sometimes admire from their accomplished ministers, when the suddenness has not been a chosen circumstance.... The best ministers in New England ordinarily would blush to address their flocks without preparation." (See MINISTERS *should give themselves wholly to their work.*) Speaking of preaching with notes, he says: "No doubt, some sermons are the better composed for it; but it will require good management if they be not the less affecting.... It was very little practised or approved of in this country till of latter years."

[1] Rat. Dis. 57—61.

SIGN OF THE CROSS.—R. Parker, in his Treatise against Symbolizing with Antichrist, especially in the Sign of the Cross, says[1] the cross, surplice, &c., they say, "being consecrate to his service, they become things of God, yea, parts of God, whose worship is the worship of God." He answers the Episcopal argument, that they had changed the sign of the cross, saying:[2] "Of the things that may be changed from their abuse, the sign of the cross is none."—See CEREMONIES; HABITS.

[1] Page 8. [2] Ib. 25.

SINGING.—Cotton tells Ball[1] that the Psalms cannot be sung without the help of music, natural music at least; and so this is ordained of God, according to the light of nature, and does not fall under the general negative precept of forbidding human inventions in the worship of God; but that this does not apply to a devised form of prayer. I. Chauncy[2] says: "Some do scruple singing in a mixed congregation; but it ought not to be scrupled, any more than the church's prayers,... and they that ought not to be excluded from hearing the word, ought not to be excluded from praising God for the word of his grace." In a Brief Discourse concerning Regular Singing, published in Boston in 1725, it is argued forcibly that there is a necessity of skill in vocal music. There was a great contention between minister and people on the subject of singing, in the church in Bradford, in 1722.[3]

[1] In Han. ii. 161. [2] Divine Inst. Cong. Churches, 87. [3] Eliot, Biog. Dict. 449, 450.

STANDING COMMITTEES. — Mitchell[1] notes the fact that many of our churches have standing committees, and cautions that they be not invested with presbyterial powers, saying that he knows of instances where they are invested with such powers. "To commit the *watch* and *discipline* of the church to a permanent committee, . . . is not Congregational." — See SCRIPTURES *a sufficient guide to order;* OFFICERS, *God's gift, and not to be multiplied.*

[1] Guide, 142, 143.

SUBSCRIPTION was first enjoined in 1571, and universally enforced in three articles in 1584. The articles were — the queen's sovereign authority; that the Book of Common Prayer, and ordination of bishops, priests, and deacons, contains nothing in it contrary to the word of God; and the articles of religion, agreed upon by the bishops and archbishops in 1562, are all agreeable to God.[1] The Offer of a Conference by the Deprived Ministers in the reign of James I.[2] states, that, in about one year, three hundred ministers have been turned out of Christ's service, only for refusing such ceremonies as have their life, breath, and being from Popery; and such a subscription as the like hath never been urged under a Christian magistrate. The Canons of Convocation[3] denounced excommunication, *ipso facto*, upon all who refuse to subscribe, that the church of England is a true, apostolical church; that the Common Prayer contains nothing contrary to the word of God; that none of the thirty-nine articles are superstitious; or that there are other churches than the Episcopal, and the like.

[1] Nichols's Plea, in Han. i. 3, 4. [2] Ib. 126. [3] Ib. 121, 122.

SUCCESSION *in churches.* — This is shown by Mather and Tompson, in their Answer to Herle,[1] to be *essential*, that is, confined to the question of obeying God; not *ministerial*, i. e. by direct line from the apostles. "Such a principle would unchurch all Christian communities."

[1] In Han. ii. 170.

SUCCESSION, *ministerial, interrupted or uninterrupted?* — Barrowe, in his Refutation of Giffard,[1] shows in substance, that if those who hold it uninterrupted hold the church of Rome a true church, then are they, on their *own* principles, schismatics; if otherwise, then their ordination is through a false church. Neal[2] shows that the bishops in the English church, all save one, declined, when the act of uniformity was passed, and were deprived; and Archbishop Parker was consecrated by some who had been deprived in the late reign; so that the Papists made him and his coadjutors doubt the validity of their own ordination, till Parliament confirmed it about seven years after. English bishops, therefore, have their succession through deposed bishops, and *ex post facto* Parliament laws; and not in an unbroken chain from Peter, with authority to bind and loose. All this, to say nothing of the question, through which of the contemporaneous rival Popes they received the transmission of apostolical succession. — See BISHOPS; ORDINATION *by ministers; by direct succession.*

[1] In Han. i. 58. [2] Hist. Puritans, i. 78.

SUSPENSION, *pastoral condemned.* — Barrowe, in his Description of a False Church,[1] says: "They add new devices of their own, as pastoral suspension from the sacraments." Baillie[2] says: "The Independents denied the lawfulness of all such censures."

[1] In Han. i. 46. [2] Ib. ii. 256.

SUSPENSION, *church; is it lawful?* — Mitchell[1] thinks that it is, though he says that some doubt it. The compiler is of that number. Johnson, who was presbyterially inclined, is the only writer among the early Congregationalists, who, to my knowledge, advocated it. (See his views in Hanbury, i. 318.) The authors of the Congregational Manual[2] make it a kind of probation, and what the church may do pending the trial of one accused. Isaac Chauncy[3] says: "Suspension is unwarranted by Christ, and the member has a right to church privileges, till fully convict before the church. Hence, brethren sin greatly in withdrawing from communion on account of the supposed sin of a member." — See Letchford, Punchard, and Upham, in article ADMONITION.

[1] Guide, 104. [2] Page 36. [3] Div. Inst. Cong. Churches, 129.

SUSPICION *not a ground for discipline.* — Bradshaw, in his English Puritanism,[1] says: "By virtue of these keys, they are not to examine and make inquisition into the hearts of men, nor to molest them upon uncertain fame, but to proceed only upon open and notorious crimes." — See ACCUSATION; DISCIPLINE.

[1] In Neal's Puritans, i. 249.

SYNODS *not juridical.* — Goodwin has the fourth, fifth, sixth, and seventh chapters of his fifth book on Church Government against the subordination of synods to exercise jurisdiction. He argues against it, "because there is no warrant for it in the Scriptures. . . . It would introduce a foreign ecclesiastical power in every state and kingdom. . . . There is no standing rule by which it should be managed. . . . It requires representations arising from representations, for which there is no Scripture warrant. . . . And Acts xv. and the analogy of Matt. xviii. do not prove such a subordination and juridical power." The Savoy Confession[1] disallows the power of all stated synods, presbyteries, &c., over particular churches, but admits that such assemblies may meet to give advice, without exercising any jurisdiction. Jacob's Church, in their Confession, art. v.[2] say: "On occasion there ought to be a consociation . . . of churches, but not a subordination, or surely not a subjection, . . . under any higher spiritual authority, only Christ and the Holy Scriptures." Paget[3] complains of Davenport, saying: "This is no more than Mr. Jacob did give to classes and synods for counsel and advice." Davenport, in his Power of Congregational Churches, says:[4] "God hath enjoined entireness of jurisdiction . . . to a particular church. Who, then, shall sunder it from such a church, and place it in classes and supreme judicatories where God never put it?" Richard Mather, in his Answer to Rutherford,[5] shows that the parallel does not hold, so that classes have jurisdiction over churches, as the Jewish Sanhedrim had over the synagogues. And[6] he shows that other churches may not take power even from an erring church; for who gave them this authority? Welde, in his Answer to Rathband,[7] shows that delegating representatives to do church work does not imply a jurisdiction in them over the churches. The Desires of the Independents[8] craves "that congregations may not be brought under the government of classical, provincial, or national assemblies, in respect of ecclesiastical jurisdiction." Bartlett's Model[9] inquires, "Where do these men read, in all the New Testament, of these greater assemblies, with authoritative power?" Secretary Cook, in his What the Independents Would Have, says:[10] "I shall tell you in one word what will content every Independent in England, viz. — an entire exemption from the jurisdiction of prelates and ecclesiastical officers other than themselves shall choose." Milton, in his Answer to Salmasius,[11] says: "They which we call Independents are only such as hold that no classes or synods have a superiority over any particular church." Cotton, in his Keys,[12] shows that, if it be granted that a synod may better understand the rule of proceeding, they are further removed from the knowledge of the facts and of the spirit of the offender than a particular church; and [13] that the church is not now to be under tutors and governors, as in her Jewish nonage. Cambridge Platform [14] says: "It belongs to synods and councils to determine controversies of faith and cases of conscience; to clear from the word holy directions, for the worship of God and good government of the church; to bear witness against maladministration in any particular church, and to give directions for the reformation thereof; *not to exercise church censures, in way of discipline, nor any act of church authority and jurisdiction, which that (the Antioch and Jerusalem) presidential synod did forbear.*" In the Appendix to Hooker's Survey,[15] those who sent the book to be printed after his death say: "This is known to be the author's mind, which the whole discourse doth manifest, that he denies a synod hath juridical power, . . . and grants a synod that hath power of counsel." Samuel Mather, in his Apology,[16] urges to find where Christ placed the final termination of causes, and rest the case there. He says: "It is to be hoped the brethren in these churches . . . will never think of placing juridical power in councils and synods." He shows [17] that a synod or consociation is not a "church of churches, as Mr. Cotton once spoke, though he *afterward spoke and thought otherwise.*" Increase Mather, in his Disquisition on Ecclesiastical Councils,[18] shows that a New England Platform synod cannot exercise any authority; that the nature and power of synods is only decisive, not authoritative, i. e. judicial. He cites Norton's Catechism: "Ques. What is the power of a council? Ans. To declare truth, not to exercise authority." Davenport, in his Apologetical Reply,[19] states the power of a classis to be, not juridical, but ministerial, stewardly, like that of ambassadors. Cotton Mather, in his Ratio Disciplinæ,[20] says: "The synods of New England pretend to no juridical power, nor any supremacy, but what is merely instructive and suasory. . . . When they have done, all the churches are at liberty to judge how far their doctrine is to be followed." This from one of the most stringent men of his day, and one who in early life had strongly advocated the "Proposals" for a standing juridical council. (See Wise's Quarrel of the Churches Espoused, p. 79.) Hubbard, in his History of Massachusetts,[21] though he complains of both the church and civil government as too popular, still asserts it as a principle of the New England Churches, that "there is no jurisdiction to which particular churches ought to be subject." The Synod of 1637 refused to name the persons who held the doctrines they condemned, because that assembly (not owning themselves to have any judicial power) had not to do with persons, but doctrines only.[22] Isaac Chauncy, in his Divine Institution of Congregational Churches,[23] affirms that synods and councils are not juridical.—See Appeals; Councils.

[1] In Neal's Puritans, ii. 179. [2] In Han. i. 295 [3] Ib. 542. [4] Ib. ii. 64. [5] Ib. 180. [6] Ib. 184. [7] Ib. 300. [8] Ib. iii. 44. [9] Ib. 240. [10] Ib. 251. [11] Ib. 372. [12] Page 17. [13] Ib. 106, 107.

[14] Chap. xvi. sect. 4. [15] Part iv. 43. [16] Page 128. [17] Pages 19—24. [18] Pages 29, 30. [19] Page 229. [20] Pages 172, 173. [21] Page 184. [22] Winthrop's Journal, i. 238. [23] Page 136.

SYNODS, *of whom constituted.* — Cambridge Platform[1] says: "Synods are to consist both of elders and other church members, endued with gifts and sent by the churches, not excluding the presence of any brethren in the churches." Increase Mather[2] maintains the right of private members to sit in councils and synods, because all agree that they sit not by virtue of their office, but their delegation, and have no rule of jurisdiction. — See COUNCILS, *of whom composed.*

[1] Chap. xvi. sect. 6. [2] Disq. Ecc. Councils, 25—28

SYNODS *not legislative.* — Watts, in his Foundation of a Christian Church,[1] shows that a synod has no power to make laws; if it had, then others might be deputed to act in larger synods, and they may depute all to the Pope, "so we are at Rome ere we are aware." Punchard, in his History,[2] shows that general synods, with legislative power, were actually one great source of corruption to the primitive churches. — See COUNCILS; LEGISLATION.

[1] Works, iii. 220—222. [2] Page 21.

SYNODS, *for what purposes lawful, and for what unlawful.* — Goodwin, in his Church Government,[1] argues that it is lawful to ask needed advice even of synods assembled for further and unauthorized purposes, but not to subject ourselves to them. He says: "If any new cases fall out, let the churches advise;" but maintains that they have no need to advise where they know the rule and the facts, much less to subject themselves to synod, where God has made their duty plain and positive. Davenport, in his Power of Congregational Churches,[2] says: "If a church, when first gathered, had complete power, and by the rising up of other churches should be deprived of it, then the neighborhood of churches should not be a benefit but a disadvantage to them. If the church want sufficient light or consent for the sentence, then they are to seek light from others, by their consent and counsel; but still preserving the power of censure in the church, where Christ placed it." Mather and Tompson, in their Answer to Herle,[3] say: "Let a church have entireness of jurisdiction before she hath neighbors, and be deprived of it when God sends such neighbors, and by this means she sustains a loss by having neighbors." They show that a synod should not be a power of government and jurisdiction, but a power of doctrine. The matter debated in Acts xv. was a matter of doctrine, therefore it was no matter of jurisdiction. The Synod at the College in New England, about 1643, decided that consultative synods are very comfortable and necessary for the peace and good of churches.[4] The Reasons of the Independents in the Grand Debate in the Westminster Assembly[5] say: "The scope and end of Acts xv. were to give satisfaction to the offended brethren at Antioch, and dogmatically to declare their judgments in a difficult case of conscience, not to put forth any act of juridical power upon any." In their Dissent from the Propositions of the Assembly concerning Synods,[6] they say: "Although we judge synods of great use for finding and declaring truth in difficult cases, . . . yet . . ." And they go on to give reasons at length against subjection to synods. So Burroughs, in his Irenicum;[7] Savoy Confession;[8] Cotton's Keys;[9] Cambridge Platform;[10] Higginson's and Hubbard's Attestation to the same;[11] and Hutchinson's History of Massachusetts.[12] Cotton Mather, in his Magnalia,[13] says: "The design of the Synod of 1637 was not *jus dare*, but only *jus dicere*." — See book ii. sect. 4, at length.

[1] Pages 139—145. [2] In Han. ii. 65. [3] Ib. 173, 174. [4] Letter from a minister in New England to one in Old England, in Reply to A. S. (Simon Ash), in ib. 343. [5] Ib. 483. [6] Ib. 497. [7] Ib. iii. 111. [8] Ib. 548. [9] Pages 6, 7. [10] Chap. xvi. sect. 1, 2. [11] Ib. 70. [12] Vol. i. 372. [13] Vol. ii. 443.

SYNODS *have no power to excommunicate churches.* Goodwin shows this at length, book v. chapter xi.: "They receive their power to become a church from Christ alone, and he only can remove their candlestick out of its place." So Cambridge Platform, chapter xv. section 2.

SYNODS, *standing, denounced.* — Goodwin,[1] after stating his grounds of dissent from juridical synods, proceeds to answer objections, as that the neighbor-churches have an interest indirectly in the decisions. Ans.: "So have all the churches in the world." In the multitude of counsellors there is strength. He replies: Let them, then, have the use of counsellors only, and we deny it not; men will not go for counsel, unless there be need. Is it inquired, May we not submit to such synods for the sake of peace? Ans.: If it be an indifferent matter, we may submit, but may not submit not to do our own duty, nor give away our own liberty. It is asked, Will it not be better to have a standing council, of whom to ask advice beforehand, and prevent offence? He shows from Jerome that this has been tried, and all at last referred to one man, and so prelacy was set up. Barrowe, in his Discovery of a False Church,[2] denounces their "select classis of ministers, and their settled supreme council." Savoy Confession, chapter on Institution of Churches, article xxvii.,[3] says: "Besides these occasional synods or councils, there are not instituted by Christ any stated synods."

[1] Ch. Gov. 147—149. [2] In Han. i. 46. [3] Ib. iii. 548.

SYNODS, *cautions concerning*. — Cotton, in his Keys,[1] after recommending occasional consociations, councils, or synods, with limited powers, says: "Give us leave to add this caution, — to see that this consociation be not perverted either to the oppression or diminution of the just liberty and authority of each particular church." Davenport, in his Apologetical Reply,[2] urges the same caution, in nearly the same words.

[1] Page 105. [2] Page 225.

SYNODS, *subordination of, denounced.* — See SYNODS *not juridical.*

SWEARING. — See OATH.

TEACHER or DOCTOR, *his office.* — The True Description of the Visible Church, &c.[1] makes it, to build, upon the true groundwork, gold, silver, precious stones; to take special care to keep the church free from errors, revealing the wood, hay, and stubble of false teachers; and to declare his doctrine so plainly, simply, and purely, that the church may grow thereby. Bradshaw, in his English Puritanism,[2] though he makes the pastor the main officer in the church, says: "There should also be, in every church, a doctor to instruct and catechize the ignorant in the main principles of religion." Hooker, in his Survey,[3] says: "Many confine the teacher's work to the school." But he argues that it extends to perfecting the whole body of the church; that, with the pastor, he has a right to administer the sacraments; the aim and scope of the doctor is to inform the judgment, deliver fundamental points of Christian faith, and handle controversies between the church and her adversaries. — See OFFICERS; TEACHER *distinct from pastor.*

[1] In Punchard's Hist. 368. [2] In Neal, i. 249. [3] Part ii. 20—22.

TEACHER, *is his office distinct from pastor?* — Goodwin, in his Church Government,[1] answers the plea that they were one and the same, by insisting that the Greeks used *kai* disjunctively at the end of a disjunctive enumeration, and applies it to Eph. iv. 11. (*Query*, Is the enumeration strictly disjunctive?) Cambridge Platform[2] says: "The office of pastor and teacher appears to be distinct." (See ib. on PASTOR, *his office.*) Johnson, in his Treatise on the Reformed Churches,[3] argues that they are distinct, from Eph. iv. 11; 1 Cor. xii. 5, 6; with Rom. xii. 7, 8. He says that the distinctive particle is used in Eph. iv. 11 in the Syriac translation, which is the oldest. Baillie[4] says: "The Independents were for a doctor in every congregation, as well as a pastor. . . . The absolute necessity of a doctor was, however, eschewed (by the Westminster Assembly); yet, where two ministers could be had, one was allowed, according to his gift, to apply himself more to teaching, and the other to exhortation, according to the Scriptures." Cotton Mather, in his Ratio Disciplinæ,[5] says that, "when there were two ministers to a church, one of them was formerly distinguished by the name of teacher. . . . More lately, the distinction is less regarded; their being mentioned so as they are together in the Sacred Oracles (Eph. iv. 11) pleaded for little short of an identity between them." The distinction has now gone into practical disuse. (See Punchard's View, 80.) I. Chauncy[6] contends that "the pastoral office comprehends the whole ministry of the church; but if, by reason of infirmity, or the size of the church, the pastor is unable to do the whole work, he may have aid or helps,—a teacher to aid him in preaching, or a ruling elder to assist in ruling. He that is called to concur with the pastor in teaching, waits on that service, 1 Pet. iv. 10, 11; and he that is called on to concur with him in ruling is to wait on that work especially." And[7] "a church that hath a pastor and deacon is fully organized, the church requiring no more to edification; the pastoral office containing in it all the teaching and ruling charge, and the deacon's all that concerns the care of the church as to externals." Eaton and Taylor, in their Defence,[8] say: "There must be pastors distinct from teachers." Letchford, in his Plain Dealing:[9] "They generally hold *pastor and teacher distinct.*"

[1] Page 288. [2] Chap. vi. sect. 5. [3] In Han. i. 316. [4] Ib. ii. 217. [5] Pages 42, 43. [6] Divine Inst. Cong. Churches, 61. [7] Ib. 62. [8] Page 69. [9] In Hist. Soc. Col. series iii. vol. iii. 65.

TITHES, *involuntary ones unlawful.* — Jacob's Church, in their Confession, art. xxvi.,[1] say: "We believe tithes for the pastor's maintenance under the gospel are not the just and due means thereof." They, however, assert that they do not deem them unlawful, if they remain voluntary. "And so of other set maintenance established by temporal laws." They recommend that it be done "by voluntary conscionable contributions." The Army Scruples[2] say: "*They* should pay ministers who employ them. . . . They should not be paid by forced tithes." Roger Williams, in his Hireling Ministry None of Christ's,[3] says: "The civil authority cannot lawfully enforce the payment of tithes, nor *prevent* those who choose." — See MINISTERS, *maintenance of.*

[1] Han. i. 301. [2] Page 16. [3] Page 26.

TOLERATION *desired.* — A committee of Presbyterians, in the Westminster Assembly, say,[1] with apparent surprise, that it seems to them "the Independents desire liberty of conscience not only for themselves, but for all men." Mr. Burroughs replied, if they might not have liberty to govern themselves in their own way, as long as they behaved peaceably towards the civil government, they were resolved to suffer, or to go to some other place of the world where they might enjoy their liberty. "But, while men think the civil sword an ordinance of God to determine all controversies of divinity, and that it must needs be attended with fines and imprisonment to the disobedient, . . . there must be a base subjection of men's consciences to slavery, a suppression of much truth, and great disturbances in the Christian world." An Independent writer,[2] in Answer to the London divines, says: "The ministers say, if we tolerate one sect, we must tolerate all. . . . True, . . . and men have as good a right to the liberty of their consciences as to their clothes or estates, no opinions being cognizable by the civil magistrate any further than they are inconsistent with the civil government. . . . Can Bedlam or the Fleet open men's understandings, and reduce them from error?" So he goes on with equal point and truth. Edwards, in his Gangrænæ,[3] classes together "denying the Scriptures and pleading for toleration of all religions." He[4] puts the Independents at the head of all sectaries, because "they were for the toleration of all Christians who agreed in the fundamentals of religion." The ordinance in the time of the Protectorate[5] provides, art. xxxvi., "that none be compelled to conform to the public religion by penalties or otherwise." Art. xxxvii. protects all men in the profession of their faith, and exercise of their religion, "so as they do not abuse this liberty to the civil injury of others, and the actual disturbance of the public peace; provided this liberty do not extend to Popery or Prelacy, or to such as, under profession of Christ, hold forth and practise licentiousness." Considering what Popery and Prelacy had done, it is not strange that the first legislators for liberty did not distinguish between tolerating principles and tolerating overt acts of iniquity. Burton, in his Answer to Prynne, says:[6] "The magistrates may not tolerate open Papacy and idolatry to be set up in the land; but the conscience of a Papist they are no masters or judges of. . . . Evil *actions* he must punish." Baillie, writing from the Westminster Assembly,[7] says: "The Independents had nearly carried a toleration of their way; but the legerdemain, being perceived, was crushed." He says:[8] "They plead for the toleration of other sects as well as their own." (!) Lord Brooke, in his Discourse on Episcopacy,[9] says: "So long as the church, in her church tenets, intermeddleth not with state matters under the notion of religion, I suppose the state is not to interpose." — See two next succeeding articles.

[1] In Neal's Puritans, ii. 17. [2] Ib. 19. [3] Ib. 37. [4] Ib. 38. [5] Ib. 135. [6] In Han. ii. 402. [7] Ib. 547. [8] Ib. 558. [9] Ib. 126.

TOLERATION, *why not universal at first in New England.* — In the work entitled The Independents

Accused and Acquitted, by a member of John Goodwin's Church, it is said:[1] "I suppose it is easier to affirm than to prove that any in New England were imprisoned and banished *merely* for their consciences." Welde, in his Answer to Rathband,[2] denies that "any have been dealt with for dissenting from us in matters of discipline." Katherine Chidley, in her Answer to Edwards (wounding him as with a millstone from a wall), says:[3] "It may be, that there be some there who have taken it upon them to bend men's consciences, as you and your fellows do here." She suggests that "there might be fear, that, upon complaint made for disorder, in suffering the liberty of the gospel there, they might have been sent back, . . . and committed to the same stinking prison here in London, there to have been murdered, as divers of the Lord's people have been of late years." This Hanbury represents as throwing "a blaze of light on their conduct, which seemed to be inexcusable with their principles and profession." Radcliffe, Gardner, and Morton, who had been sent back for misdemeanors, were actually in 1633 petitioning the king and council against them, and representing them as seditious.[4] Besides, most of the Massachusetts Planters had been educated to believe in the necessity of purifying the church with the sword. They had not yet learned that it was lawful to tolerate any who did not hold the essentials of religion; and, even in this, they had advanced beyond almost all who had preceded them since the commencement of the dark ages. Yet there are who seem vexed with them for not learning every thing in an hour. Such persons might as well term the ancient Greeks and Romans besotted savages, because they had no railroads or steamboats, and Newton and Franklin dolts, because they never discovered the magnetic telegraph nor the electro-magnetic light. They wonder that those who had already bared their necks to the halter, and their breasts to the sword, should not have made sure their own execution by retaining within their patent those whose conduct would surely have affixed on them the imputation of doctrines which themselves did not believe, and practices which they could not approve, though they would many of them have gladly tolerated these things if they could. Chimney-corner soldiers of this day would have fought the battle of liberty better than they did. Some, moreover, demand that the principles of Congregationalism should cure all the depravity and Diotrephesian spirit of all who hoist its colors, or take hold of its skirts, or live near where it is professed; forgetting the saying of Luther, "Every man has a little pope in his own belly." But, with all its faults, or rather the faults of its professors, we fearlessly challenge the showing of equal fruits of civil and religious liberty, growing out of any other principles, since the world was made. — See next preceding and next succeeding articles.

[1] In Han. ii. 545. [2] Ib. 298. Ib. 112. [4] Hubbard's History Mass. 153.

TOLERATION, *how far should it be practised by*

a state? — Burroughs, in his Irenicum,[1] says: "The devil must not be let alone because he is got into men's consciences; . . . if a man's error be dangerous to the state, he may be cut off; . . . errorists, who by any means do not serve the state, may be deprived of some privileges." He acknowledges it "hard to cut in the right joint" in this case. The difficulty, doubtless, lay in not distinguishing between mere error and seditious overt acts, as ground for punishment. Hanbury[2] describes at large the doings of the London ministers in the Westminster Assembly against toleration. The case of Roger Williams has been much insisted on, as an instance of the anti-tolerating spirit of our fathers. It, however, needs proof that the main cause was ecclesiastical. Winthrop[3] says the governor and assistants were doubtful of the lawful use of the cross, but condemned the manner of Mr. Williams's proceedings; therefore they wrote to Mr. Downing in England, excusing themselves, expressing their dislike of the thing, and their determination to punish the offenders. As for his Baptist principles being the cause, it was an afterthought. He was converted to these after he went to Rhode Island in 1638, and renounced his connection with the Baptist order in 1639.[4] Dunster and Chauncy, the first two presidents of Harvard College, held, one to believer's baptism only, and the other to immersion. It is, therefore, preposterous to assert that even a supposed leaning of Williams that way could have been the cause of his banishment. "He spoke dangerous words against the patent."[5] Professor Knowles, in his Life of Williams,[6] says: "He was charged with insisting that the charter ought to be returned to the king." This, he says, "would have been very unwise; but we can hardly believe that he would carry his opposition to this unreasonable length." And is it credible, both that this positive testimony was false, and that he was banished for an opposition which was not "unreasonable"? Knowles condemns cutting the cross out of the king's colors, but says: "We have no evidence that Williams advised to it." What, then, are we to think of the accusations of his cotemporaries, which Williams did not deny? Probably Williams would have scorned to have even put them upon the proof of the fact. Knowles believes the true reason of his banishment to have been the doctrine that the civil power had no control over conscience. But this doctrine, though not universal, was no novelty at that time; Professor Knowles to the contrary. He shows[7] that "Cotton and his associates argued that they ought to promote truth and oppose error by all the methods in their power." This was their true error. In the end he gives the righteous verdict, that Williams was unnecessarily scrupulous, and his opponents thought it duty to vindicate what they thought to be truth. He might have added their necessity, from the operations of their enemies with the company, king, and parliament, at the very time that an insult had been offered to the king's colors. Williams himself, in his Bloody Tenet,[8] shows that God's ministers are able to kill "spiritual wolves only with spiritual weapons." Cotton, in his Bloody Tenet Washed,[9] affirms that "fundamentals are so clear, that a man cannot but in conscience be convinced of them, after two or three admonitions." He undertakes to show,[10] that the prosperity of the church is inseparably connected with the civil power. Williams, in his Answer to Cotton's Letter, says,[11] that one of the magistrates, on summing up the case, said: Mr. Williams holds these four things: "1. We have not our land by patent from the king, but the natives are the true owners of it;* and we ought to repent having received it by such a patent. 2. It is not lawful to call a wicked man to pray or swear, as being contrary unto God's worship. 3. It is not lawful to hear any of the ministers of the parish assemblies in England. 4. That the civil magistrates' power extends only to the bodies and goods and outward estates of men, &c." Cotton, in his Answer,[12] denies that these four things were the cause of his banishment, and knows not what magistrate asserted it. The two first, many if not most, of the colony admit; and there are many who hold the two latter, who are still tolerated

* John Q. Adams, in his Plymouth Anniversary Oration, page 23, says: What right has the huntsman of the forest to the thousand miles over which he has accidentally ranged in quest of prey? Shall he not only resist civilization himself, but prevent the cultivation of whole countries? He shows that our fathers fairly bought what they took from the natives. He also demonstrates the same truth, in a masterly manner, in his Second Century Oration at Boston, in Historical Society's Collection, series iii. vol. ix. 196, 197. But not so, as he shows elsewhere in this oration, was the seizing their *cultivated* country, and forcing them beyond the Mississippi, by the present generation.

here. He asserts[13] that "it was for his *tumultuous* carriage against the patent, and his violently withstanding the oath of fidelity." Cotton denies having had a hand in his banishment, but not that the magistrates may punish for sins against conscience. Williams says, in his Answer to Cotton's Letter,[14] that personally he honors and loves Cotton, and speaks of him as, otherwise than his persecuting tenets, an excellent and worthy man. He complains[15] that Cotton addresses him as beloved in Christ, and "denies him a common air to breathe." Cotton was evidently wrong in supposing that men may be civilly punished for the alleged crime of sinning against their own consciences; and Williams, in supposing that he might act against the charter, thereby endangering the charter privileges of his fellow-citizens, and not be molested by the civil law. (For a succinct account of this controversy, see Remarks on the History of Salem, in Historical Society's Collection, series i. vol. vii. Prefix iii.—v.) Upham's Life of Sir H. Vane, the Younger,[16] says: "It was for religious freedom, in a peculiar sense, that our fathers contended. They were faithful to the cause, as they understood it. The true principle of religious liberty, in its wide and full comprehension, had never dawned upon their minds." Callender, in his Historical Discourse,[17] says: "It was not the *peculiar* fault of the people of Massachusetts to think themselves bound in conscience to use the sword of the civil magistrate to open understandings. . . . All other Christian sects acted as though they thought this the very best service they could do to

God." Philip Nye, in his Lawfulness of the Oath of Supremacy, &c.,[18] says: "All men are by nature equal;" yet he argues the right of kings to govern in ecclesiastical affairs. He asserts[19] that no ruler, civil or ecclesiastical, has power to enforce the soul, and still[20] maintains that the magistrate is keeper of both tables.* Wisner, in his History of the Old South Church, says no instance existed in the days of our fathers, without an established religion. Instead of railing at them for their blindness, we should wonder that they were so far advanced. How natural to say, Go, plant your principles somewhere else. He quotes Magnalia, book vii. 24: "Even the Quakers would say, if they had gotten into a corner of the world, and at great toil and charge made a wilderness habitable, on purpose to be there undisturbed in their worship, they would never love to have the New Englanders come among them, and disturb their public worship." This the Quakers did in the New England Congregations:[21] women came into the congregations; some blacked, others naked. These were overt acts, which would ensure civil interference at this day. Our fathers, in their act against them, assign as a motive a fear that the "scenes of Munster might be repeated here." Alden Bradford, in his Plymouth Anniversary Oration,[22] asserts that the severities of persecutions were never known in New Plymouth Colony. Still there were then severe laws against Quakers. (See Plymouth Colony Laws.) Even in Rhode Island, the rights of Protestant citizens were not

* Our fathers saw not the full consequences of their tenets.

extended to Catholics till 1783.[23] * Cartwright, on Toleration,[24] argues that "the blasphemer and stubborn idolater ought to be put to death." He argues at length for the perpetuity of Moses's law; and that for a magistrate to tolerate a seducer was to undo the word of God where he sat in judgment. Ward, in his Simple Cobbler of Agawam, argues that it is treason against God to tolerate error in fundamentals. Locke, in his Letters on Toleration,[25] shows that the argument, founding the right of magistrates to enforce religion on that of parents and instructors to prescribe and enforce studies, fails; because this right continues only during minority of children. He shows[26] that, if one magistrate may use force, then all may use it, and ought to use it, to enforce the religion they believe to be true. He asserts[27] that a right to use force in this matter implies that he who uses it is an infallible guide. And, if he ought to use it to induce to believe, then still more to induce to embrace the true religion. He says:[28] To punish for rejecting the true religion, the magistrate must judge what the true religion is. So, if the true religion is every where the national, they must punish differently in different countries. Again:[29] "You tell us that, by the law of nature, magistrates are obliged to promote

* Professor Gammell, in his Biography of Roger Williams (in Sparks's Am. Biog. ser. ii., vol. iv. 210), sets down the clause excepting Catholics from citizenship, as an interpolation of the Rhode Island Records. He does this on negative evidence. Rev. J. B. Felt has pointed the compiler to the law itself, published in 1744, of which an entire copy is in the library of the Massachusetts Historical Society.

the true religion. What, then, is the Emperor of Peru obliged to do, who was not so much as within hearing of the Christian religion?" — See last two succeeding articles.

[1] In Han. iii. 109—112. [2] Ib. 97—125. [3] Journal, i. 150. [4] Ib. 293—307; and Hubbard, 207, 208. [5] Hubbard, 206. [6] Pages 60—80. [7] Ib. 76. [8] Page 115. [9] Page 9. [10] Pages 10, 11. [11] Page 375. [12] Page 26. [13] Page 27. [14] Pages 367, 368. [15] Page 370. [16] In Sparks's Am. Biog. iv. 147. [17] Page 16. [18] Page 17. [19] Page 32. [20] Page 43. [21] Page 86. [22] Page 10. [23] Repeal of Act of Disability, in Hist. Soc. Col. series iii. vol. v. 243, 244; and R. I. Laws, 1744. 3, 4. [24] Page 4. [25] Pages 161, 162. [26] Page 265. [27] Pages 289, 290. [28] Page 303. [29] Page 399.

TRADITION (*i. e. example*), *apostolic*, *binding*. — Jacob's Church, in their Confession, art. xvii.,[1] say that every ordinance or institution apostolic, out of the Scriptures, is of divine authority.

[1] In Han. i. 298.

TRADITION, *superstitious*. — John Robinson, in his Posthumous Work,[1] represents some as so carried away with their former guides, that they think it half-heresy to call in question any of their declarations or practices. "We must not think that only Pharisees and Papists are superstitious, and addicted to the traditions of the elders and the authority of the church."

[1] In Han. i. 452; and Works, iii. 355, 356.

TRANSLATION. — Hanbury [1] asserts that the Congregationalists complain that King James required the translators to use the old ecclesiastical words; as, for instance, to put *church* for *congregation*, thus making the translation a sectarian one. The Defence of the Petition for Reformation[2] complains that, while the Geneva and former church translation renders Acts xiv. 23, "And when they had ordained them elders *by election*," our new translation leaves out the words "by election;" and that in 1 Cor. xii. 28, where it was formerly *governors*, it is now translated *governments*. So Doddridge *in locis;* see also Dr. Bacon's Church Manual, 21; and for a learned and critical handling of the question, Coleman's Primitive Church, chap. iv. — See ORDINATION, *imposition of hands*.

[1] Han. i. 2, note. [2] Address to the Reader, in ib. i. 131.

TREASURY, *what may be put into it?* — Smith, after his defection, maintained[1] that "they that are without, if they would give any thing, must lay it apart severally for the treasury, and it must be employed to common use." Ainsworth replied, that goods gotten by violence, extortion, murder, theft, or the like evil way, may not be put into the treasury, even though the members of the church do offer them. He supposes that the example of Matt. xxvii. 6, 7, will not bear us out in appropriating to common use all unbelievers' gifts.

[1] Han. i. 184.

TYPES. — Goodwin, in his Church Government,[1] shows that an Old Testament one applies to an institution under the New, just so far as God applies it, and no farther; otherwise we are led away by endless fanciful analogies. — See Dr. Emmons's Sermon on Heb. x. 9, in Works, v. 427.

[1] Page 173.

UNANIMITY, *is it necessary in church acts?* — Welde, in his Answer to Rathband,[1] shows that in the admission of members, if some few be dissatisfied, they used to submit to the rest, and sit down in their acts. Letchford, in his Plain Dealing,[2] says: "In Boston, they commonly rule by unanimous consent, if they can; in Salem, by majorities." Punchard, in his View,[3] says: "It is not common to settle questions of great importance by the vote of a bare majority. A greater degree of unanimity is usually sought, and generally obtained." In a note he informs us, from Rev. A. Carson's Reason for Separating from the Synod of Ulster, that Congregationalists in "Ireland consider entire unanimity indispensable." It may be easily perceived that this doctrine puts a veto into the hands of any ill-disposed member. — See MAJORITIES; MINORITIES.

[1] In Han. ii. 302. [2] In Hist. Soc. Col. series iii. vol. iii. 74. [3] Page 170.

UNIFORMITY, *how far attainable and desirable.* Goodwin, in his Church Government,[1] argues it prejudicial to oblige either to a national or presbyterial uniformity, and oblige, for uniformity's sake, to the same pitch and model that one church should not practise further than another. The apostle's rule is, that, *so far as we have attained*, we should all walk by the same rule. And the churches may establish a common rule among them, so far as they have attained; but, if any be otherwise minded, they should wait till God shall reveal this in its time. Otherwise the churches will grow corrupt, because the greater part is still more corrupt. The general Scripture rule is made in favor of the weak, not against them. The Desires of the Independents[2] argues uniformity attainable, so far as described in Phil. iii. 16; and that, beyond this, all efforts at it will prove perfect tyranny. C. Upham, in his Century Sermon,[3] thinks that uniformity might be lost by a coercive course, if that could be lost which was never gained. Cotton Mather, in his Ratio Disciplinæ,[4] condemns those who, with Phaetonic fury, would set the world on fire to promote it. He quotes Irenæus: "A diversity in lesser matters commends a church persevering in the unity of the faith." Dr. Bacon, in his Church Manual,[5] says: "The only security for uniformity is dead indifference. The only security for brethren that think and inquire is love and liberty."

[1] Page 236. [2] In Han. iii. 64, 65. [3] Page 55. [4] Page 185. [5] Page 177.

UNION, *scriptural, what.* — Dr. Isaac Barrow, in his Treatise on the Pope's Supremacy, published in 1680,[1] shows that it does not consist in being under one government politically, but in union of spirit. Congregationalists agree to these arguments of this powerful Episcopal writer. Indeed, they usually apply all the arguments of Episcopalians against Popery, to prove Congregational principles, as they do those of Presbyterians against Prelacy. Robinson, in his parting address to the Pilgrims,[2] says: "Study union with the godly people of England in all things, where you can have it without sin, rather than in the least measure to affect a division or separation from them." — See note on the efforts of Drury, on this point, in Eliot's Biog. Dict. 342. The original of Norton's letter there referred to, with the signatures, is in the Antiquarian Library, Worcester. — See SEPARATION.

[1] In Han. i. 11, 12. [2] Ib. 394, note.

UNION *of Christians.* — Neal, in his History of the Puritans,[1] shows the happy effects of the meetings of ministers of different denominations in Worcestershire and the West of England during the protectorate, upon general principles, not to meddle with politics nor the subject of the keys. He shows, too, how these meetings were opposed by the bigoted of the various sects. Had Baxter, the prime mover, always thus promoted peace-principles, instead of advocating civil non-resistance, he had done still more good in this contentious world. — See RESISTANCE.

[1] Vol. ii. 137.

UNITY, *church, what.* — Goodwin, in his Catechism,[1] shows it to consist in being of one mind and one heart, though every man must speak as he judgeth, and not prevaricate. Still we must be of one heart, of a heart to draw as close to another as may be, and to drive it as far as truth will bear.

Lord King, in his Enquiry,[2] shows that it does not consist in uniformity of rites and customs, nor of consent to the non-essential points of Christianity; and that whoever undertakes to enforce either of these to promote the unity of the church, only thereby violates the church's unity and concord; but that it does consist "in a harmonious consent to the essential articles of religion." Neander, in his Planting and Training of the Church,[3] strongly intimates the same from the decision of the apostolical assembly at Jerusalem. The Defence of Matthew Henry's Brief Enquiry into the Nature of Schism[4] says: "Moral unity of the church consists in love, not in adherence to the ministry; for this would render it impossible for the laity to reform the churches." Polhill, on Schism, shows that the unity of the church is a divine thing, and does not consist in human rites, liturgy, diocesan Episcopacy, nor the civil laws of magistrates. He says:[6] "In the first or golden age of the church, there was little of ceremony, but much of unity." Sir Edwin Sandys, in his Europæ Speculum,[7] shows the insurmountable obstacles to complete outward unity in his day.

[1] Pages 33, 34. [2] Part i. 156, 158. [3] Page 83. [4] Pages 4—6. [5] Pages 1—23. [6] Ib. 10. [7] Pages 194—210.

UNITY, *when perfect.* — Burroughs, in his Irenicum,[1] says: "The unity of the faith and the perfect man go together, Eph. iv. 13. When that is done, our work is done for this world."

[1] In Han. iii. 123.

USURPATION, *ecclesiastical, to be resisted in the beginning.* — Wise, in his Quarrel of the Churches Espoused,[1] urges the maxim, *Obsta principiis* (Resist beginnings), as a reason for rejecting the famous Juridical Proposals of 1705. These he compares to Aaron's calf (the work of a good man for a bad object), and thinks they should be treated as that calf was, Exod. xxxii. 20. He thinks that the beast with seven heads and ten horns was once just about such a calf, till the potentates of the earth reared it on the choicest royal cows, and at length tipped his horns with iron and shod his hoofs with brass, till few of them dare take it by the horns, it was grown so pompous and furiously mad. Well have Congregationalists, in general, followed his advice. "In deference to some good men" (or their prospective votes), "the proposals were never carried beyond the bounds of mere proposals."[2] So have fared the subsequent proposals, having all died in their birth. The Connecticut Consociationists did not claim to be strict Congregationalists in the beginning,[3] and have ever been divided on the vital question, whether the consociätion has juridical or only advisory power.[4]

[1] Page 138. [2] C. Mather's Rat. Dis. 183, 184. [3] Trumbull's Hist. Con. i. 486. [4] Dr. Stiles's Con. Serm. 74—80.

VETO. — See Pastor, *has he a negative vote?*

VOTERS, *who are, in the church?* — Robinson, in his Apology,[1] argues the privilege to all of voting in church judgments; "by which," he says, "we do not understand, as it hath pleased some contumaciously to upbraid us, to include women and children, but only men, making account that as children by their nonage, so women by their sex, are debarred the use of authority in the church."

[1] In Punchard's Hist. 348, 349; and Works, iii. 43.

VOTERS, *restriction of affected ecclesiastical affairs.* — In 1631, the General Court of Massachusetts "made an order that for time to come none should be admitted to the freedom of the body politic, but such as were church members.[1] In 1646, the subjects of these restrictions in Massachusetts and Plymouth petitioned "that civil liberty and freedom be granted to all English." In 1657, the disaffected endeavored to get redress by claiming their rights to the Lord's Supper.[2] This resulted in the adoption of the Half-way Covenant, by the Synod of 1662.[3] In 1664, the order was repealed; but "the minister was to certify that the candidates for freedom were of orthodox sentiments, and of good lives and conversation." The bearings of these restrictions on the efforts to establish the Half-way Covenant and the Church-membership of the baptized may be learned from Trumbull's History of Connecticut, and Wisner's History of the Old South Church, Boston. — See CONSOCIATIONS, *origin of;* HALF-WAY COVENANT.

[1] Hutchinson's Hist. Mass. i. 30. [2] Wisner's Hist. Old South Church, Boston, 4, note. [3] Ib. page 5.

WAR. — Burroughs, in his Irenicum, says: "The

apostle doth not here (James iv. 1) condemn wars simply. This was the error of the old Manichees, raised up again by some among us (the Anabaptists). There can be no reason given why our civil right to our religion may not as well be maintained by the sword, as our civil right to our houses and lands. This answers all the objections from the practice of the primitive Christians: . . . they never had any civil right to the practice of their religion. The wars meant in the text are contentions, jars, divisions among Christians." He says:[2] "Dividing terms are not broad among the army; . . . soldiers united in love, and hating that which is vile, are exceedingly strengthened in valor. Ever since our armies have been united, God hath wonderfully blessed them. A rare instance, but still a *real* one, in which an army can be cited as a model of a collection of Christians. — See RESISTANCE.

[1] In Han. iii. 116. [2] Ib. 120, 121.

WESTMINSTER ASSEMBLY, *no ecclesiastical authority.* — Neal, in his History of the Puritans,[1] shows that their confession never was adopted by the English Parliament, nor did it become the law of the land; but was forthwith made the test of the kirk of Scotland. Parliament called them to sit,[2] with the express injunction that "this ordinance shall not give them, nor shall they in this assembly *assume* or *exercise*, any jurisdiction, power, or authority ecclesiastical whatsoever." — See SAVOY CONFESSION.

[1] Vol. ii. 41. [2] Ib. i. 458.

WIDOWS, *their office.* — Robinson, in the Appendix to Mr. Perkins,[1] makes it "to afford to the sick and impotent in body, not able otherwise to help themselves, their cheerful and comfortable help." So the True Description of the Visible Church;[2] Cambridge Platform;[3] Cartwright's Answer to Whitgift.[4] This was obviously a very necessary office in the times of persecution, but, so far as I know, is now universally laid aside, as of special origin and institution. The True Description of the Visible Church[5] says they must be at least sixty years of age, &c. Isaac Chauncy, in his Divine Institution of Congregational Churches,[6] says: "And there may be women's helps, called deaconesses." — See Neander's Church History, vol. i. sect. 2, p. 188; Punchard's View, 85. Some suppose the widows to have been taken into the number to be provided for; widows indeed, having none to provide for them; received, both in charity and to promote their usefulness.

[1] In Punchard's Hist. 353. [2] Ib. 369. [3] Chap. vii. sect. 7. [4] Page 191. [5] In Punchard's Hist. 367; and Works, iii. 429. [6] Page 62.

WITCHCRAFT. — The early New England Congregationalists are often stigmatized as having been peculiar in their delusions concerning witchcraft. But the same delusion prevailed all over the Christian world. Scotland, with her semi-infallible kirk, was even then doing more work of the same kind than was done in the New England colonies. The King's Bench in England, with Sir

Matthew Hale at the head, drove forward the same business, and employed a witch-hunter by profession.[1] But, lo! in Essex county, Mass., it is discovered that the supposed ordeal for detecting the guilty may be defective. Judge Sewall, with tears, bewails the wrong he has been superstitiously inflicting on the unhappy accused, condemned, and executed; the world are publicly informed of the discovered error; and the multitude now agree to cast the obloquy on the first discoverers and forsakers of the wrong. And (O shame!) Congregationalists, and some of them in high standing, carelessly perpetuate the obloquy, by commingling their false invectives against the first reformers on this subject with the truthful history of our country. As well might we disparage the sagacity of Columbus, because he was once ignorant of the existence of the Western World. Witchcraft was almost the only subject upon which the Christian world was agreed, till our fathers discovered their own error therein, and led the way which has since been universally followed. A letter from T. Brattle, F.R.S., Oct. 8, 1692,[2] though expressing a disbelief in witchcraft, attributes the matter to Satanic influence; and says it was "proved a slander that more than forty men in Andover could raise a witch as quick as any astrologer." He expressly acquits Increase Mather from being in favor of the prosecutions, and reckons him among those who took the same ground with himself; being dissatisfied with the course pursued. Eliot, in his Biographical Dictionary,[3] art. Calef, Robert, speaks of Increase and Cotton Mather as identified with a defence of the course; an insinuation from which such testimony as the above from Brattle (an opponent of the Mathers') ought for ever to free, — at least the father. J. Moody defended and aided the accused in their escape, at his own peril.[4] Dr. Watts, in a letter to Cotton Mather in 1719—20,[5] cannot believe that the spectral evidence is sufficient for conviction, though he is convinced "that there is much agency of the devil in these affairs, and perhaps there were some real witches too." Even Calef, one of the earliest opposers of the mode of testing witches, seems to have but very confused notions on the subject; sometimes seemingly admitting, and anon denying, special possession. (See his work entitled Wonders of the Invisible World.) Doubtless, ministers were many of them equally confused in their views, in those practically fearful times. Yet it is worthy of note, that the opposers of Mr. Parris, one of the greatest agents in the tragedies, represent his principles as "differing from the opinion of the *generality* of orthodox ministers in the country."[6] This was in 1693. Increase Mather, in his Cases of Conscience,[7] gives many cautions against condemning on insufficient testimony. He inveighs against the trial by water, and reduces the points of evidence to two, viz.: Voluntary confession of sane persons; and two witnesses to the doing of that which none can do but by supernatural power. For a lucid view of the Scripture doctrine concerning witchcraft, see Kitto's Cyclopedia of Biblical

Literature. He demonstrates that it refers to pretended supernatural powers.

[1] Pond's Mather Family, 110—130. [2] In Hist. Soc. Col. series i. vol. v. 61—79. [3] Page 95. [4] Eliot, Biog. Dict. 328, 329, note. [5] In Hist. Soc. Col. series i. vol. v. 202. [6] More Wonders of the Invisible World, 126. [7] Pages 34, 38.

WITHDRAWING *communion; the extent of the power of churches respecting each other.* — Cambridge Platform[1] takes this ground, and asserts that churches have no more power over each other than one apostle had over another. See Upham's Rat. Dis. 143. — See CHURCHES *discipline each other, &c.;* EXCOMMUNICATION, *one church has not power of, over another.*

[1] Chap. xv. sect. 2.

WITHDRAWING *from communion, what have churches to do with those?* — Bradshaw, in his English Puritanism,[1] says: "If . . . offenders will voluntarily withdraw from communion, the church have no further concern with them." The Congregational Manual[2] says of such: "The church may withdraw fellowship from him, and esteem and declare itself discharged from any further watch and care over him." Mitchell[3] holds the contrary, saying: "The gospel knows no such rule; it supposes no separation from the church, but by regular dismission to another church or by excommunication." Yet[4] he quotes approvingly from Saybrook Platform, that the church may simply disown or cease to know him as a member: he having thereby cut himself off from the church's communion, the church may justly esteem and declare itself discharged from any further inspection over him." Owen, in his Nature of a Gospel Church,[5] uses nearly the words last quoted, and says: "Some say that this is enough;" and adds: "It is sufficient for those who own no office-power in excommunication." Owen maintains that the church have further duties to do, which they owe both to themselves and the offender. Isaac Chauncy, in his Divine Institution of Congregational Churches,[6] says of one departing to non-communion, or to communion with another church: "He doth disfranchise and excommunicate himself." He asserts,[7] that, if a member thus withdraw, the church ought to declare, that he, being sinfully departed from them, is no longer under its watch, and is not to return till he has given satisfaction to the church. The Heads of Agreement by the United Congregational and Presbyterian Ministers[8] says: "It may sometimes come to pass, that a church member, not otherwise scandalous, may fully withdraw. . . . He having cut himself off from that church's communion, the church may justly esteem and declare itself discharged from any further inspection over him."

[1] In Neal's Puritans, i. 249. [2] Page 35. [3] Guide, 117. [4] Ib. 116. [5] Works, xx. 558. [6] Pages 116, 117. [7] Ib. 128. [8] In Congregational Order, 257, 258.

WITHDRAWING *to other churches, when deniea a dismission.* — Watts, in his Terms of Communion,[1] asserts, that, if a church refuse to dismiss a member to another church, he may withdraw. — See AFFINITY; DISMISSION; MEMBERS, *may a church receive, without dismission?*

[1] Works, iii. 253.

WOMEN'S RIGHTS. — Robinson, in his Reply to Bernard,[1] enumerates, among their ecclesiastical rights, making profession of faith and confession of sin; saying amen to the church's prayers; singing psalms vocally; accusing a brother of sin; witnessing an accusation, or defending themselves being accused; and, where no man will, reproving the church rather than it should go on in sin. He holds them debarred from voting and ordinary prophesying (i.e. publicly expounding and exhorting), but not from simple speaking. Ainsworth, in his Reply to Clyfton,[2] says: "And although woman, in regard to her sex, may not speak or teach in the church, yet with other women, and in her private family, she openeth her mouth in wisdom, and the doctrine of grace is on her tongue. Miriam was a guide to the women of Israel, and Priscilla helped to expound the way of God more perfectly to Apollos." Robinson [3] advocates the same in his Letter to the Church in London. The Synod in Boston, in 1637, condemned the proceeding of a public meeting, where some sixty or more were present weekly; and one woman took upon her the whole exercise in a prophetical way.[4] Isaac Chauncy, in his Divine Institution of Congregational Churches,[5] says: "Women may not speak or exercise authority in the church." Eliot, in his Ecclesiastical History of Massachusetts,[6] says Cotton would not consent that his wife should make an open confession of her faith, when she joined the church, considering it as against modesty; but she was examined by the elders. John Milton, in his Treatise on Christian Doctrine,[7] after advocating the right of every brother to teach and expound the gospel, adds: "Women are, however, enjoined to keep silence in the churches." See Neander's Church History, i. 104.— See PREACH, *who may?*

[1] In Han. i. 214, and Punchard's Hist. 331; and Works, ii. 215, 216. [2] Han. i. 281. [3] Ib. 450. [4] Winthrop's Journal, i. 240. [5] Page 105. [6] In Hist. Soc. Col. series i. vol. ix. 22. [7] Vol. ii. 204.

WORSHIP, *instituted, a church may not impose additions to.*— Owen, in his Catechism,[1] says: A church may not impose additions to instituted worship. Bradshaw, in his English Puritanism,[2] says: "The Puritans hold it to be high presumption to institute, and bring into divine worship, such rites and ceremonies of religion as are acknowledged to be no parts of divine worship at all." See also his general arguments, proving that the ceremonies imposed upon the Puritans by the prelates were unlawful.[3]

[1] Works, xix. 490. [2] In his Treatise on Worship and Ceremonies, 36. [3] Ib. 51—81.

BRIEF NOTICES

OF SOME OF THE

PRINCIPAL AUTHORS, TREATISES, AND ASSEMBLIES,

REFERRED TO IN THIS DICTIONARY.

ABBREVIATIONS.

In the following notices, —

H. U. . . stands for . . graduated at Harvard University.*
Y. C. . . . . Yale College.
B. U. . . . . Brown University.*
D. C. . . . . Dartmouth College.
W.C. . . . . Williams College.
N. H. . . . . Nassau Hall.

(1) implies that the work thus noted may be found in the —
Library of American Antiquarian Society.
(2) . . . Library of Brown University.
(3) . . . Library of Harvard University.
(4) . . . Library of Boston Athenæum.
(5) . . . Library of Massachusetts Historical Society, Bost.
(6) . . . New England Library, Old South Church, Boston.
(7) . . . Library of the Theological Seminary, Andover.
(8) . . . Commonwealth Library, Boston, State House.
(9) . . . Library of Yale College.
(10) . . . Connecticut Hist. Society's Library, Hartford.
(*a*) . . . Massachusetts Historical Society's Collection.
(*b*) . . . Historical Memorials, by Hanbury.
(*c*) . . . History of Congregationalism, by Punchard.
(*d*) . . . History of the Puritans by Neal.

D. died. æt. aged.

When several figures occur within the same parenthesis, — thus (1, 2, 4, 8), or (3, 1, 2, 4), the first of the series is of the edition quoted in this Dictionary; the rest may be of another edition: in that case, the pages may not correspond with the notes in the Dictionary.

* The present names of these institutions are used in this work.

NOTICES.

ADAMS, HANNAH, a woman of rare literary merit and great worth. D. 1831, æt. 76. History of New England, Dedham, 1799 (1, 3, 4, 9).

ADAMS, J. Q., sixth President of the United States; H. U. 1787. D. 1848, æt. 81. Anniversary Plymouth Oration, Bost. 1802 (1). Oration before the Massachusetts Historical Society (*a*).

ADAMS, SAMUEL, the celebrated revolutionary politician, remarkable for his piety, patriotism, and Puritanism. H. U. 1740. Governor of Massachusetts, 1794—1796. D. 1803, æt. 82.

ADAMS, ZABDIEL, a very respectable minister of Lunenburg. H. U. 1759. D. 1801, æt. 61. Treatise on Church Government, Bost. 1773, maintaining veto power in ministers (1).

ÆRIUS, presbyter of Sebastia, flourished about A.D. 385. He maintained that there should be but one order of the clergy, and was the leader of a sect essentially Congregational.

AINSWORTH, HENRY, one of the exiles to Holland, and teacher of the church in Amsterdam, sustained by Robinson and Brewster. A great, learned, and good, but imperfect man. Arrow against Idolatry (*b*); Answer to Clyfton, Amst. 1613 (1); Answer to Paget (*b*); Controversy with Broughton (*b*); Answer to Smith, Amst.

1609 (1); Communion of Saints, Lond. 1641; Reply to Johnson (*b*).

Alasco, or à Lasco, John, a Polish nobleman. Gathered a church of Polish refugees in London in 1550. Was in great esteem with Erasmus and Peter Martyr; was banished by Mary; returned on the accession of Elizabeth, but could not get his charter for an Independent church re-established.

Allen, William, D.D., formerly President of Bowdoin College, now a resident of Northampton, Mass. American Biographical Dictionary, valuable; Bost. 1832 (1, 2, 3, 7, 8, 10).

Allin, John, first minister of Dedham. A courteous man, full of Christian love, bold against error, a diligent student and good scholar. D. 1671, æt. 71, having been twenty-four years at Dedham. Defence of Answer to Nine Positions (with T. Shepard), Lond. 1648 (1, 6).

Allyn, John, a highly respectable pastor of Duxbury. Ordained 1788. Anniversary Plymouth Sermon, Bost. 1802 (1, 10).

Ames, William, D.D., educated at Cambridge, England; exiled to Holland; Professor of Divinity at the University of Franeker; removed to Rotterdam, and was co-pastor with Hugh Peters. D. 1633, æt. 57. Preface to Bradshaw's English Puritanism, Lond. 1660 (1); Fresh Suit against Human Ceremonies, Lond. 1633 (1, 4, 6); Cases of Conscience, Lond. 1643 (3); Marrow of Sacred Divinity (translation), Lond. 1642 (3).

Ames, William, jun., D.D., son of the famous Professor of Franeker, came to New England when a child. H. U. 1645. Settled co-pastor with his uncle in Wrentham, England, 1648; afterwards ejected. A very holy and excellent man. D. 1689, æt. 65. Legislative Power Christ's Prerogative, Lond. 1656 (1).

Answer of the Divines to His Majesty's Reasons why he cannot Abolish the Episcopal Government (Compiler, *d*).

Answer of New England Elders to Nine Positions, Lond. 1643, a very able work, usually ascribed to the pen of John Davenport, though some have attributed it to Richard Mather (1, 6).

Appleton, Nathaniel, D.D., a distinguished minister of Cambridge, Mass. H. U. 1712; ordained, 1717. D. 1784, æt. 90. Sermon at Ordination of Missionaries, Bost. 1753 (1).

Backus, Isaac, ordained over Congregational Church, Middleborough, 1743; became a Baptist, 1756. D. 1806, æt. 82. An author of considerable merit. History of New England, with special reference to Baptists, Bost. 1777 (1, 2, 3).

Bacon, Leonard, D.D. Y. C. 1820; installed pastor, First Church, New Haven, 1825. A distinguished divine, excelling both in logical and forensic talents. Church Manual, New Haven, 1833; Historical Discourses, New Haven and New York, 1839; exceedingly valuable documents, from which much more valuable matter should have been extracted for this work, had they been seasonably possessed.

Bagshawe, Edward, a respectable lawyer of the Middle Temple; author of Arguments in Parliament against the Canons, for which he was obliged to retire into the country. He appears to advantage in Hanbury, ii. 140—147. Blake notices a minister of the same name, who was so violent, that he was imprisoned for his nonconformity in 1671. *Query*, Was it the same individual?

Baillie, Robert, one of the Scotch commissioners in the Westminster Assembly; a man of great talents. His letters to Spang, in Hanbury, however, show him not very tolerant in his religious views, invoking a Scots army, 15,000 strong, to enforce his arguments. Still he was, doubtless, a very amiable man. D. 1662. Author of a powerful treatise against the Erastians, entitled Aaron's Rod that Budded, &c.; Dissuasive from the Errors of the Times, Lond. 1646 (*b*).

Balch, William, pastor of Second Church, Bradford. H. U. 1724; ordained, 1728. Was disciplined with his church by a neighbor-church in 1743. Council censured the complainants. D. 1792, æt. 87. Vindication of Second Church, Bradford, Bost. 1746 (1, 3).

Ball, John, an English Nonconformist divine, yet greatly opposed to separation John Robinson had a controversy with him on some points, on which he held Robinson to be too great a Separatist. D. 1640, æt. 55.

Bancroft, Richard, D.D. Archbishop of Canterbury, first broached the doctrine of the divine right of Episcopacy. A violent member of the High Commission Court, covetous and cruel. D. 1610, æt. 66.

"Here lies his Grace in cold clay clad,
Who died for want of what he had."

Barrington (Lord), John Shute, a celebrated lawyer, a learned Puritan, and a peer of the realm. D. 1734, æt. 65.

Barrow, Isaac, D.D., a learned Episcopal divine and mathematician. Held many professorships in the University of Cambridge, and became Master of Trinity College. D. 1677, æt. 47. Treatise on the Pope's Supremacy, in which he admits the independency of the primitive churches (*b*).

Barrowe, Henry, usually styled a Brownist. Punchard asserts that he was not one. He was a lawyer of Gray's Inn; was hanged with Greenwood, in 1793, for "nonconformity to the rights and ceremonies of the English Church." Brief Discovery of a False Church, 1590 (*b*); Answer to Giffard, 1591 (*b*).

BARTLETT, WILLIAM, minister of the gospel at Wapping. Hanbury, in a note, iii. 236, says that he was formerly of the University of Oxford. This is all which, with considerable effort, I have been able to learn of him; but his work is a sufficient biography: where that is known, his fair fame will not decay. Model of the Primitive Congregational Way, 1647 (*b*), (1, 9).

BASTWIC, JOHN, M.D., a physician of Colchester. Excommunicated, fined £1,000, and imprisoned for writing a book against the Roman Episcopate, which offended the English bishops, because it denied their divine right. On charge of writing other books in prison, he was pilloried and lost his ears, in company with Prynne and Burton, in 1636. A violent Presbyterian. Treatise on Church Government, 1645 (*b*).

BAXTER, RICHARD, a great and good man, whose character is too well known to require description, and too well established to need panegyric. He was a Nonconformist, but agreed strictly with no sect of them concerning ecclesiastical polity. Ejected from Kidderminster; retired to Coventry. Chaplain both to Cromwell and Charles II., but agreed with neither. Imprisoned repeatedly, and last by Jeffries, for his Commentary. D. 1691, æt. 76.

BAYLIES, FRANCIS, a gentleman of political note and literary merit. He has recently deceased. Has published a good History of New Plymouth Colony, Bost. 1830 (2, 3, 9, 10).

BAYNES, PAUL, educated at Christ's College, Cambridge, of which he became Fellow and Lecturer. Put down, at the instance of Bancroft, for not subscribing.

A divine of uncommon learning, clear judgment, ready wit, and much communion with God and his own heart, but was reduced to great poverty and want. D. 1617. Diocesan's Trial, Lond. 1641 (1, 3).

Bellarmine, Robert, a celebrated Jesuit of Italy, but did not adopt all the tenets of the Jesuits. His admissions and demonstrations are frequently quoted to sustain certain Congregational principles. D. 1621, æt. 79.

Bellamy, Joseph, D.D., minister of Bethlem, Conn. Y. C. 1735 ; ordained, 1740. Was one of the most able divines of the country. D. 1790, æt. 71. Works, New York, 1812 (1, 2, 3, 4, 7, 9, 10).

Bentley, William, D.D., pastor of Second Church, Salem, Mass. H. U. 1777 ; ordained, 1783. D. 1819, æt. 81. Donor of a collection of books to Meadville College, Penn., and another to the American Antiquarian Society. History of Salem (*a*).

Bernard, Richard, rector of Batecome, in Somersetshire. A conforming Puritan ; once well affected towards Separatists, but relapsed, and used much invective against them. Separatists' Schism about 1608, answered by Ainsworth and Robinson (*b*, *c*).

Bradbury, Thomas, a facetious dissenting minister of Stepney, and Fetter Lane, near London. Some speak of his wit as consecrated to Christ, while others censure it in no measured terms. He had certainly unbounded popularity with his own people. D. 1757, æt. 80. The Ass and the Serpent, Lond. 1712 (1, 2, 3, 4, 5) ; Lawfulness of Resisting Tyrants, Lond. 1714 (1, 3, 4) ; Non-resistance without Priestcraft, Lond. 1715 (1, 3, 4).

Bradford, Alden, H. U. 1786. Several years a clergyman of Wiscasset, Maine ; afterward Secretary of State of Massachusetts. D. 1843. Anniversary Sermon, Plymouth, Bost. 1805 (1, 4, 5, 8, 10); History of Massachusetts, Bost. 1822 (1, 2, 3, 9, 10).

Bradford, William, second Governor of Plymouth Colony, and one of the first settlers; had only a common school education; was imprisoned at eighteen years of age for attempting to go over into Holland with the Puritans; was among the most daring of the explorers for a place of settlement; Governor, except five years, from 1621 till his death, 1657; æt. 69. Dialogue in Young's Chronicles of the Pilgrims.

Bradshaw, William, educated at Emanuel College; Fellow of Sidney College; suspended from his ministry in Kent for non-subscription in 1601; Lecturer of Christ's Church, London, but obliged to leave the city on account of his Treatise on Worship and Ceremonies, Lond. 1660 (1). He also published English Puritanism, — clear, powerful, and very instructive, Lond. 1642 (1). D. 1618, æt. 47

Brattle, Thomas, an eminent merchant of Boston. H. U. 1676. Treasurer of the College from 1693 to his death, 1713, æt. 55. Letters in (*a*).

Brewster, William, the first and a distinguished ruling elder of the church in Plymouth; was educated at the University of Cambridge, England. He frequently preached, but would never consent to become pastor. D. 1644, æt. 84.

Bridge, William, one of the Westminster Assembly; Fellow of Emanuel College; minister in Essex and Norwich; silenced by Bishop Wren; was excommunicated, and became pastor of the English Church at Rotterdam; returned in 1642, and became minister of Great Yarmouth, whence he was ejected by the Bartholomew Act. D. 1670, æt. 70. Wounded Conscience Cured, Lond. 1642 (1, 2, 5); Sermon to Volunteers of Norwich and

Yarmouth, Lond. 1642 (1, 2, 5); Sermon before House of Commons, Lond. 1643 (1); Vindication of Ordinances (4).

BROOKE, ROBERT, one of the English lords who signally defended the Puritans; afterward commander of the Parliament army; killed in storming a close, 1643. Treatise on Episcopacy (*b*, *d*).

BROUGHTON, HUGH, a learned but ill-tempered divine; minister of the English Church at Middleburg. D. 1612, æt. 63. Controversy with Ainsworth on Silk and Wool (*b*).

BROWN, ROBERT, leader of the sect of Brownists. An active, persevering, headstrong reformer; advocated Congregational principles in the main, but was a rigid Separatist; at last reverted back to the Episcopal Church. D. 1630, a rector of Northamptonshire; in prison for the abuse of a magistrate; æt. 80, boasting that he had been an inmate of thirty-two prisons.

BUCER, MARTIN, formerly a monk, afterward a celebrated reformer; twenty years Professor of Divinity at Strasburg; came to England on invitation of Archbishop Cranmer, and was Professor at Cambridge: he would not wear a square cap because his head was not square. D. 1551, æt. 60. Remarks on the Habits, and on Ecclesiastical Discipline (*d*). His bones were dug up and burned in Mary's reign.

BURROUGHS, JEREMIAH, one of the Independents in the Westminster Assembly; educated at Cambridge; pastor at Rotterdam; afterward preacher, at Stepney and Cripplegate, to two of the largest churches about London. D. 1646, æt. 47. Glorious Name of the Lord of Hosts, Lond. 1643 (1); Answer to Ferne, Lond. 1643; Irenicum (*b*).

BURTON, HENRY, B.D., Clerk of the Closet to Prince

Henry and Charles I.; imprisoned, fined, pilloried, and cropped, with Prynne and Bastwick, for his sermons against Episcopacy. He embraced the Independent views. D. 1848, æt. 69. Answer to Prynne's Twelve Considerable Questions, Lond. 1644 (1, *b*). A Modest Answer to Prynne's Full Reply to Certain Observations on the Twelve Considerable Questions, Lond. 1645.

Byles, Mather, D.D., H. U. 1725; ordained first pastor of Hollis-street Church, Boston, 1733. D. 1788, æt. 82.

Calef, Robert, a merchant of Boston; author of one of the earliest treatises against the prevalent notions concerning witchcraft, about the beginning of the last century. More Wonders of the Invisible World, Salem, 1796 (1, 4).

Callender, John, an eminent Baptist minister of Newport, R. I.; H. U. 1723. D. 1748, æt. 41. Historical Discourse concerning Rhode Island, Bost. 1739 (1, 2, 3, 5, 9, 10).

Cambridge Platform, the Rules of Church Order and Discipline adopted by the Synod at Cambridge, 1648, as pointing the churches to the Scripture directions, which are the only authority acknowledged by Congregationalists, Bost. 1808 (1, *et al.*).

Canne, John, a distinguished Brownistical Baptist; pastor of the Brownist Church at Amsterdam; author of valuable Notes on the Bible.

Cartwright, Thomas, one of the chief of the Puritans; Fellow of Trinity College; one of the most learned and acute disputants of the age. D. 1603, æt. 68. Reply to Whitgift (2, 4, 5, 6).

Charles I., King; Answer to the Divines attending his Majesty's Parliament, concerning Abolishing Episcopacy, Lond. 1648. (The Compiler, *d.*)

Chauncy, Charles, D.D., educated at Westminster and Cambridge; minister of Ware; prosecuted by Laud before the High Commission for preaching against the Book of Sports; recanted, but repented his recantation, and came to New England in 1638; was sixteen years pastor of the church in Scituate, and seventeen years President of Harvard College; very learned and very industrious, — always rose at four o'clock. D. 1671, æt. 82. Anti-synodalia (4, 5).

Chauncy, Charles, D.D., great-grandson of the President; H. U. 1721; ordained colleague with Mr. Foxcroft of the First Church, Boston, 1727; figured in the Episcopal controversy about his Dudlean Lecture; wrote and published much in favor of the doctrine of universal restoration; received the first diploma from Edinburgh ever given to an American divine. D. 1787, æt. 82. Dudlean Lecture, Bost. 1762 (1, 4, 5, 9).

Chauncy, Isaac, son of Pres. Charles; H. U. 1651; minister of a Dissenting church in London; Dr. Watts became his colleague in 1698. Chalmers quotes Calamy: "He so tormented his hearers with declamations on church government that they left him." If they were episcopally inclined, they doubtless were "tormented" by his lucid demonstrations; nor could they have been much relieved under the castigations of his successor. Divine Institution of Congregational Churches, Lond. 1697 (1); Gospel Order, Lond. 1690 (1, 2).

Chrysostom, John, Bishop of Constantinople; one of the most illustrious of the fathers; attributed the power of electing and deposing pastors to the people. D. 407, æt. 53.

Clemens Romanus, a companion of Paul; Bishop (i.e. pastor) of Rome. D. 100. Epistle to the Corinthians, Lond. 1647 (1, 2, 7).

Cleveland, John, minister of Ipswich; Y. C. 1745; ordained, 1747. D. 1799, æt. 79. Narrative of the Fourth Church, Ipswich, Bost. 1767 (1).

Coleman, Benjamin, D.D.; H. U. 1692; ordained in London for the new church in Brattle-street, 1699, which led Dr. Mather to call the church a "Presbyterian brat;" elected President of Harvard College, 1724. D. 1747, æt. 73.

Coleman, Lyman; Y. C. 1817; ordained pastor of the Congregational Church, Belchertown, 1825. A distinguished scholar. Primitive Church, Bost. 1844.

Concord, Result of Council in 1743 (1).

Congregationalism as contained in the Scriptures and explained by the Platform, an anonymous pamphlet of considerable merit, Bost. 1794 (1, 4).

Congregational Manual, the work of a sub-committee of ministers, of which the venerable Dr. L. Woods was chairman. The committee was chosen at a meeting informally called in Boston, 1844; the sub-committee first sent an "Unfinished Report" to the several associations, where it was variously received. The Manual is the mature result of the labors of that sub-committee, published on their own responsibility in 1846. It seems to advocate juridical power in councils.

Congregational Order, such a treatise as the name announces, by the General Association of Connecticut, Middletown, 1843.

Congregational Union of England and Wales, such an association of Congregational ministers as its name imports, acting also as an efficient publishing board. Declaration of Faith; Church Order and Discipline, Lond. 1833 (*b*).

Convention of Congregational Ministers in Massachusetts; an assembly, meeting annually on the last Wednesday in May. It is now conducted mainly as a charitable association for the relief of the indigent widows of deceased clergymen. Many attempts have been made to induce it to do ecclesiastical work; but they have usually been failures.

Cook, John, Cromwell's principal Secretary; executed, 1660. What the Independents would Have, Lond. 1647 (*b*); Monarchy no Creature of God, Waterford, 1652 (*b*).

Cooper, Samuel, D.D.; H. U. 1743. Ordained successor of his father in Brattle-street, Boston, 1746; chosen President of Harvard College, 1774. Fellow of the American Academy of Arts and Sciences, and first Vice-President of the Society. D. 1783, æt. 58.

Cooper, William, father of the preceding. H. U. 1712; ordained colleague with Dr. Coleman, 1716. Chosen President of Harvard College, 1737, but declined. His hearers, instead of admiring and praising his sermons, went home silent as the grave. D. 1743, æt. 49.

Corbet, John, an eminent divine, graduated at Magdalen College, 1639; rector of Bramshot in Hampshire, and ejected in 1662. Baxter preached his funeral sermon, and expressed a high opinion of his learning, piety, and humility. Had a considerable share in compiling the first volume of Rushworth's Historical Collections; Principles and Practices of Several Nonconformists, Lond. 1682 (1).

Cotton, John, Fellow of Trinity College, a great linguist and scholar; minister of Boston, England. Fled from the High Commission Court, and became teacher of the church in Boston, New England. His controversy with Roger Williams has been much misrepresented. Though his principles of toleration did not come up to our standard, yet he was very far in advance of his age.

Because he was a very great man, his errors and inconsistencies appear the more conspicuous. No man of any age ever swayed greater influence in Massachusetts, save during the Hutchinsonian Controversy. His waning then shows that our fathers were only influenced by his reasons, not controlled by his dictation. D. 1652, æt. 67. Bloody Tenet Washed, Lond. 1647 (1, 2, 3, 6); Reply to Williams, Lond. 1647 (1, 2, 5, 6); Keys of the Kingdom, Bost. 1843, Lond. 1644 (1, 2); Way of the Churches, Lond. 1645 (1); Way of the Churches Cleared, Lond. 1647 (1, 3, 5); Holiness of Church Members, Lond. 1650 (1, 2, 3, 5, 6).

Cranmer, Thomas, D.D., Archbishop of Canterbury, a celebrated reformer. At first, superstitious and persecuting, but continually growing more tolerant and republican. One of the martyrs of Mary's reign, 1555, æt. 67.

Creeds, Seasonable Thoughts on, a pamphlet containing very much sound and some false logic, attributed to Hon. John Lowell. It gives the Unitarian view of the subject. Bost. 1813 (1, 3, 5).

Cromwell, Oliver (Protector), than whom no man has been more abused. To no individual does England owe so much for her freedom and her grandeur; yet, through the restrictions and corruptions of the press after his decease, he was "damned to everlasting fame;" but, by the labors of Carlyle, Merle D'Aubigne, and others, he now rises to a glorious immortality. D. 1658, æt. 59.

Cyprian, Thascius Cælius, one of the principal Fathers. Beheaded at Carthage, 258.

Davenport, John, B.D., educated at Brazenose College, Oxford, Vicar of St. Stephen's, Coleman-street, London. Preached and visited constantly in London during the plague; fled to Holland from the persecution of Laud; had a controversy with the Dutch divines about baptizing the infants of those not professing experimental religion; came to Boston 1637, and sat with the Synod at Cambridge; declined an invitation to be one of the Westminster Assembly; principal founder of the colony of New Haven; was threatened with royal vengeance for concealing the regicides, preaching to the people from Isa. xvi. 3, 4; came to Boston in 1657, without a dismission from New Haven, being most deeply interested against the Half-way Covenant: this caused the organization of a new church. D. 1770, æt. 73. Apologetical Reply (6); Power of Congregational Churches, Lond. 1672 (1, 3, 6); Royal Edict for Military Exercises, Lond. 1629 (1).

Declaration of Ecclesiastical Discipline, a work published anonymously (of necessity) in 1574. It is a powerful treatise, and was probably from the pen of Udall, though the histories do not give exactly this title to Udall's work (6).

Denison, Daniel, Maj.-Gen., a very influential inhabitant of Ipswich. D. 1682. Irenicon, or Salve for New England's Sore (1).

Dorchester, Votes of Church and Result of Council in, 1773 (1, 4); Remarks on Result of Council in, Bost. 1774 (1, 5).

Dunster, Henry, first President of Harvard College, from 1640 to 1654; resigned on account of his opposition to infant-baptism. The ministers and magistrates were anxious for his continuance, if he could be persuaded not to propagate his peculiarity; but he was too conscientious to compromise. Revised the New England Version of the Psalms. D. 1657, in perfect harmony with, and bequeathing legacies to, those who removed him from the College.

Dwight, Timothy, D.D., LL.D.; Y. C. 1769.

Taught Grammar School two years; was tutor six years, farmer five years. Ordained at Greenfield, Conn., 1783. President of Yale College, 1795. D. 1817, æt. 64. Works, in 4 and 5 vols. (9, 10).

EATON, SAMUEL, one of the first settlers of New Haven, Conn., afterwards returned and was teacher of a church in Dukinfield, in Cheshire. D. 1665. Defence of Sundry Positions and Scriptures said to Justify the Congregational Way (with T. Taylor), Lond. 1645 (1, 3).

ECKLEY, JOSEPH, D.D.; N. H. 1772. Ordained minister of the Old South Church, Boston, 1719. A Semi-arian, but held all the other points of the Orthodox faith. D. 1811, æt. 60. Artillery Election Sermon, Bost. 1792 (1, 10); Dudlean Lecture, Bost. 1806 (1).

EDWARDS, JONATHAN; Y. C. 1720. Ordained, Northampton, 1727; dismissed, 1750. President of Princeton College, N. J., 1758, and died a few months afterwards, æt. 54. Probably the first of American divines. Treatise on Full Communion, Bost. 1749 (1, 4, 5, 9, 10).

ELIOT, JOHN, D.D.; H. U. 1772. Ordained pastor of New North Church, Boston, 1779. Contributed much to the historical learning of our country. D. 1813, æt. 58. Biographical Dictionary (1, 2, 3, 7, 10).

EMERSON, WILLIAM; H. U. 1787. Ordained pastor of Church in Harvard, 1792. Installed, First Church, Boston, 1799. D. 1811, æt. 42. Piety and Arms, Artillery Election Sermon, Bost. 1799 (1).

EMMONS, NATHANAEL, D.D.; Y. C. 1767. Ordained, 1773, pastor of Church in Franklin (then the Second Church in Wrentham). D. 1840, æt. 95. Thus he was sixty-three years in the pastoral office, and has a name as a writer and a theologian that will never perish. Works, in 7 vols. Bost. 1842.

Endicot, John, sixteen years Governor of Massachusetts. Came to Salem in 1628, and is styled Governor of Naumkeake settlement. He was ardent, and sometimes violent: cut the cross out of the king's colors, after Williams had preached against that symbol. D. 1665, æt. 75.

Euring, William. Hanbury says that we know no more of him than he tells us in the preface to his work, viz. that he was not brought up among the muses, but the mariners. Robinson speaks of his assistance with respect, in Han. i. 53. Answer to Drake's Ten Counter Demands, 1619 (*b*).

Eusebius, Pamphilius, styled the Father of Ecclesiastical History. D. 340. Ecclesiastical History.

Felt, Joseph B., formerly pastor of Congregational Church in Sharon and in Hamilton; now a learned and laborious antiquarian; Librarian of the Massachusetts Historical Society. Annals of Salem, Salem, 1827 (1, 3, 4, 5, 8).

Ferne, Henry, D.D., Bishop of Chester, son of Sir John, Fellow of Trinity College. D. 1661, æt. 59. Resolving of Conscience; Conscience Satisfied (*b*); Tract against the Lawfulness of Subjects to take up Arms in any case whatever, triumphantly answered by William Bridge (1) and Jer. Burroughs (1).

Fish, Elisha, minister of Upton, Mass. H. U. 1750; ordained, 1751. D. 1795. An acute reasoner and firm patriot. Art of War Useful and Necessary, Bost. 1774 (1).

Fitchburg, Facts and Documents concerning an Ecclesiastical Controversy in; doubtless from the pen of Dr. Samuel Worcester, Bost. 1802 (1); Comments on the same, Wor. 1804 (1).

Foxcroft, Thomas, H. U. 1714. Ordained colleague

with Mr. Wadsworth, 1717. Dr. Chauncy was settled as his colleague, 1727. Polite, eloquent, and universally admired; a very devout and edifying preacher; author of numerous valuable treatises. D. 1769, æt. 72. Sermon at his own Ordination, Bost. 1718 (1, 2, 3, 4, 5, 10); Sermon Preparatory to the Choice of a Minister, Bost. 1727 (1, 10); Century Sermon on the Beginning of New England, Bost. 1730 (1, 4, 5, 6, 7); Sermon at Ordination of a Deacon, Bost. 1731 (1, 2, 3, 5, 6).

Frankfort, Troubles in, 1575 (6).

Fuller, Andrew, an eminent English Baptist divine; a very lucid, powerful, and valuable writer. D. 1815, æt. 61. Works, Bost. 1833 (2, 7, 9, 10).

Fuller, Samuel, a physician of Plymouth, and one of the first settlers; deacon in the church with Gov. Carver. Successfully showed Governors Endicot and Bradford, and the churches of Plymouth and Salem, that they were agreed on the subject of church government and discipline; whereas, from the misrepresentations, each had been jealous of the other.

Fuller, Thomas, D.D., an eminent English historian and divine. D. 1661, æt. 55. Church History of Britain, 1656.

Genevan Disputations. Theses on various Points of Doctrine and Discipline Disputed and Maintained by Select Scholars at Geneva, before Beza and Faius (translation), Edinb. 1591 (Compiler).

Giffard, George, a conforming Puritan of the sixteenth century, minister of Malden: figured largely in the controversy with Greenwood and Barrowe (*b*).

Goodwin, Thomas, D.D., educated at Catherine Hall, Cambridge; left in 1639, being dissatisfied with conformity, and went to Holland; returned at the sitting of the Long Parliament, and was the master-spirit among the Independents in the Westminster Assembly; President of Magdalen College, which he left at the Restoration; and preached in London till his death, 1679–80, æt. 79. His Works are published in five large folios; half of vol. iv. is on Church Government, Lond. 1697 (2, 9).

Gospel Order Revived; an anonymous publication in answer to Increase Mather's Gospel Order. It is levelled chiefly against requiring experimental religion in candidates for church membership; probably from the pen of Mr. Stoddard, of Northampton. Bost. 1700 (1, 5).

Greenhill, William, a distinguished member of the Westminster and the Savoy Assemblies. He acted in concert with the Independents.

Greenwood, John, a university scholar; took his first degree, 1580; hanged at Tyburn, 1593, for "nonconformity to the rights and ceremonies of the English Church." A godly, devoted minister of Christ. Refutation of Giffard (*b*, *c*).

Hall, Edwin, D.D., pastor of the Congregational Church, Norwalk, Conn. Puritans and their Principles, N.Y., 1846, a work of unusual worth.

Hall, Joseph, a learned Bishop of Norwich. D. 1656, æt. 82. John Robinson had a controversy with him on Church Government (*b*, *c*).

Hall, Robert, a very eminent Open-communion Baptist. His writings and his spirit are universally admired, even by those who do not adopt them; educated at Aberdeen; ordained 1780; declined the title D.D. D. 1831, æt. 67. Works, in 3 vols. 8vo (9, 10).

Hampshire Narrative, a controversial work concerning the ordination of Mr. Breck at Springfield, Bost. 1736 (1); Answer to the same, attributed to the pen of

Dr. Cooper, of Boston, 1736 (1, 4); Rejoinder, Bost. 1737 (1).

HANBURY, BENJAMIN, deacon of the First Congregational Church, London. Historical Memorials, Lond. 1839, for the Congregational Union of England and Wales; — an invaluable digest of the works of the old Puritans, in 3 vols. 8vo, compiled with great care, but wants distinctness of typographical arrangement (9).

HARRIS, THADDEUS MASON, D.D., a distinguished and very learned Unitarian minister, of Dorchester, Mass.; H. U. 1787. D. 1842, æt. 74. Sermon on Covenant Engagements, Bost. 1801 (1, 5).

HART, WILLIAM, minister of Saybrook, Conn.; Y. C. 1732. D. 1784. Remarks on Mr. Dana's Ordination, New Haven, 1759 (1, 4, 5).

HAVEN, SAMUEL, Hon., son and grandson of ministers of Dedham; Judge of County Court; a professed Swedenborgian. Proceedings of the First Church and Parish of Dedham, Cambridge, 1819 (1, 2).

HAWES, JOEL, D.D., minister, Hartford, Conn.; B. U. 1813; was soon ordained at Hartford, where he remains, one of the distinguished ministers of the country. Tribute to the Pilgrims, Hart. 1830 (2).

HEADS OF AGREEMENT between Congregational and Presbyterian Ministers in London, A. D. 1690; — a kind of confession of faith, embodying the general points on which the denominations are agreed. They were adopted by the Saybrook Convention as a part of their Platform. They may be seen in Congregational Order, Upham's Ratio Disciplinæ, *et al.*

HEMMENWAY, MOSES, D.D., minister of Wells, Me.; H. U. 1755; ordained, 1759. D. 1811, æt. 84; — a learned theologian. Controversy with Dr. Emmons on the Sacraments, Bost. 1794 (1).

HENRY, MATTHEW, a learned divine and noted commentator. D. 1714, æt. 52. Defence of his Enquiry into the Nature of Schism, Lond. 1692 (1).

HIGGINSON, FRANCIS, first minister of Salem; educated at Emanuel College in Cambridge; became minister of Leicester; fled from the High Commission Court, and came to New England, 1629. D. 1630; — a truly great, learned, and good man. Confession of Faith for the Church in Salem (5).

HIGGINSON, JOHN, son of the preceding; was assistant preacher some fifteen years at Guilford, Conn., and ordained at Salem by lay brethren (as his father had been before him), 1660; one of the most popular and influential preachers in the country. D. 1708, æt. 93. Attestation (with William Hubbard), in Appendix to Cambridge Platform.

HIGH CHURCH POLITICS, a work setting forth some of the glaring pretensions of high churchmen, Lond. 1792 (3, 1, 7).

HISTORICAL SOCIETY OF MASSACHUSETTS, instituted 1791; has accomplished much for the advancement of historical knowledge; has published three series of ten volumes each, consisting of rare treatises, chiefly on the early history of New England. The Society has a fine library over the Savings' Bank, Boston.

HOLMES, ABIEL, D.D., LL.D.; Y. C. 1783; ordained at Midway, Georgia, 1785; installed at Cambridge, Mass., 1792; dismissed, 1832. D. 1837, æt. 74. Was son-in-law of President Stiles. One of the very best of historians, and a great patron of historical learning. Dudlean Lecture, Camb. 1810 (1); Anniversary Plymouth Sermon, Camb. 1806; Second Century Sermon, Camb. 1821 (1, 3, 4); American Annals, Camb. 1805 and 1829 (1, 3, 4, 5, 7, 8, 9, 10).

Holt, John (Lord Chief Justice), first a lawyer of Gray's Inn; a great and upright judge. D. 1709, æt. 67.

Hooke, William; Oxford, 1620; Vicar of Axmouth, in Devonshire; fled for nonconformity, and was first pastor of Taunton; afterward colleague with J. Davenport, in New Haven. Returned to England, and was chaplain to Oliver Cromwell, his near kinsman. His wife was sister to Judge Whalley. D. 1678, æt. 77.

Hooker, Richard (called "The Judicious"), educated at Corpus Christi, Oxford, where he was a Fellow; took orders, 1581; Lecturer of the Temple, 1584, where he came in uncomfortable contact with Travers; became rector of Kent, 1595. D. 1600, æt. 46. Ecclesiastical Polity, — a work in high repute with Episcopalians.

Hooker, Thomas, educated at Emanuel College, Cambridge; Lecturer at Chelmsford, 1626; silenced for nonconformity, 1630; fled to Holland, and was assistant to Dr. Ames; came to New England, and had lay ordination at Cambridge, 1633; removed to Hartford, 1636; the most influential man in the colony of Connecticut. D. 1647, æt. 61. Survey of Church Discipline, Lond. 1648.* His corrected copy was lost at sea, and his first draft was sent over and published after his death. This work, with many blemishes, shows great research, and probably the corrected copy was an unequalled production (1, 5, 6, 9, 10).

Hopkins, Samuel, D.D., an eminent theologian from whom the Hopkinsians derive their name; Y. C. 1741; ordained, Great Barrington, 1743; installed at Newport,

* On page 121, note, it is stated that some authors ascribe the fourth part of this work to J. Cotton. At the suggestion of Rev. E. Hooker, D.D., I have examined the subject so as to be fully convinced that the whole work is Hooker's. See Dr. Hooker's Life of T. Hooker, pages 280, 281.

R.I. 1770. D. 1803, æt. 82. System of Divinity, 2 vols. Bost. 1811.

HOWE, JOHN, educated at Cambridge; Cromwell's domestic chaplain, and minister at Torrington and Silver-street, London; was silenced by the act of uniformity. D. 1705, æt. 74. He possessed talents of the highest order, with unfeigned and exalted piety. Dr. Emmons styled him the very best English divine. His writings most felicitously combine wit and dignity. Works, N. Y. 1835.

HUBBARD, WILLIAM; H. U. 1642, in the first class; an eminent preacher of Ipswich. He was for more stringency of the civil law in enforcing religion than most of his brethren. D. 1704, æt. 83. History of Massachusetts (belonging to all the town-libraries in the State): it borrows very largely from the third volume of Winthrop's manuscripts, without giving credit, for which he has been much censured, probably without good reason, as the work was not published till after his death. It is unfair to blame the author for what his survivors did not do. Attestation (with John Higginson), in Cambridge Platform.

HUME, DAVID, a celebrated English writer of great power. He was an atheist and sceptic, but sustained an unblemished personal character. D. 1776, æt. 65. History of England.

HUTCHINSON, THOMAS, LL.D.; Governor of the Province of Massachusetts from 1771 to 1774; H. U. 1727. In early life was a popular magistrate, but by his Tory preferences became very obnoxious as the crisis of the Revolution approached. D. 1780, æt. 69. History of Massachusetts, Salem, 1795 (1, 2, 3, 8, 9, 10); Massachusetts Collection of State Papers, Bost. 1769 (1, 2, 3): both are valuable productions.

INDEPENDENTS IN THE WESTMINSTER ASSEMBLY: Thomas Goodwin, Philip Nye, William Bridge, Jeremiah Burroughs, and Sidrach Simpson; and, usually, William Greenhill and William Carter acted hand in hand in favor of Independency in that assembly. To these, Baillie adds Caryl, Phillips, and Sterry. To their efforts, small minority as they were, we are, under God, indebted for much of the ecclesiastical liberty which we now enjoy. A Scots army, fifteen thousand strong, was invoked to make the arguments of their opposers respected. Several of their very valuable papers are quoted in this work, from Hanbury, Punchard, and Neal.

JACOB, HENRY, an eminent early Nonconformist divine; educated at Oxford. D. 1621, æt. 60. At first he wrote against the Separatists, but at length embraced Semi-separatist principles, and wrote with great power in their defence; was a companion of Robinson in Holland; became pastor of the First Congregational Church, England. D. 1621, æt. 60. Defence of Church and Ministers of England, Middleburg, 1599 (*b*); Divine Beginning of Christ's Visible Churches, 1610 (*b*); Reasons for Reforming our Churches in England, 1604 (*b*); Humble Supplication for Toleration, 1609 (*b*); Attestation of Godly Divines, that Church Government should be by the People's Consent, 1613 (*b*, 1); Church Confession, 1616, prefaced "*Vide et fide, fide sed vide*" (*b*).

JEWELL, JOHN, Bishop of Salisbury, educated at Christ's Church College, Oxford. He held to absolute obedience to the sovereign, and so adopted the habits, though against his own convictions of right, and bore hard on the consciences of those who would not comply. D. 1571, æt. 49. Apology for the Church of England (*b*, *d*).

JOHNSON, FRANCIS, a Brownist preacher in Holland;

once associated with H. Ainsworth; held the absolute rule of the elders (*b*, *d*).

Junius, Francis, Divinity Reader in Leyden and Middleburg. Had some controversy with the exiled Puritans, though Ainsworth says (Hanbury, i. 172), that he neither approved the English Church, nor condemned the Separatists' practice. D. 1602, æt. 57. Letters to the English Church at Amsterdam, 1602.

King, Peter (Lord Chancellor), a writer of great ability and candor. D. 1734, æt. 65. Enquiry into the Discipline, &c. of the Primitive Church, by an Impartial Witness, Lond. 1719 (1, 9).

Kippis, Andrew, D.D., F.R.S., educated under Dr. Doddridge, minister at Boston, Dorking, and Westminster; editor of Biographia Britannica. An eminent scholar. D. 1795, æt. 70. Vindication of Dissenting Ministers, 1773 (3).

Knowles, James D., late Professor of the Theological Seminary at Newton. Columbia College, 1824. D. 1838, æt. 40. Life of Roger Williams, Bost. 1734; valuable, and generally candid, but sometimes given to special pleading (1, 2, 4, 8, 9).

Latimer, Hugh, Bishop of Worcester, was a great reformer; derided the habits, and so became an early object of the vengeance of the Conformists to all things, in Queen Mary's reign. Burnt 1555, æt. 85.

Laud, William, Archbishop of Canterbury, the great persecuting prelate. Himself proved the truth of the assertion, "They that take the sword shall perish by the sword." Beheaded 1645, æt. 72.

Letchford, Thomas, a lawyer from London. Lived in Boston, New England, from 1638 to 1640. He was disgusted with the requirement of experimental piety for church membership. Wrote Plain Dealing (*a*), in which he gives a very candid and fair account of the ecclesiastical usages of New England.

LILBURNE, JOHN, an enthusiastic Nonconformist. Styled the most sincere and most imprudent of men. Was often in prison; yet, by his boldness and energy, he accomplished considerable for the cause of liberty. D. 1657, æt. 49. Answer to a Gentleman, 1639 (*b*).

LOBB, STEPHEN. I am unable either to learn much of this gentleman from those biographical works to which I have access, or to recall what I have somewhere read in his praise. Happily, there is little need of it, as his works praise him, and commend themselves to reflecting minds. True Dissenter, 1685 (1). He was a voluminous writer.

LOCKE, JOHN, the well-known philosopher. He refused political preferments for the quiet of the study, in which he greatly enlightened and benefited mankind. D. 1704, æt. 72. Letters on Toleration, Lond. 1695 (3, 1, 2, 8, 9).

LOW COUNTRY EXILES. The Nonconformists, who, in the latter part of the sixteenth century, went over to Holland, after banishment had been decreed against them, and the prisons were thrown open, where such multitudes of them had suffered, and so many perished. Johnson, Ainsworth, and Robinson were among the leaders of these exiles. Confession, Amst. 1598 (1, *b*).

MACAULAY, THOMAS BABBINGTON, the celebrated living English historian. History of England, Bost. 1849.

MACCARTY, THADDEUS. H. U. 1739; ordained pastor of the First Church in Worcester, 1747. D. 1784.

MARTYR, PETER, a distinguished Florentine commentator on the Bible. D. 1562, æt. 62.

MATHER, COTTON, D.D., F.R.S., son of Dr. Increase Mather; H. U. 1678. Ordained colleague with his father, 1684. D. 1728, æt. 66. He was one of the most remarkable men of this or any other country. His reading was immense, and the number of his publications almost or quite unparalleled. He examined every subject, though often superficially, and came to conclusions and wrote treatises in a corresponding manner. No student of our country's history and customs can do without his works; yet no one can safely depend on him for any thing but naked facts, where superstition and imagination had little chance to bias his judgment. Sermon to an Artillery Company, Bost. 1687 (1, 4, 5); Magnalia, Hartford, 1820 (1, 3, 4, 5, 7, 8, 9, 10); Sermon to the Forces engaged in a Just War, &c., Bost. 1689 (1, 4, 5); Ratio Disciplinæ, Bost. 1726 (1, 3, 4, 9, 10).

Mather, Increase, D.D., President of Harvard University, son of Richard. H. U. 1656; ordained pastor of North Church, Boston, 1664. Chosen President, 1681, but his church refused to part with him; rechosen, 1684, after the death of President Rogers. He exerted an all-controlling influence both in church and commonwealth. D. 1723, æt. 85. First Principles of New England concerning Baptism, Camb. 1675 (1, 3, 4, 5, 6); Discourse concerning the Lawfulness of Common Prayer Worship, &c., Lond. 1689 (1); Order of the Gospel practised in the New England Churches Justified, Bost. 1700 (1, 3, 5); Concerning the Maintenance Due to Ministers, Bost. 1706 (1, 4, 5); Disquisition concerning Ecclesiastical Councils, Bost. 1716 (1, 5); Sermon at Ordination of Mr. Appleton, Bost. 1718; Dissertation against Encouraging the Unsanctified to Approach the Table of the Lord, Bost. 1708 (1); Cases of Conscience concerning Witchcraft (1, 6).

Mather, Nathaniel, second son of Richard, and

brother of President Increase Mather; H. U. 1647. Settled in Barnstable, England; ejected in 1662, went to Holland, and was minister at Rotterdam; succeeded his brother Samuel at Dublin; afterward removed to London, and was pastor of a Congregational church there, where he died, 1697, æt. 67. Lawfulness of a Pastor's Administering Seals in another Church, Bost. 1730 (1, 6).

MATHER, RICHARD, the progenitor of the whole race in America. Educated at Oxford. Suspended for Nonconformity in 1633, restored, and again suspended. Came to New England, 1635; ordained pastor of the church in Dorchester, 1636. He was a distinguished ornament of the churches. Cambridge Platform was chiefly from his pen. Church Government and Church Covenant Discussed in Answer to Thirty-two Questions, Lond. 1643 (1, 6); Apology of the New England Elders for Church Government, Lond. 1643 (1); Answer to Herle, Lond. 1644 (1, 3, 5).

MATHER, SAMUEL, D.D., son of Cotton; H. U. 1723. Ordained over the same church to which his father and grandfather had ministered, 1732, as colleague with Mr. Gee. He has been less praised than some of his ancestors, and in many respects needed less. He was less dazzling, but usually more careful to be correct, than any of them, save Richard the patriarch. Apology for the Liberties of the New England Churches, Bost. 1738 (2, 3, 4, 5, 9).

MAUDUIT, ISRAEL, some time an English dissenter; afterwards a successful merchant and writer of political pamphlets. Even Chalmers admits that he was a temperate advocate for civil and religious liberty. D. 1787, æt. 79. Case of Dissenting Ministers, a work of considerable merit, Lond. 1772, and Bost. 1773 (3, 1, 2).

Mayhew, Jonathan, D.D.; H. U. 1744. Ordained, 1747, pastor of the West Church, Boston. A powerful preacher and acute reasoner. D. 1766, æt. 45. Thirtieth of January Sermon, 1750 (*d*, 1).

Milton, John, the poet and politician; Latin Secretary to Cromwell. Educated at Christ's College, Cambridge. D. 1674, æt. 66. Treatise against Prelacy, in Works (2, 1, 9); Christian Doctrine, Bost. 1825 (2, 9); Eikonoklastes, Amst. 1690 (1, 2, 9).

Minot, George R.; H. U. 1778. First clerk of Massachusetts House of Representatives under the Constitution, and clerk of the Convention which adopted the Constitution of the United States. D. 1802, æt. 43. Continuation of History of Massachusetts, 1798—1803 (1, 2, 3, 4, 5, 8, 9).

Mitchell, John, formerly a pastor in Connecticut; afterwards in Northampton, Mass. Church Member's Guide, Northampton, 1838; a work of considerable research and merit, yet not always correct, particularly on the church membership of ministers. Leans to Consociationism, but is honest and candid.

Mitchell, Jonathan, a distinguished minister of Cambridge, Mass.; H. U. 1647; ordained, 1650. The Result of the Synod of 1662 was chiefly from his pen. D. 1668. He overcame Increase Mather in the Half-way Covenant Controversy.

Moody, Joshua, H. U. 1653; minister of Portsmouth, N.H., 1660. Imprisoned by George Cranfield, for not administering the Lord's Supper in the way of the Church of England. Preached to First Church, Boston, from 1684 to 1693. Harbored and succored those accused of witchcraft, at his own peril. Was chosen President of Harvard University, but declined. D. 1697, æt. 65.

Moody, Samuel, the powerful, pious, and eccentric minister of York, Me.; H. U. 1697. D. 1747, æt. 70. Remarkable stories are told of almost miraculous interpositions for his temporal sustenance.

Mornay, Philip, an illustrious Protestant French nobleman. D. 1623, æt. 72. Mystery of Iniquity, Lond. 1612 (1); Treatise on the Church (*b*).

More, Stephen, pastor of the church in Deadman's Place, London. His congregation were most of them apprehended and sent to prison; but the House of Lords interposed, and Mr. More was afterwards promoted. Sermon before Parliament (*b*, *d*); Preacher Sent (*b*); Wise Gospel Preacher (*b*).

Morton, Nathaniel, one of the first planters of New Plymouth. A correct and valuable author. New England Memorial, Bost. 1826 (1, 2, 3, 4, 5, 8, 9).

Mourt, George, supposed to be one of the merchant adventurers to New England. Relation of Beginning and Proceedings of the English Plantation at Plymouth, in New England (*a*).

Neal, Daniel, pastor of an Independent Church, London. D. 1743, æt. 65. History of New England, Lond, 1747 (1, 2, 4, 5, 7, 9); History of the Puritans, New York, 1844. The latter work is an invaluable production, probably the best on the subject (1, 2, 4, 5, 7, 8, 9, 10).

Neander, Augustus, D.D., a celebrated German scholar, recently deceased. Planting and Training the Christian Church, Philad. 1844; Ecclesiastical History, Bost. 1847.

Newman, Samuel, pastor of the church in Seekonk (formerly Rehoboth), Mass. He had been obliged to flee seven times in England, to avoid persecution. Author of the Cambridge Concordance. D. 1663, æt. 62.

Nonconforming Ministers, Letter of, Lond. 1702 (1).

Nonconformity, History of, Lond. 1701. A somewhat valuable anonymous work (3).

Norris, Edward, teacher of the church in Salem, with Hugh Peters as pastor; afterwards had the sole charge eighteen years; ordained, 1640. D. 1659.

Norton, John, educated at Cambridge, England; pastor of the church in Ipswich, and removed to Boston (with some difficulty) by advice of council. Persuaded Boston Church to send delegates to the Synod of 1647. He was famous as a divine, but met with the usual changes as a politician. D. 1663, æt. 57. Answer to Apollonius, Lond. 1648 (1); Catechism.

Nowell, Increase, one of the first magistrates of the Massachusetts Colony, and a ruling elder of the church in Charlestown, till it was decided that it was inconsistent for the same person to hold both offices, when he resigned the eldership.

Nye, Philip, one of the Westminster Assembly; educated at Magdalen College, Oxford, and was curate of St. Michael's. Fled from Laud's persecution; was principal manager of the meeting of ministers at Savoy. Blake has spoken disparingly of him, following the author of Hudibras; but Neal gives him a good character. Doubtless he was an eyesore to high churchmen; but he certainly had the confidence of contemporaneous dissenters. Lawfulness of Oath of Supremacy, &c., Lond. 1683 (1). D. 1672, æt. 76.

Oakes, Urian; H. U. 1649; pastor of church at Cambridge, 1671; President of Harvard University, 1675. D. 1681, æt. 49. A distinguished scholar.

Origen, a distinguished father in the church. D. 254. æt. about 70. Some of his writings savor of Universalism.

Osgood, David, D.D.; H. U. 1771; ordained at Medford, 1774. D. 1822, æt. 74. One of the most distinguished preachers of Massachusetts. Dudlean Lecture, Camb. 1802 (1, 3, 4, 7).

Owen, John, D.D., educated at Queen's College, Oxford, and left as a Nonconformist. Became Cromwell's chaplain, and Vice-Chancellor of Oxford. One of the most learned of the Independent divines. D. 1683, æt. 69. Works, in 22 vols. Lond. 1826 (2, 10), containing, in vol. xix., Duty of Pastor and People, Nature of Schism, Catechism, Vindication of Independents in Answer to Stillingfleet; and vol. xx., Original of Churches, Answer to Stillingfleet's Unreasonableness of Separation, and True Nature of a Gospel Church.

Paget, John, a semi-conforming Puritan of considerable ability. Wrote Arrow against the Separation of the Brownists, Amst. 1618 (*b*). This was stoutly opposed by H. Ainsworth and J. Davenport.

Paræus, David, D.D., a famous professor at Heidelburg. Author of various Expositions of Parts of the Bible. D. 1622, æt. 74.

Parker, Robert, a Wiltshire divine, educated at Cambridge, England; father of Thomas Parker, first minister of Newbury, Mass. Fled to Holland, and became chaplain of the garrison at Doesburg, where he died, 1630. Increase Mather styles him the Incomparable Parker. Against Symbolizing with Antichrist, &c., Lond. 1607 (1, 6); Ecclesiastical Polity (6).

Pemberton, Ebenezer, pastor of Old South Church, Boston. A distinguished divine. D. 1717. Sermon at Ordination of Mr. Sewall, Bost. 1718 (1).

Penry, John, one of the martyrs for Congregationalism, styled the Apostle of Wales, being the first that preached the Gospel to the Welsh; Oxford, 1586.

Wrongfully suspected of being the author of the Mar-Prelate Pamphlets. Apprehended as an enemy to the State, and hanged 1593.

Peters, Hugh, educated at Trinity College, Cambridge, where he spent nine years. The early companion of Hooker and Davenport; was colleague with William Ames in Rotterdam; came to Salem, Mass., 1635, and succeeded Roger Williams; assisted Vane, Winthrop, Cotton, and Shepard, in framing the Fundamentals of Massachusetts; was sent on important business to London by the General Court of Massachusetts. Here he figured greatly in the Revolution as a divine, a politician, and even a military commander. After the Restoration, he was hanged and quartered with savage cruelty, on accusation of having compassed the king's death, 1660, æt. 61. No man has been more, or more unjustly, calumniated. See Mr. Felt's Memoirs of his Life.

Pierce, James, an eminent Presbyterian divine of Exeter; an Arian. D. 1730. Vindication of Dissenters, Lond. 1718 (2, 3, 9).

Polhill, Edward, Esq., a learned gentleman of Berwash, in Sussex, in constant communion with the Church of England, zealously concerned for truth, and not for party. Discourse on Schism, Lond. 1694 (1, 4).

Polycarp, Bishop of Smyrna, one of the eminent Fathers. Burnt, 167.

Pond, Enoch, D.D.; B. U. 1813. Minister of Ward (now Auburn), Mass.; a distinguished professor of Bangor Theological Seminary. The Church, New York, 1837; The Mather Family, Bost. (Mass. S. School Soc.), 1844.

Price, Richard, LL.D., pastor at Newington Green and Hackney. A great philosopher and an Arian divine. D. 1791, æt. 67.

PRINCE THOMAS; H. U. 1707. Travelled extensively. Ordained pas.or of Old South Church, Boston, 1718. D. 1758, æt. 71. Was one of the most learned and useful men of his age. He founded the New England Library, the portions of which that escaped the Vandalism of the British soldiery are still an invaluable treasure. Chronology, Bost. 1736 (1, 2, 3, 4, 7, 8, 10). This work shows almost unbounded research, and the most scrupulous accuracy; yet he could not procure subscribers for a second volume, and only a small portion of it was ever published. Callender said at the time, that it was "an honour to the country, though he wished for his sake that he had taken less pains to serve an ungrateful age. . . . Sooner or later, the country will see the advantage of his work, and their obligation to him." Remarks eliciting more of discernment than of the spirit of prophecy. D. 1758, æt. 71.

PRINCIPLES OF THE PROTESTANT RELIGION; a work by the Ministers of Boston to meet the insinuations of George Keith, Bost. 1690 (1, 3).

PROPOSITIONS TO PARLIAMENT FOR GATHERING INDEPENDENT CHURCHES; an anonymous valuable tract, 1647 (*b*).

PRYNNE, WILLIAM, a distinguished English Presbyterian lawyer; educated at Oriel College, Oxford; removed to Lincoln's Inn, 1620; lost part of his ears for writing Histrio-mastix, and the remainder of them for satirizing Laud, besides being pilloried, fined, and branded. He, in turn, became the chief manager of Laud's trial, being then member of the Long Parliament. D. 1669, æt. 69. Histrio-mastix, Lond. 1633 (1, 3, 4, 9).

PUNCHARD, GEORGE, formerly pastor of the church at Plymouth, N.H., now editor of the American Traveller. History of Congregationalism, Salem, 1841; View of Congregationalism, Andover, 1844; — works which deserve to be better known and prized.

RAINOLDS (Raynolds, Reynolds, *et al.*), JOHN, King's Professor at Oxford, and President of Corpus Christi, a reforming and conforming Puritan. Opposed Bancroft's claims to *jure divino* Episcopacy, and plead the cause of the Puritans in Hampton Court Conference (*b*, *d*). A great scholar and living library. D. 1607, æt. 68. Overthrow of Stage Plays, Middleburg, 1600 (1).

RATHBAND, WILLIAM, a great opposer of the Independents. Published an account of the sentiments of the New England Churches, which he did not well understand, 1644. Thomas Welde stripped him of every feather in his Reply (*b*).

ROBINSON, JOHN, educated at Cambridge. At first, a conforming Puritan and minister at Norwich, and fled with his people to Holland in 1608–9, whence a portion of them came to Plymouth, and commenced the settlement of New England. A wise and far-seeing man, and a shrewd and sound divine. His positions are always strong, and hard to be overthrown. D. 1625, æt. 50. Several of his treatises are referred to in this Dictionary, quoted from Hanbury and Punchard. His complete works are now just published by the Congregational Union of England and Wales, and the American Doctrinal Tract Society. They are invaluable to those who would understand Congregationalism.

ROGERS, JOHN, first martyr in Queen Mary's reign. Prebend of St. Paul's; refused to wear the habits, and so disturbed the disguised Papists, who brought him to the stake in 1555. Assisted Coverdale in translating the Bible into English.

RUTHERFORD, SAMUEL, one of the Scots Presbyterian Commissioners to the Westminster Assembly, and Profes sor of Divinity in the University of St. Andrews. Author of several treatises against Congregationalism, answered by Cotton, Hooker, and others.

SAINT'S APOLOGY; an anonymous tract, 1645, containing a succinct representation of a visible church under the gospel (*b*).

SANDYS, SIR EDWIN, son of the archbishop; was prebend of York. Travelled extensively, and published the result of his observations entitled Europæ Speculum, Lond. 1687; from the author's edition, 1599 (4). He most evidently leaned to and sustained Congregational views. Some of the Robinson Church were of his household. Educated at Corpus Christi, Oxford. D. 1629, æt. 68.

SAVOY CONFESSION; a declaration of the faith and order owned and practised in the Congregational churches in England, agreed upon by the synod at the Savoy, Oct. 12, 1658; essentially the same as the Westminster Confession, and adopted by Boston Massachusetts Synod, 1680. Goodwin, Owen, Nye, Bridge, Caryl, and Greenhill were the committee who revised it.

SAYBROOK PLATFORM; the Confession of Faith, Heads of Agreement, and Articles of Discipline, adopted by the Assembly of ministers and messengers of the churches at Saybrook, 1708. This Platform embodies the consociation plan, and is the generally but not universally received directory of the Connecticut churches.

SACHEVERELL, HENRY, educated at Oxford. A zealous, fiery advocate for non-resistance, and contemner of the toleration of Dissenters, for which he was impeached by the House of Commons, and found guilty in the reign of Queen Anne.

SCOTTOW, JOSHUA, an eminent merchant of Boston; admitted to the First Church, Boston, 1634. Lived to a great age, and published Old Men's Tears, &c., Bost. 1691 (1). Narrative of the Planting of Massachusetts Colony, Bost. 1694 (1).

SEWALL, JOSEPH, D.D.; H. U. 1707. Ordained colleague with Mr. Pemberton, pastor of the Old South Church, Boston, 1713. Distinguished for his piety. Sermon at Ordination of Messrs. Parker, Hinsdell, and Secomb, as missionaries to the Indians, Bost. 1733 (1).

SHEPARD, THOMAS, educated at Emanuel College, Cambridge. Silenced by Laud. He came to New England in 1635, and succeeded Hooker at Cambridge. Esteemed one of the first divines of New England. D. 1649, æt. 43. Matter of the Visible Church (1, 6); Church Membership of Children, Camb. 1663 (1, 5); Defence of Answer to Nine Positions (with John Allin), Lond. 1648 (1, 6).

SIMPSON, SIDRACH, B.D., one of the Independents in the Westminster Assembly, and of the Committee for digesting the Savoy Confession. Fled from Laud's persecution, and was minister of an Independent Church at Rotterdam; afterward Master of Pembroke Hall, and was one of the triers of the ministry during the interregnum. Even Baillie acknowledges him a discreet, learned, and zealous man, well skilled in cases of conscience. D. 1658. Fast Sermon (1, 3, 4, 6, *b*); Anatomist Anatomized, Lond. 1644 (*b*); Lond. 1643 (1).

SMITH, JOHN, pastor of the original Separatist Church in England; organized, 1602, from which Robinson's Church colonized. He endured great sufferings and imprisonment in England, escaped to Holland in 1606, and settled at Amsterdam. Here he became a Baptist, and immersed himself. Hence he is sometimes called a Se-Baptist. He then immersed Helwisse, his associate, and other disciples. D. 1610.

Sparke, Thomas, D.D., Professor of Divinity, Oxford. A famous Nonconformist divine, who figured, with Travers, at the Conference of Lambeth, and plead the cause of the Puritans in the Hampton Court Conference (*d*).

Sparks, Jared, LL.D.; H. U. 1815. A distinguished scholar, and late President of Harvard University. American Biography (1, 2, 4, 5, 8, 9, 10).

Stiles, Ezra, D.D.; Y. C. 1746. One of the greatest scholars the college had ever produced; ordained, Newport, R.I., 1755; President of Yale College, 1778. D. 1795, æt. 68. Convention Sermon, Bost. 1761 (1, 2, 4, 5, 9, 10); a most lucid exposition of the several interests which operated in the construction of the Cambridge and Saybrook Platforms, and of Congregational principles and practices generally. It should be republished, and in the possession of every friend of religious liberty. Election Sermon, New Haven, 1783 (1, 4, 5, 7, 9, 10).

Stillingfleet, Edward, Bishop of Worcester. An elegant writer. D. 1699, æt. 64. Irenicum, 1659 (*b*); Unreasonableness of Separation.

Stoddard, Solomon; H. U. 1662. Ordained, 1672, pastor of church at Northampton, Mass., where he preached without interruption fifty-six years. He was presbyterially inclined in his views of church government, and in favor of admitting all baptized persons to the communion. D. 1729, æt. 86. Instituted Churches, Lond. 1700 (1, 3); Right of Visible Saints to the Lord's Supper, though destitute of a Saving Work in their Hearts, Bost. 1709 (1). See Gospel Order Revived.

Strype, John, a learned editor. D. 1737, æt. 94. Ecclesiastical Memorials; Annals of Reformation (2, 3, 8, 9).

Stubbes, Philip; Anatomie of Abuses, Lon. 1583 (1).

TAYLOR, NATHANIEL, minister of the Gospel in London; author of several valuable treatises. Vindication of Dissenters, *v.* Dr. Sherlock, Lond. 1702 (1).

TAYLOR, TIMOTHY, pastor of a church in Dukinfield, in Cheshire (with Samuel Eaton). Defence of Sundry Positions, Lond. 1645 (1, 3).

THACHER, PETER; H. U. 1696. Ordained at Weymouth; removed to Boston, 1720, and was installed pastor of the New North Church; colleague with Mr. Webb. His removal caused great excitement, on the ground that it was robbing the church in Weymouth, and derogating from the character of the ministry. D. 1739, æt. 61. Objections to his Ordination, Bost. 1720 (3, 6); Declaration (with John Webb) in behalf of themselves and the New North Church, Bost. 1720 (1, 5).

TOMPSON, WILLIAM, pastor of the church in Braintree called by Dr. Mather one of the American pillars. Ordained, 1639. D. 1666, æt. 68. Answer to Herle (and R. Mather), Lond. 1644 (*b*).

TRAVERS, WALTER, B.D., Fellow of Trinity College, Cambridge. Ordained at Antwerp, 1578; was one of the defenders of the Puritans at the Lambeth Conference; silenced for life for Nonconformity; went into Ireland, and became Provost of Trinity College, Dublin. One of the worthiest divines of the age.

TRUMBULL, BENJAMIN, D.D., minister of North Haven, Conn.; Y. C. 1760. D. 1820, æt. 85. History of Connecticut, New Haven, 1818, a work of great value (1, 7, 8, 9, 10).

TURNER, CHARLES; an esteemed minister of Duxbury; H. U. 1752. Ordained, 1755; dismissed, 1775. Afterwards settled at Turner, Me. D. 1818, æt. 81. Plymouth Anniversary Sermon, Bost. 1778 (1, 5).

UDALL, JOHN, minister of Kingston-upon-Thames.

Silenced for Nonconformity; sentenced to die for writing the Mar-Prelate Pamphlets, which he solemnly denied, and died of broken heart in Marshalsea Prison, 1592. The witnesses in his favor were denied a hearing in court, "because they were against the queen's majesty." Demonstration of Discipline (probably Declaration of Discipline), 1574 (5).

UPHAM, CHARLES W.; H. U. 1821. For several years minister in Salem, more recently has figured in political life. Is now mayor of Salem. Dedication Sermon, Salem, 1826 (1, 3, 4); Second Century Sermon, Salem, 1829 (1, 3, 4).

UPHAM, THOMAS C., Professor in Bowdoin College, Me. Ratio Disciplinæ, a work of great research, and generally correct, Portland, 1844.

VANE, SIR HENRY, the younger, Governor of Massachusetts, 1636. Returned to England, was active for Cromwell, and hanged and quartered for high treason; with Hugh Peters, after the Restoration, 1662, æt. 50. Imbibed many errors, but had clear views of ecclesiastical liberty.

WARE, HENRY, Jun., D.D.; H. U. 1812. Pastor of church in Boston, and afterward Professor of Sacred Rhetoric in Harvard University. History of Old North and New Brick Churches, Boston, Bost. 1821 (1, 3).

WATTS, ISAAC, D.D., the poet, philosopher, and divine. Assistant to Dr. Isaac Chauncy, in London, 1698, and succeeded him in 1701–2. Mr. Price was chosen his assistant in 1703. Had feeble health till his death, 1748, æt. 74. Works in 7 vols. (2, 3, 7, 9, 10); Terms of Christian Communion; Foundation of a Christian Church, in Works.

WEBB, JOHN, first pastor of New North Church, Boston; H. U. 1708; ordained, 1714; survived one colleague (Mr. Thacher), and enjoyed the assistance of another (Dr. Eliot) eight years, who pronounced him one of the best of Christians and of ministers. Sermon at the Ordination of a Deacon, Bost. 1731 (1, 6). — See THACHER, PETER.

WELDE, THOMAS, first pastor of the church in Roxbury; refused to submit to the ceremonies, and came to New England, 1632; was sent to England with Hugh Peters, 1641, and returned to his former parish, Durham; from which, Eliot says, he was ejected, 1662; though Blake says that he died 1660. A very judicious minister. Answer to Rathband, Lond. 1644 (*b*).

WELLS, NOAH, D.D., minister of Stamford, Conn.; Y. C. 1741; ordained, 1746. D. 1776. A theologian of great renown; author of several valuable treatises against the Episcopate, also of other works.

WEST, SAMUEL, a famous Arminian divine; H. U. 1754; ordained at Dartmouth about 1764. D. 1807, æt. 77. Plymouth Anniversary Sermon, Bost. 1778 (1, 5).

WHITE, JOHN. H. U. 1698. Pastor First Church in Gloucester. D. 1760. Lamentations (in Wise's Vindication), Bost. 1772.

WHITGIFT, JOHN, Archbishop of Canterbury; a talented but severe governor of the church, pressing conformity with rigor. In early life he was against the habits, and run the usual race of the relapsed from reforms. D. 1603, æt. 73. Controversy with Cartwright (*b*, *d*).

WICKLIFFE, JOHN, D.D., educated at Merton College; called the Evangelical Doctor; Professor of Divinity, Oxford, and had the highest reputation in the university; a great opposer of the mendicants. He sustained Edward III. in his refusal to pay tribute to the Pope, and openly appealed to the word of God as the rule of faith and practice, and met the thunders of the Vatican for his presumption; yet he died in his bed, 1384, æt. about 60. He maintained the great, leading principles of Congregationalism with great success in that dark age, and was the grand means of planting principles of religious freedom in England.

WILLIAMS, ROGER, educated at Oxford, was a minister of the Church of England; became a Separatist, and came to New England, 1631; became pastor of the church in Salem; sentence of banishment was denounced against him, and he fled to Providence, where he afterwards became a Baptist, and subsequently a Seeker; renouncing his immersion because it had not been performed by one who had himself been immersed in regular succession. He was certainly in advance of his brethren on this side the water on some points of religious liberty, though the commonplace representations of his case are as much at variance with his own version of the matter as with that of his opponents. D. 1683, æt. 84. (See art. TOLERATION, in Dictionary.) Bloody Tenet (2, 3, 5, 6). Answer to Cotton's Letter, Lond. 1648 (1). Hireling Ministry none of Christ's, Lond. 1652 (1).

WILLARD, SAMUEL, Vice-President of Harvard University; minister of Groton, and Old South Church, Boston; H. U. 1659; a devoted Christian and sound divine. D. 1707, æt. 68. Election Sermon, Bost. 1694 (1); Discourse concerning Laying the Hand on the Bible in Swearing, Lond. 1689 (1, 6).

WINSLOW, EDWARD, Governor of Plymouth Colony; united with Robinson's Church in Leyden. He was a very laborious and serviceable magistrate, and a daring adventurer. D. 1655, æt. 61. Good News from New England (*a*).

WINTHROP, JOHN, many years Governor of Massachusetts Colony; expended a fine estate and endured great privations for the benefit of the colony; was for mild and tolerant measures in religion. D. 1649, æt. 60. Journal, Bost. 1825, in the town-libraries of Massachusetts (9, 10).

WISE, JOHN, minister of Ipswich; H. U. 1673; was zealously attached to civil and religious liberty; was imprisoned by Andros for remonstrating against the taxes. D. 1725, æt. 73. A learned scholar and an eloquent orator. Quarrel of the Churches Espoused, and Vindication of the Liberties of the New England Churches. Bost. 1772 (1, 2, 4, 7).

WISNER, B. B., D.D.; Union College, 1813; ordained pastor of Old South Church, Boston, 1821; afterward Secretary of the American Board of Commissioners for Foreign Missions. D. 1835, æt. 40. History of Old South Church, Boston, Bost. 1830 (1, 3, 5, 6, 7, 8, 9).

WITHERS, JOHN. I can learn nothing of this author, save his book, which ought to render his name immortal. History of Resistance in the Church of England, Lond. 1710 (1).

WREN, MATTHEW, Chaplain to Charles I. and Bishop of Hereford and Norwich. D. 1667, æt. 81. Articles of Visitation (*d*).

YOUNG, ALEXANDER, D.D., pastor of New South Church, Boston; H. U. 1820; ordained, 1825. Chronicles of the Pilgrims (1, 2, 4, 5, 8, 9); a work of merit and research. Chronicles of Massachusetts (1); Dudlean Lecture, Bost. 1846 (1, 2), in which he breaks up the fallow ground of Episcopacy.

THE END.

www.ingramcontent.com/pod-product-compliance
Lightning Source LLC
LaVergne TN
LVHW021142110826
845150LV00005B/1099

* 9 7 8 1 4 2 5 5 4 7 7 6 9 *